A
Twentieth
Century
Lady

Enjoy reading

A
Twentieth
Century
Lady

The Story of
Katharine Sinclair Minor

by Mary Minor Evans

Mary Minor Evans
July 20, 1999

M C M E Publishers
1832 E. Fifth Street
Duluth, MN 55812-1341
218-728-4146
revans@d.umn.edu

Printed in the United States of America by Tri-State Printing Co.
157 N. Third Street, P.O. Box 1119
Steubenville, OH 43952
740-283-3686

First printing
10 9 8 7 6 5 4 3 2 1

ISBN 0-9668088-C-0

Library of Congress Catalog Card Number 98-96896

Front cover photograph - Katharine Sinclair in the 1920's.
Back cover photograph - Mary Minor Evans in her mother's dress with
Katharine Sinclair Minor in 1995.
Both covers - photograph of Steubenville, Ohio in 1998.

Special thanks to Albert Tezla and James Evans for reading the manuscript.

A Twentieth Century Lady

The Story
of
Katharine Sinclair Minor

Katharine was raised by a mother who was born in 1862 and she lived in every decade of the 20th century. She had four children but sometimes it is hard to believe it when someone in Chautauqua, New York or Steubenville, Ohio walked up to her and said, "Hi Mom." One man said she was Ohio Mother of the Year, so he called her "Mom." Another just adopted her, so she called her "Mom." Of course all her children called her Mom.

Katharine Sinclair Minor was a person who combined the Victorian Age with the Scientific and Information Ages. These are the recollections of my mother about her life, either written down or told to me by her. I have embellished and confirmed data through writings by my uncle Dohrman J. Sinclair II, my aunt Wilma Sinclair LeVan Baker, newspaper articles, histories of the Steubenville area, letters and my own recollections. It has been a great opportunity and an exciting adventure to relive the past in this special way. This is her story.

This book is dedicated to my four sons, John, Jim,
Alan, and Matt who learn from the past and carry
their knowledge to the future.

Mary Minor Evans

CONTENTS

Thomas S. Sinclair
(1835-1865)

Catherine B. (Dohrman) Sinclair
(1838-1907)

Dohrman J. Sinclair
(1860-1915)

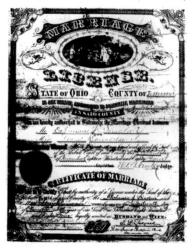

Sinclair-Donaldson Marriage Certificate
Dohrman J. Sinclair and Mary Donaldson were married on the
19th of November 1884 by E.D. Ledyard, Pastor of the Second
Presbyterian Church, Steubenville, Ohio. At that time, the bride
and groom were 22 and 24 years old respectively.

Mary (Donaldson) Sinclair
(1862-1940)

William B. Donaldson
(1837-1916)

Emelda (Junkin) Donaldson
(1840-1922)

I.

Birth In The New Century

*A*s the massive black steam driven locomotive of train number 399 cut its way along the Ohio River between the hills of Ohio and West Virginia on a hot summer early evening in August of 1915, an event that would reshape the history of the Ohio Valley and a young daughter's life occurred. Dohrman J. Sinclair, a pivotal business figure in the emerging early history of Steubenville, Ohio, happened to be in the wrong place at the wrong time. This dynamic individual and wizard bank financier of Market Street who was in the prime of his personal and professional life looked up from a landscape blue print of the Cleveland and Pittsburgh Railroad yard of the La Belle mill only to see the grill of the westbound "Flyer" approaching. Whether frozen by pain of the still lodged bullets in his abdomen or the surprise of an obstacle keeping him from his plans of yet another project, the outcome was nonetheless tragic. The life of this builder of the first steel frame high-rise office building in Steubenville, philanthropist, banker and humanist was cut short at age 55. Thousands from this small town turned out to express their sorrow in the ensuing days.

Dohrman James Sinclair had lived most of his life in Steubenville, Ohio, and it was to this early Ohio settlement that he brought his visions to reality. Time after time he saw the possibilities for making his hometown a thriving area. He brought businesses to the region, helped men find jobs, created parks, and made the area a safer, healthier place to live.

In 1865 Dohrman came to Steubenville with his mother, Kate (Catherine) Brooks Dohrman Sinclair. Kate's twenty-nine-year-old pharmacist husband, Thomas Sinclair, had died in January while visiting his brother William in Milwaukee. Feeling that Erie, Pennsylvania was too far from her family, Kate brought her young son back to her hometown. She had been born in Steubenville to Peter and Margaret Garrett Dohrman, and her roots went back to the very early days when her Dutch - Portugese grandfather, Arnold

1

Henry Dohrman, was given a tract of land as the first civilian recipient of the American Revolution land grants in 1787. During the Revolutionary War, Arnold Henry Dohrman had frequently received into his own house in Lisbon, Portugal whole crews of Americans from the prison ships. The sick and wounded Americans would be sent to the hospital and the others, aided with supplies of food, medicine, clothing, and the means of transporting the captive seamen, to America.

Kate Sinclair later married Henry Arnold Dohrman, who had served in the Civil War, and in 1871 she gave birth to a second son, Horatio Garrett Dohrman, nicknamed Rash. Kate Dohrman, an accomplished musician, for thirty years played the organ as a volunteer in the Congregational Church in Steubenville. In her home she was very proud of the Circassian walnut upright piano which she had purchased with the first money her son, Dohrman Sinclair, earned.

D.J. Sinclair started his working career at The Union Deposit Bank, which was one of the oldest banking institutions in Steubenville. It had its inception in the Union Savings Institute organized in 1854, of which Horatio G. Garrett was Treasurer. The bank was long and favorably known as Garrett's Bank, and after nineteen years of successful business was merged into the Union Deposit Bank in 1873. Mr. Garrett was also cashier of this institution until his retirement in 1887. Mr. Garrett was the brother of Dohrman's grandmother. When Dohrman's step-father died, forcing him to quit school and support his mother and half-brother at the age of thirteen, it was H. G. Garrett who gave him the job of sweeper at the bank. Dohrman worked his way through jobs as sweeper, teller and cashier within a few years' time. He learned quickly and well. Later he completed a course in financial law and became an advisor to the bank without completing his formal schooling.

The 1897 Steubenville Centennial Souvenir listed the bank officers as William R.E. Elliott, President; D.J. Sinclair, Cashier; H.G. Dohrman, Teller; John P. Edgar, Bookkeeper; H.C. Cook, Assistant Bookkeeper; J.W. Matheus, Messenger. The directors were W.R.E. Elliott, D.J. Sinclair, J.M. Cook, W.B. Donaldson, Wesley Permar, and H.G. Dohrman. Under this management the bank did a steadily increasing business, having a large line of savings deposits upon which it paid interest, in addition to doing an extensive general banking business.

At the age of 24 Dohrman James Sinclair married Mary Donaldson on November 19, 1884, in the bride's home at 332 N. Fourth Street on the southeast corner of Dock Street. D.J. Sinclair was working in the bank the day of his wedding, and one of the customers asked, "Where are all those carriages going?" Dohrman looked out and confessed, "I believe they are going to my wedding. I should think about leaving myself." He did leave and made the wedding and the reception which followed. Afterwards, as they were beginning their honeymoon by train to New York, Dohrman fell asleep. It was his first chance to catch some sleep after a sleepless night and a very busy day. He worked long hours his entire life. His great friend, A.C. Lewis, gave Sinclair a grandfather's clock with the message "From one old fool to tell another old fool when it is time to go home."

Mary Donaldson also had deep roots in the Steubenville area. Her mother, Emelda Junkin, was born in Steubenville. Emelda's father, Matthew Junkin, served as Justice of the Peace for years before becoming mayor of Steubenville in 1863, serving until 1866. Emelda married William B. Donaldson, who was also born in Steubenville. The ceremony took place on Christmas Eve in 1861. Their first daughter, Mary, was born October 30, 1862. Nearly eighteen years later, William and Emelda had a second daughter, Florence. William's parents were William and Margaret Murphy Donaldson. They lived in Jacksonville, now very much a part of Steubenville, in a big red brick house, on the corner of Market Street and Wildon Avenue. The avenue was named for Mary's grandfather, using the first three letters of his first and last name. William's grandfather and Mary's great grandfather, John Donaldson, died September 10, 1854. John held the dubious honor of being the first adult buried in the Union Cemetery, which had been dedicated July 4, 1854. The pall bearers brought along wooden horses on which they placed the casket while they rested on the way to the grave. The Donaldson plot soon added John's son William, who died October 8, 1855 at the age of 67 years, and William's infant son George, who was moved to the new cemetery in 1856 as were many other bodies from earlier cemeteries.

In the 1880's three children were born to the Sinclairs. Marie arrived in 1885, Wilma in 1887 and Frank in 1889. These three grew up with family living nearby. Dohrman's mother lived next door. Dohrman's half brother, Horatio Garrett Dohrman, wife Carrie Pettit and son Frank Sinclair Dohrman lived on the southwest corner of Fourth and Clinton Street at 539 N. Fourth Street. Mary Donaldson Sinclair's parents lived two blocks away from the Sinclairs at Dock and N. Fourth Street.

The Sinclair home was a lovely house built in 1865 by the builder of the Pennsylvania Railroad Bridge, Maximilian Joseph Becker. He had come to Steubenville to build the first Panhandle railroad bridge across the Ohio River and had built a home for himself as well. In the Centennial souvenir book of 1897, the home is described as "a two-story brick structure of colonial architecture, and it contains ten rooms all artistically finished and equipped with modern appliances." In 1900 Dohrman bought his old home from his mother and did a great deal of remodeling. The family lived in the

The Sinclair Homestead, 523 N. Fourth Street, Steubenville, Ohio

house next door while work was being done on their new house. An attic and a new wing were added at this time as well as the bowling alley in the basement. It took from November to May to do the hand-carved stairway and install indirect lighting in the built-in china closet with shelves of mahogany for the dishes. The carpenter asked Dohrman why he wanted the best wood where no one would see it. Dohrman's reply was, "But you will know and I will know." The dining room ceiling had twelve-inch-wide mahogany beams. The dining room saw many festive dinners and luncheons around the big mahogany dining room table with the call button on the floor to alert the kitchen when something was needed. One of the novelties was a frosted glass fountain, a product of the Jefferson Glass Company. It usually appeared as the centerpiece when entertaining was done. The water supply came from the basement and the display was quite impressive. Many were the dignitaries from Washington, D.C., ambassadors from foreign countries, and powerful people from around the country who enjoyed the hospitality of the Sinclairs.

After selling her home to Dohrman, Kate Sinclair Dohrman lived six months with one son and six months with the other. On April 15, 1907, the day after she died, the following appeared in the newspaper.

> *Always the same, wherever met, she carried a personal grace that attracted and held all hearts - she was full of love for humanity, and humanity returned her love. In society she was bright, cheery and captivating, with a quick intelligence and well-stored mind that made her company a delight. But the truest test of the finer qualities of any one is in ordinary life, and here the goodness of Mrs. Dohrman shone. Ask anyone with whom she came in contact in matters of trade; hear the testimony of Steubenville's salesladies, as to her kindly courtesy and sweet ways when she met them across the counter. Ever and always she was the same gentle woman. And was there ever a woman so young? Mother of two of Steubenville's prominent businessmen, yet young in spirit as the most youthful matron in the town; and feeling young, the years did not mark her with their signs. This secret of perennial youth all have not solved, nor can it be solved by rule. But the well-spring of love in the heart, making other lives sweet because of its ever growing and extending sweep, is this fountain of perpetual youth. And Mrs. Dohrman was ever young because she loved others, and loved to do good. Her life was a benefaction, and the world is better because she lived and loved.*

When Mary and Dohrman Sinclair's children were in their teens a new son, Dohrman, arrived. Four years later on Thursday morning, July 23, 1908, their youngest daughter, Katharine Emelda Sinclair was born at the family homestead. Her life would not be the same as her older sisters and brothers, for tragedy would enter her younger brother's and her lives.

Katharine was named after her two grandmothers, Kate Dohrman, whom young Katharine never knew, and Emelda Donaldson, just as the author, Katharine's daughter Mary, was named after her two grandmothers, Mary Donaldson Sinclair and Carrie Holland Minor.

The substantial brick home, at 523 N. Fourth Street, had a wide center hall which was flooded with sunlight through the three large stained-glass windows on the landing at the far end of the hall. There was a hospitable living room and a music room. The parlor wall had large pink silk-brocaded panels, edged in white beading and framed by a foot wide white border. The woodwork was white, and an elaborate gold edged mirror hung between the two front windows. The furniture was ornate rose wood or mahogany, upholstered in pink satin. The parlor was seldom used. Into this home with its grand staircase containing deep five-inch-high steps, which led to the landing with the stained-glass windows and then turned to reach the second floor, came the cheerful little baby girl, Katharine, who learned to first crawl up the steps and then walk up them.

Tiffany Stained-glass Windows in the Sinclair Homestead   *The Garden at the Homestead*

After the remodeling, each principal room on the first and second floors had modern gas heaters in the fire places. They consisted of upright sheets of asbestos with rows of holes for gas to radiate heat when lit. These modern gas heaters were guaranteed to be cleaner than coal grates. The homestead was wired for electricity before Katharine's arrival, but there must have been some question in her father's mind whether that method of lighting was here to stay, because the gas jets were left just in case they were needed. Katharine says, "Many times I saw my mother curl her hair with her curling iron which she heated on the wall jet next to the mirror on her dresser." The upstairs center hall contained the recessed electric fuse box housing the main switch, which Katharine's father pulled at night before going to bed. It served as a safeguard against the danger of fire from the electric current.

An ample pantry, a lavatory, and a spacious kitchen completed the first floor. "Next to the sink there were drawers which I'd pull out to form steps and climb up, so I'd be tall enough to help dry dishes, which didn't happen often," relates Katharine. There were also two stairways to the second floor and two to the basement in addition to the outside steps down to the basement. From upstairs, people could communicate with the kitchen by what looked like an old-fashioned telephone mouthpiece.

Katharine remembers the large front porch with the customary golden oak swing. Walking to and from work, in those early decades, friends frequently stopped as they passed and exchanged *pleasantries*. At night a policeman on the beat usually rested, unseen, on their swing, because the house was in the middle of the block and the arc lights at Logan and Clinton Streets cast only a faint eerie glow through the thick growth of the maple trees. On national holidays or similar occasions the Sinclair's enormous 10 by 15 foot flag would be displayed.

Out in the yard a landscaper from Pittsburgh created a sun dial with 14 different kinds of irises. This lovely yard had flower beds bordering the walks and lawn in geometric design. There were colorful and fragrant roses, hollyhocks, irises, lilies of the valley, pinks, jack in the pulpits, ferns, oriental poppies, bachelor buttons, and many other species.

The family often gave yard parties, sometimes to raise money for organizations such as Martha Manor, a home for the aged. Decorations included Japanese lanterns with lighted candles inside which hung from clothes lines around the yard. These were kept on the third floor in the box seats with tops which lifted to store the lanterns. Guests would sit around the ballroom on these seats when lovely dances and parties were held by the family for their friends.

"My two sisters, Marie and Wilma, were married at the homestead. Marie was married in the Music room, Wilma in the beautiful formal landscaped garden in the back yard. Marie married Harry Grant before I was born, and Nana carried me to Wilma and Garry Le Van's wedding before I was two years old," states Katharine. After their marriage the Le Vans lived in a white cottage on the northwest corner of N. Fourth and Dock Streets in Steubenville. It was here that their son, Garrett, Jr., was born. According to family legend, many years before, Wilma's great-grandparents, Peter and Margaret Garrett Dohrman, had started married life in the same cottage. On the mantle in the bedroom there was a hand-fashioned nail on which Peter Dohrman is said to have hung his watch each night.

Katharine remembers the square pergola with a red tile floor, three Doric columns at each corner, two matching Doric columns at each end, and an over-head rose trellis in her back yard. The pergola housed rustic furniture and the longstanding porch swing. The yard also contained a delightful wooden one-room playhouse with a concrete step. Marie, Wilma, and Frank had had a roller coaster which Dohrman and Katharine were still able to use. There was also a trapeze set with a swing, two rings, and a bar in the back yard, where Katharine and her friends played. The basement bowling alley, which was used for the enjoyment of family and friends, had to be extended outside the house when it was installed to be the proper length. The top of the extension was the bottom of Katharine's sandbox.

There was one big back yard for the two houses owned by Dohrman J. Sinclair at 523 & 525 N. Fourth Street. A two-story building contained the laundry. It had been a barn with stalls when Katharine was young. There was also a very ornate stucco garage with leaded glass windows at the south end of the lot where their Peerless car was kept. It contained an incinerator as well. When Frank was young he threw rocks at the stucco garage trying to see how close he could come to the windows without breaking the glass. He managed to break the windows!

Katharine states, "My brother Dohrman and I had a nurse, Mrs. Hannah (Nana) Cunningham, who came to live with us when he was born. Nana had come from Germany through Ellis Island." In the latter part of this century, when that area was being restored, Katharine sent money in memory of her Nana to help the restoration. "Nana stayed with us for eleven years, until my father's death. Her salary, I believe, was $3.00 a week, and our black cook, Helen Jackson, who was with us for twelve years, received around $2.00 a week with every other Sunday off. Our chauffeur, Charlie Triplet, lived with his wife and two daughters in a house behind us and always had an inexhaustible supply of penny candy in his pockets. His daughter Minnie and I were close friends. The maid at the house was from Mt. Pleasant, Ohio. Helen Saunders was a Black and she had a son called Douglas. Everyone in the family referred to her as Peddy-Dink. Just as the old song of the time went, Peddy-Dink did the washing on Monday, the ironing on Tuesday and on Friday she polished silver.

Picture taken 1909 of Mary D. Sinclair, her husband, and 5 children.
Top tow - Dohrman J. Sinclair, Katharine E. Sinclair, Mary D. Sinclair. Middle row - Marie Sinclair, Frank D. Sinclair, Wilma Sinclair. Foreground - Dohrman J. Sinclair, Jr.

Sibling Activities

Mrs. E.Y. Daugherty was a friend of Katharine's mother. They exchanged Christmas presents and played 500 and later Mah Jong together. The Daughertys lived in the north end of town, in a lovely home overlooking the river. Mrs. Daugherty always referred to her husband as "Mr. Daugherty," never by his first name. Katharine remembers that they had two sons, one her brother Frank's age. "Once my mother took the boys for an 'over nighter' at a fancy hotel, what today we would call a Five Star hotel. At breakfast, in the elegant dining room, they were seated and each given a formal breakfast menu. Donald studied every word, then put it aside, and in utter disgust said, 'No one in the world can eat that much.'"

Marie Sinclair graduated from Cleveland, Ohio's Mittleberger's School for Girls in 1903 and attended Ogontz School at Elkins Park, Pennsylvania for a year where Wilma was at school. In 1904 the sisters traveled to Europe together with Miss Dora Hill, who served as their chaperone. Miss Hill lived across the street and taught them French. Frank, who was still in school and attending Culver Military Academy in Andover at the time his sisters set out for Europe, climbed out the window of his dorm to come home and see Marie and Wilma off on their trip.

Frank attended Cornell University before he traveled by steamer to South America. The passengers on the ship thought he was related to Harry Sinclair, the oil tycoon, and therefore very wealthy. Of course, Frank let them believe it. Frank had wanted to bring back a horse but there was no room. He did bring back three monkeys. At the time he was working at the Union Bank, so he took one monkey to the bank and put it in the window with a sign which said, *"This monkey is too dumb to save money, how about you?"* One monkey was a wedding present. The third one was at the house, and it was put in the downstairs lavatory at night. The monkey jumped over to the light fixture and saw himself in the mirror, which made him laugh and laugh. He also unrolled the toilet paper and it was all over the place when the door was opened.

Phones

Fifty years before the beginning of the 20th century, a man in the patent office resigned because he said, "Everything had been invented." He was of course wrong. Phones, which today are taken so much for granted, had not been invented. In 1876 Alexander Graham Bell patented a phone. Dohrman J. Sinclair had one of the early phones installed in his home as soon as companies formed to provide service. In fact, he installed a phone from the Phoenix Company and one from the National Company. The wall-type phones were located in the back hall on the first floor, and when one picked up the receiver the operator would say, "Number please." People could call only those who subscribed to the same company, which caused hopeless confusion to both people and "centrals" (operators), with whom one placed the call. Many neighbors used "the other" phone at the house, and a small stool covered with red carpet was kept at the phones for short neighbors. Later there was only one company and the number was changed to 45. The police department was 55. Mistakes were frequent. Often the Sinclairs would get calls, usually at night, from hysterical women, to send the police right away to S. Sixth Street where someone was beating his wife! The calls meant someone had to come down in the middle of the night if the phone happened to ring. As the number of phones reached 100 there were three digits in the numbers. Party lines became popular. County phones added "rings" such as 7202 ring 15 for a certain party which in the case cited was the Wells' farm number. This was done with a long ring for the 10 and then 5 short rings after that.

Katharine and her mother

Katharine

The 1900-1909 Era

During the first decade of the twentieth century the Boer War was being fought in South Africa and the Boxer rebellion broke out in China. England ruled one-fifth of the globe in 1906. The Simplon Tunnel, a twelve-mile railway tunnel between Switzerland and Italy opened. Queen Victoria and Verdi died. Mrs. Carrie Catt presided at the International Woman's Suffrage Alliance in London. It was discovered that yellow fever was carried by mosquitoes.

The New York subway opened in 1904, forty years after London's, and so did the Plaza Hotel. Hawaii became a territory of the United States. Cuba was forced to give the United States naval bases, and later Taft promised to keep Cuba a republic. America's Great White Fleet peacefully entered Tokyo Bay and a naval base was started at Pearl Harbor. McKinley won the presidency, was shot, and Teddy Roosevelt became president. He settled the coal strike, and his daughter, Alice Roosevelt, married Nicholas Longworth, Speaker of the House in 1906. The Pure Food and Drug Act was passed. The San Francisco earthquake killed nearly a thousand. Immigration through Ellis Island continued to increase with five thousand three hundred and thirty-five immigrants passing through on May 4, 1907. Reno became the divorce center. Booker T. Washington encouraged those of his own race to work for advances in education and jobs.

It took 51 days by auto to drive from San Francisco to New York, and the Wright brothers flew 850 feet in a heavier-than-air plane. The rough Peking-Paris 8,000-mile auto race was run in 1907. The first English Channel flight succeeded, and explorer Robert Peary reached the north pole.

The 36-pound Davis cup became a tennis trophy at the beginning of the century. The second modern Olympic games were held in Paris with some participants avoiding Sunday races; it was followed by the 1904 Olympics in St. Louis and the 1908 games in London. The Belmont race track was opened.

Rudyard Kipling won the Nobel Prize for literature. Caruso made his first recording in America, and the Italian Coloratura soprano Mme. Tetrazzini was signed by the Manhattan Opera House in 1908. Cubist art was born with Picasso's Les Demoiselles d' Avignon, and John Singer Sargent dominated the London art exhibit.

J.P. Morgan formed U.S. Steel, the Eastman Kodak company was incorporated, and Henry Ford formed an auto company in Detroit. Gillette marketed the double-edged disposable blade, and a form of plastic was invented. The New York Stock Exchange moved into a new building at Broad and Wall Street, the St. Louis' Exposition opened, and in 1907 John D. Rockefeller was the world's richest man, at $300 million.

The 1910-1919 Era

While Katharine was growing up in Steubenville, the world was changing. Paris was flooded and the Louvre was threatened in 1910. King Edward VII of England and Tolstoy died. Japan annexed Korea, France took over Morocco and the Chinese regime became a republic in 1912. Archduke Franz Ferdinand, heir to the throne of Austria-Hungary, was assassinated in Sarajevo, war flared up as Germany invaded Belgium and France and aerial combat started. The Lusitania was sunk with 124 American lives lost, and war raged in Europe. 1916 saw the Germans attack Verdun, the Allied forces retreat from Gallipoli, and the Italians join the French and British. In Dublin the Nationalists staged a bloody uprising. Germany declared total submarine warfare. In 1917 the U.S. Congress voted to enter the war, and the War Department reported that it took $156.30 to provide an infantryman with arms, clothes and eating utensils. The Russian Czar abdicated, the Bolsheviks seized power in Russia and the Russian Reds signed a peace treaty, then civil war gripped Russia. In 1918 Lloyd George became Britain's Prime Minister and Lady Astor become the first woman in Parliament. United States' Eddie Richenbacker recorded 26 downed German planes. The armistice was signed by the Germans at 11:01 on November 11. The League of Nations was created at Versailles but the U. S. Congress rejected it. The influenza epidemic raged across the world killing 20 million or more.

In 1911 U.S. Senators choose direct election by voters, and Wilson was elected president. New York City had a shirtwaist factory fire that killed 146, and in 1913 New York's Grand Central Station opened. The income tax was passed, and Wilson opened the Panama Canal. The Federal Reserve began in 1914.

During the decade, the Tango dance arrived in New York. Edison invented talking pictures. The first full length color film, *The World, the Flesh and the Devil* was released and *Birth of a Nation* opened in New York. Henry Ford established the first assembly line. The zipper was perfected and in 1915 Einstein developed the theory of relativity. Speed in different forms found Atwood flying the 1,365 miles from St. Louis to New York in a record 28 hours 31 minutes, the Indianapolis 500 occurring for the first time, and Sir Barton claiming the first triple Crown in horse racing. Amundsen reached the South Pole ahead of Scott. An iceberg caused the Titanic to sink, drowning 1,595.

II.

Growing Up In
The Second Decade

$\mathcal{T}$he second decade of the 20th century found Steubenville bursting with optimism, according to the book, *STEUBENVILLE, OHIO,* published in 1911 by the Chamber of Commerce. The Ohio River town had an estimated 25,000 inhabitants and was less than 40 miles from Pittsburgh, Pennsylvania if you traveled by train or road instead of by river. It had twenty-four miles of paved streets, three hundred arc lights, twenty-one miles of sewers, the most complete water works along the Ohio River, and a splendid fire department. It had eight banks and four building-and-loan associations, twenty-four churches, fourteen school buildings and a business college. Sixty-four trains caring 4,000 passengers a day ran through the town. One hundred and seven trolley cars clanged up hill and down dale, to Mingo, Brilliant, Toronto, Empire, Wellsville and East Liverpool.

Steubenville is the first and oldest continuous organized community in Ohio and the Northwest Territory. The first white child born in Steubenville was James Hunter, in 1798. Fort Steuben was built in 1786 to protect those living in the Steubenville region and the civil engineers surveying the land. The Land Ordinance of 1785 was passed by Congress, and the First Federal Land Office in the United States to own its own building was located in Steubenville. The office promoted the sale of land west of the Ohio River, including Ohio, Indiana, Illinois, Michigan, and part of Minnesota and Wisconsin, for one dollar an acre. The Point of Beginning, which was used for surveying purposes, is now in the Ohio River near East Liverpool, Ohio. Near Alikanna just north of Steubenville, the Ohio River obtains fresh water from a spring located under a ledge, making the Steubenville water purer.

The village around the fort became Steubenville in 1797. By 1810 Steubenville had 112 frame and brick homes and 900 inhabitants. The Female Seminary, well known for educating young girls, drew from a wide area, with many arriving by boat on the Ohio River. The first United States woolen mill was located in Steubenville. There were flocks of sheep grazing everywhere in the area. Steubenville was called the Merino Sheep capital of the country. Early in Steubenville's history, Bezaleel Wells had brought a few sheep from a nobleman in New England who had purchased the sheep in Portugal to start a herd. In 1897 the United States Merino Sheep Breeding Association held a meeting in Burgettstown, not far from Steubenville. During the Civil War, Steubenville's Edwin M. Stanton was President Lincoln's secretary of war, and President Woodrow Wilson's family lived in Steubenville in a home not far from Katharine Sinclair's childhood home. James Wilson, the grandfather of President Wilson, owned the *Western Herald* from 1815-1828.

Downtown Steubenville

During the early years of the century, the downtown business district was a thriving and busy hub of activity. On Saturdays the shopping area was crowded with people not only from the city but from all the surrounding country. Most of the stores were located on Market Street between Third and Sixth Streets. Munger's grocery was located at Third and Market next to the Union Deposit Bank at 106 S. Third Street. On the south side of the street across from the bank stood the H.C. Cook Printing Shop and the Harvey motorcycle shop. They were located on the half-block long street back of the present day city building. The street is now gone and is part of a parking lot. Other stores included Reiner's, Munker's ladies' store, Sulzbacher's, Cooper-Kline's woman's clothing, the elegant Hub, Denmark's, McCrory's 5 & 10 cent store with merchandise at those prices, Shannon Jewelers, May & Leopold furniture store, McCauslen's Florist, Fiest Confectionery which later became Seltzer, Woepert's grocery store, Spies' fine jewelry store, and McCoys' shoe store. Some of these stores had balconies where cash change was made. A silver two-inch by three-inch box slid up to the bookkeeping department on wires where change would be put into the box and sent down again. In the 100 block of N. Fourth was the McGowan Insurance Company and the *Herald-Star* newspaper.

Near Fourth on Market Street was a tobacco store that had a life-size Indian statue in front, complete with head gear, bow and arrow. Native Americans had introduced tobacco to the American invaders, and thus such a statue would immediately identify the store. Some of the other stores included Erwin's Complete Stationary Store, Robinson's Music Store,

Isaly's, Mosel-Johnson's wholesale groceries, and the popular Central Drug.

One bright summer day, Katharine's brother Frank and another bank teller, Earl Vance, from the Union Savings Bank and Trust Company at Fourth and Market went to the drug store next door. They had a long discussion on whether to have the small or large coke while the waitress stood patiently poised to take their order. Frank and Earl finally decided on two small cokes and finished them before the waitress presented the bill for the two five-cent cokes. They produced a $1,000 U.S. currency bill and asked for their change.

In the 200 block of N. Fourth Street stood the beautiful Johnson home on the northwest corner, where a fast food Hardee's restaurant is now located. Further along the street was the Masonic Temple and the Westminster Presbyterian Church. Next to the church was the church's manse in what had been the Welche's home and then the Grant School, which burned down about 1920. On the east side of the block stood the Christian Church and the house where Edwin M. Stanton was born. The house is now gone and a drive-in bank stands on the spot. Stanton later moved to Logan and Third Street. The Star Vulcanizing Store was also on that block on the southeast corner.

Newspapers in 1915 revealed prices of groceries and housewares, glowing business opportunities, and a sure cure for any known and unknown ailment. Fresh eggs were twenty-two cents a dozen; bread was five cents a loaf; hams, plain or skinned, were sixteen cents a pound, and twenty-five cents for two pounds. *Two bits* also bought six pounds of fancy sweet potatoes. Beets and onions were a penny a bunch, sweet and juicy oranges fifteen cents a dozen. Fancy Malaya grapes were ten cents. Fresh cabbage went for one cent a pound, and fancy ripe tomatoes were yours for four cents a pound.

Bathroom fixtures made of brass and heavily nickel-plated were priced for 49 cents each and included soap dishes, twenty-four-inch towel bars, bath tub soap holders, tumbler holders, white enameled bath tub seats and an eighteen-inch plate glass shelf with nickel brackets. Slop jars, sometimes called chamber pots, were 69 cents, but still a bargain against the discomfort of a trip to the back yard on a frosty night. Good quality Brussels carpet for hall or stairs cost 59 cents a yard. A 9 x 12 Axminster, Wilton, Velvet, or Colonial Velvet by Smith, Bigelow, or Sanford sold for $14.75. C.L. Mueller's offered men's regular $28.00 to $30.00 suits for $15.00. During Munkers' August blanket sale that year, one could buy comforts from 98 cents to $2.25 each, and their all wool blankets of *elegant stock* were $4.65 a pair.

The mercantile and department stores offered a tempting array of merchandise at bargain prices. The Hoover Bond Company advertised five-foot oak porch swings, "full bolt and nut construction," complete with chains and hooks for $1.98. At fabulous Sulzbacher's you could buy fine ribbed seamless hose with reinforced knee, heel and toe in black or white for ten cents for regular, fifteen cents for quality; trimmed hats were nine cents and pillow cases eight cents each.

If you wanted to explore far away places you could take the Wheeling and Lake Erie Railroad excursion to Niagara Falls and return, any Wednesday for $6.00. Or you could take their personally conducted tour to Grand Canyon, California and cities of the west all first class, twenty-two days for $186.

Newspapers advertised their classified ad rates as "three lines, six words to a line, three insertions 25 cents; six insertions, 35 cents"; and advertisements for "situations wanted" were published three insertions free. You could rent three rooms and a bath for $8 a month, or for $13 more you could rent a whole six room house with bath, porch, cellar, laundry, furnace and all modern conveniences, situated on street car line La Belle View.

Drug stores not only sold soda water called "Jagless Juice of Joy" but an endless variety of sure cures for weak stomachs and neuralgia and all summer and winter distresses. A few of these included Mott's Nervine Pills to renew the normal vigor and make life worth living, Beecham's Pills to insure Health and Happiness, The Neal 3 Day Cure to break the alcohol habit, Sentanel Laxative to guard your health, and Mr. Man at your desk! "Your brain can't work when your bowels are clogged." There were many other glowing claims. Somehow, the people survived all these sure cures.

Business Growth

In the early years, when businesses were coming to town, H.O. Hennings was looking for a possible outlet for his Chicago wallpaper store. D.J. Sinclair found out almost too late that he was in Steubenville and went to the train station where Mr. Hennings was about to catch the train home. Dohrman Sinclair had not persuaded him to locate an outlet in Steubenville when the train was ready to leave, so he boarded the train with Hennings. The train took Sinclair half way to Chicago before he felt he had convinced Hennings to bring an outlet of his wallpaper business to Steubenville by using his persuasive arguments. Hennings later brought the company home office and his family as well to this Ohio River town. Katharine knew all five Hennings children. Son Joe was a hemophiliac and died quite young. Son Herb married Mary Ellen, and their daughter Ginny became the author's best friend when she was growing up. Virginia, who was

Katharine's age, died when she was about 20. Ruth married Tom Welch and Margaret never married.

Neighbors

This was a time when most people knew not only their close neighbors but also everyone who lived on their street from Adam Street to the Railroad bridge north of Franklin Avenue. Many of the Sinclair neighbors had fascinating idiosyncrasies. One prominent couple had a little baby boy, and for a long time after the birth the mother bragged confidentially to anyone who would listen that she was a virgin since she had given birth to her son! The son grew up and became a dignified, prominent citizen. He married and died long ago, leaving no children. Another story that neighbors told was about the widow and widower who lived next door to each other. He was seen by neighbors going to the widow's back door! She was 69 and he was 76.

Mr. Steel, who was a partner in the Beall and Steel's Drug store, lived across the street from the Sinclair home. The Steels had a beautiful garden filled with brightly-colored flowers and a bird bath similar to the Sinclair's. One gloomy night the two neighbors arrived at their homes. After leaving D.J. Sinclair to enter his own home, Mr. Steel went down to the basement to fire the coal furnace. Lurking in the shadows was a man who jumped out and fired shots which killed Mr. Steel! He believed Mr. Steel owed him money for work done. The amount in question was $5. Asked just before he died if it could have been their handy man, Mr. Steel said he had not seen the man but was sure the handy man could not have done it. However, a confession by that same handy man proved him wrong. Katharine remembers the Steel daughter, Ester S. Baird, returning from Pittsburgh with her new baby and the wet nurse they had hired.

Steubenville natives liked to hear good stories, and the tale which came back from South Africa was enjoyed. A Mr. Hitchcock was in a bar and struck up a conversation with another American. When Mr. Hitchcock learned that the man was from Steubenville, he mentioned that he had dated a girl from there whose father owned a clothing store. The father was a big man with rosy cheeks whose name was Sulzbacher. Mr. Hitchcock wondered if the man knew what had happened to Sulzbacher's daughter Helen. The man replied, "I married her."

Fires

"Fire was a concern of all," recalls Katharine. "When we lived at 523 N. Fourth Street we kept a fire location card on the front of the tall desk in the living room which matched the bells with the location of a fire. The court house bell in its steeple bonged out *numbers,* i.e., one (pause) three; two (pause) five, etc., and the sound could be heard all over town. The Fire Call card translated the numbers into the locations. Our number was four (pause) two for N. Fourth Street and Logan Street our immediate neighborhood. At any hour of the day or night that bell was a signal to go where the action was. There were many fires at the old Hartje Paper Mill on the east side of Third between Madison and Ross Streets. Their number was 43 and we'd wait with baited breath for that last bong." Katharine remembers going to a number of fires in her nightgown with her father. From the time he was a boy he had gone to fires, mixing with all sorts of people and gaining information he would use throughout his life. Young Katharine went one day to the North Street Reliance Fire Station with him. The firemen at this station had made Katharine a doll cradle, which she loved. The hard-working, dependable firemen were one of her father's favorite groups, and Edward Green, who later became the fire chief, was a good friend. "While we were there the siren went off and the calmness turned into completely controlled action. We stood between the two large doors while I clutched my father's hand, knowing I would be safe with him. We watched the firemen quickly slide down the large brass rod from the opening upstairs. The alarm shrieked out the location of the fire. The fervor of excitement filled the air as the horses snorted, pranced out of their stalls, and were harnessed to the fire trucks. Excited firemen rushed to their assigned positions on the running boards and rode out the doors on either side of us. We listened to the fading sound of the fire siren. What a thrilling experience. Decades later, a new fire chief told me that my father had bought, paid for, and had delivered all the materials for a bowling alley to keep the men entertained and provide exercise while they were free but on duty," recalled Katharine.

Vacations

When Katharine was about two her father and mother took her along with her brother Dohrman to New York City and Atlantic City. In New York there was The Hippodrome, the old Knickerbocker Hotel with its red, plush upholstery, the Schwartz Toy Store, and the Aquarium. The youngsters loved it.

The Sinclairs' favorite vacation spa was Atlantic City. There the family stayed at the Strand Hotel. If their rooms did not have an ocean view, Katharine's father changed them to a suite overlooking the ocean. "My father took us over by train and would see that we were 'nicely settled,' then he returned home, to work, and we spent the next two weeks vacationing. During the day, I was mostly on the sandy beach dressed in my 'swimming

Sunday Dinner at the Donaldsons in 1911
Adults: (l to r) William Donaldson, Emelda Junkin Donaldson, Harry F. Grant, Marie Sinclair Grant, Florence Donaldson Henderson, Frank D. Sinclair, Wilma Sinclair LeVan, Garrett B. LeVan, Mary Donaldson Sinclair, Dohrman J. Sinclair. Children: (l to r) Dohrman J. Sinclair II, Katharine E. Sinclair, Catherine E. Henderson, Garrett B. LeVan, Jr.

suit' made of heavy black cotton with buttons down the front, short sleeves and bloomers that went to my knees. I had my shovel and bucket and spent many hours at work. If I ventured into the water, my swimsuit invariably filled with salt water. Now there are nylon and lycra *quick dry* bathing suits, wide board walks stretching the length of the beach and casinos located on docks."

Summers

Summers in the Ohio valley were lovely. Katharine and her companions played in the sand box or on the see-saw or trapeze or on the little roller coaster which had a little red wagon that started from a low platform and rolled down tracks and out onto the smooth cement walk. Her tricycle resembled the cart used in harness racing with a small wheel instead of a horse! A long shaft to the front wheel guided it and pedals propelled it. It had a beautiful red leather seat wide enough for two and a shiny bicycle bell on the handle bar. Katharine remembers spending hours with friends from the neighborhood roller skating and playing hopscotch on the sidewalks, marked with a soft stone, not chalk. "When we fell and skinned our knees, we put peroxide on our cuts, which would sting. When it bubbled up, we knew it was the badness coming out," recalls Katharine. The girls played jacks and jumped rope. The boys played marbles. Steubenville was "the marble capital of the world," some said. A favorite pastime for the friends was the experience of being surrounded by contentment inside the playhouse walls. Above the doorway were rambler roses climbing over a trellis arch. The little house had windows on three sides, and was brightened with a flowered paper. It was small and intimate and housed a conglomeration of childhood treasures. Looking back on the time, Katharine says, "Not realizing, in our innocence, we held heaven within our grasp."

Katharine had an indoor playhouse too, made of a collapsible canvas screen reinforced with a wooden frame. It was painted green with holly-hocks growing around the swing screen door and little lattice window with its white Priscilla curtains. A much-used mail box hung next to the door. Inside were a table, two chairs, a thirty-inch brass doll bed, a tiny electric stove that made real biscuits - one at a time! By this time, her mother had decided that electricity was here to stay.

"Of all our toys the one I liked best was the original homemade doll house," Katharine recalls. "It consisted of orange crates set on end to make a two-story house. The rooms were papered (I use the word loosely) and had various sized genuine fake oriental rugs on the floors, obtained as premiums with packs of Fatima cigarettes. The beds were the bottoms of small candy boxes, slid into the lids which formed a bottom, back and canopy. The inhab-itants, small China dolls, had moving arms and legs, attached by a heavy wire that went through each doll at the shoulders and the hips. They cost a penny at the 5 and 10 cent store - the store with the fire engine red front."

Katharine and her companions played on the grass on the cool earth, in the shade of the sickle pear tree. Bees buzzed around the roses and hollyhocks; an occasional horse-drawn wagon rattled down Fourth Street. Periodically the noise of a street car rumbling up Fourth Street was heard as it passed, and faded away on its way to the switch near Ross Street. There it waited for the southbound car to pass. The sound of a street car occasionally led to putting two crossed straight pins on the street car tracks. The metal car wheels pressed them into a beautiful pair of doll scissors on the return trip. Often they could hear someone far away practicing the *Humoresque* or McDowell's *To a Wild Rose*, or pushing a lawn mower, or a man calling, "Strawberries for Sale" as he plodded along with his cart full of freshly picked sweet, home-grown strawberries. "Why, oh why, have they never tasted sweeter?" asks Katharine. Early in the morning fresh milk and cream would be delivered to their door. If it was really cold, the liquid would freeze and extend up over the rim of the glass bottle. Yocum's ice house provided homes with ice for their ice boxes.

Family Group 1915
Couple at left: William B. & Emelda (Junkin) Donaldson; Couple at right: Dohram J. & Mary (Donaldson) Sinclair;
Seated on swing: Harry F. Grant, Frank D. Sinclair, Marie (Sinclair) Grant holding son, Dohram S. Grant, Henry H.
Henderson, Florence (Donaldson) Henderson holding daughter, Harriet Henderson, Garrett B. LeVan, Wilma
(Sinclair) LeVan; Front row: Dohram J. Sinclair, II, Catherine E. Henderson, Katharine E. Sinclair, Garrett B. LeVan, Jr.

Katharine related, "When I was young I learned a poem which guided me all my life.

> Be gentle and loving
> Be kind and polite
> Be thoughtful of others
> Be sure to do right.

Growing up meant hearing and learning old nursery rhymes, too, such as *Little Miss Muffet, Jack & Jill, Twinkle, Twinkle Little Star and Hickory, Dickory, Doc.* Life was calm, happy and peaceful."

Locust Grove

For three consecutive years Katharine's father leased a locust grove and the parsonage of the Two Ridge Church for the summer. It was about seven miles from Steubenville and away from running water and electricity as well as the heat. Each year carpenters built wooden floors, and large canvas houses were placed on them. These houses had doors and windows, or openings, and were quite comfortable. With four or five portable houses, a cooking tent, lawn furniture, etc., the Le Vans, Donaldsons, Hendersons, Grants, and Sinclairs would enjoy the summer. It was a natural spot to view a sunset. All the farmers thought Dohrman J. Sinclair was crazy to set up portable houses in a locust grove because of electrical storms, but none of the trees ever fell on them. For a four-year-old it was great fun to have lots of open space to play. There was a well which had to be pumped, but most of the drinking water came from a spring under the roots of a big oak tree.

"On Saturday evening we would drive back to town to go to church and Sunday School on Sunday morning at the Second Presbyterian Church, the current site of the old Fort Steuben Hotel. I remember the church as gloomy and forbidding, but we sang 'Jesus loves me, this I know' with off-pitch vigor and put little Japanese pellets in a glass of water and watched them unfold into beautiful flowers," recalls Katharine.

Every Sunday morning on the way to church Katharine remembers passing two maiden ladies on their front porches rocking smugly in their rocking chairs. They had gone to early Mass, all their sins had been forgiven, and they could start off a new week with a clear conscience. "We usually drove back to the parsonage on Sunday afternoon. If Charlie, our chauffeur, could get a good run for the Market Street hill, we'd often get as far as the watering trough in high gear. There was a level "thank you mam" bump there, where horses could stop and rest. The area between the top of the hill and Brady Lane was called Jacksonville, and the road beyond had few houses. We would pass Spahns, Hukill School, the imposing five-winged County Home, the blacksmith shop on the right side of the road, and a handful of homes in Wintersville on our way."

Picnics

The Sinclair family had frequent picnics. Katharine liked the ones up Wills Creek in Alikanna best because she was able to ford the creek several times. The seats would be taken out of the cars and put on the ground for the adults. The children waded in the rocky creek, which was a tributary of the Ohio River, or picked wild flowers until the sumptuous lunch was served. A big red cotton cloth was spread on the ground, with a large stone holding it down at each corner. There usually was fried chicken, hard boiled eggs pickled in red beet juice, potato salad with home-made mayonnaise, baked beans, jelly sandwiches, a big cake, fruit, a thermos jug of lemonade and a big juicy watermelon cooled in the creek. It was always a wonderful day.

The Circus

One of the big treats for growing Katharine, called "Kath" by her brother Dohrman, was to go to the circus. The train would arrive at the station and unload. The next day there would be a parade up to Brady Estates where cows meandered around the area and puddles of water stood. No one seemed to work on Circus Day. Long before (and long afterwards) gaily colored signs, announcing the date, were plastered everywhere. When the big day arrived, people put more chairs on their porches and lawns to sit and wait for the big colorful parade and to drink home-made lemonade. Finally, the parade came right down Fourth Street with its noisy band, the wild animals caged and the tame ones walking on their own, the performers in gay and shining costumes, bunches of multi-colored balloons, the clowns, and the shrill calliope. Most of the town's children trailed along beside the elephants, horse-drawn carriages and per-formers. The parade would go up Market Street and set up the big tent.

The circus had its side show featuring the perennial fat lady, the tat-tooed man and the bearded woman. There was the hot, smelly animal tent; the exciting Wild West Show, which followed the main show and for which you had to pay extra; the cold hot dogs, the dripping ice cream cones, and the watery pink lemonade; the smell of sawdust, animals, and people who never heard of a cure for body odor! All these sights, noises and smells, clothed in excitement, are unforgettable to Katharine.

Entertainment

Garrett Hall was the name of an amusement center for many years. It was located across from the Jefferson County Courthouse and hosted many vaudeville and stage shows. Since West Virginia did not have such enter-tainment on Sundays, people would often cross the Ohio River to attend a performance. Then movies began in the teens and took over the amusement area. Katharine enjoyed moving pictures at Steubenville's theaters, including the small Olympic next to the court house, which could really pack them in, the Strand, and the Rex. The youngsters were lucky if a kind lady would sit with a group and read the captions of those early black and white movies. Fred Sloop was at the piano at the Olympic and the Strand for many films and was always appropriately playing to the action. Katharine relates, "Our eyes were glued to the screen as the American Indians on horseback raced across the wilds of North Dakota. The soft romantic music in the love scenes was not nearly as thrilling. There were the hilarious antics of Charlie Chaplin, the love life and adventures of Mary Pickford, the heart throb Rudolf Valentino playing love scenes, and many others. We always saw newsreels on the current happenings and a serial. The one most remembered was *The Perils of Pauline*. The heroine was tied to the railroad tracks and the train was fast approaching when the screen flashed the devastating news 'Continued next week!'" says Katharine. In 1915 movies were ten cents for the matinee and fifteen cents in the evening. Later she went to the Capitol, the Paramount, and the Grand on S. Fourth Street, which were built about 1925. There were movie stars like Lionel

We are going to have a party!
Will you come?
Our welcome will be hearty;
Will you come?
Just coax Mamma to bring you;
Some pretty songs we'll sing you,
Close to our hearts we'll swing you;
Say you'll come!

CRADLE ROLL RECEPTION
Saturday Afternoon *June 14* 19 *13*
from *three* to *five* o'clock at *Parlor*
of Westminster Presbyterian
Church.
        Emelda B. Donaldson
                Supt.

You will see some other babies
When you come;
So now no "ifs" or "Maybes"
You must come!
We're longing to caress you,
To our loving hearts will press you
And we'll ask the Lord to bless you.
'Course you'll come!

Barrymore, Clark Gable, who was from nearby Hopedale, Spencer Tracy, Bing Crosby, Bob Hope, Helen Hayes, Katharine Hepburn, Claudette Colbert, Bette Davis, and Vivien Leigh. Fiest's ice cream parlor was the place to go after movies for a banana split with scoops of ice cream with chocolate and caramel sauces, then nuts topped off with whipped cream and a cherry, all for just a quarter.

Childhood Friends

Katharine played with three friends from her very early years, all of whom attended the Cradle Roll Reception in the parlor of the Westminster Presbyterian Church on Saturday afternoon June 14, 1913. Katharine's grandmother, Emelda B. Donaldson, was the superintendent of the Cradle Roll then and held the job for fifty years. As Eleanor Giles, Mary Peterson Chalfant, Virginia Pearce Glick, and Katharine approached 90 years of age, they still kept in touch.

Virginia Pearce lived on Logan Street in a house where the parents of Woodrow Wilson had lived. It was a large house with three bedrooms and a large yard. Eleanor Giles lived her life in the 400 block of N. Fifth Street, first in a home two doors from Martha Manor and now at Martha Manor. Eleanor's father died on Christmas when she was very young. Mary Peterson lived on the north side of Market Street between Sixth & Seventh Streets next to McEldowney.

"Little girls among the crayon set in the second decade of the 20th century wore panty-waists, a harness-like affair made of white twill and muslin onto which panties, with elastic at the knees, were buttoned," said Katharine. "The panty-waist had long white supporters (never called garters) that extended from the waistband and held up long black or white cotton stockings. During the cold winter mornings, huddled close to the fire, we pulled on long-legged and long-sleeved union suits. The cuffs were folded over at the wrists, and at the ankles so the stockings would fit smoothly and the high black shoes could be buttoned. The wool content was unknown, but after each washing they were smaller and stiffer and harder to pull on, and very scratchy! Petticoats, never slips, were of outing flannel and often had *feather stitching* along the top of the hem line. Little ladies were asked to kneel and the correct dress length was marked where the dress touched the floor. Dresses, of wool or gingham, were *S.S. & G.* (Sweet, Simple, and Girlish), and often covered with a practical pinafore with ample pockets. The dresses were frequently smocked by hand across the upper front. This completed the high fashion for the crayon set. Little ladies wore black patent leather shoes with one strap that buttoned on the side. They were called *Mary Janes*. Later the girls wore black dresses with two inch lace collars around their neck. They were the forerunners of the turtle neck shirts." Katharine wore her hair in long curls which her mother would brush into shape. Eleanor Giles wore braids and her mother wound them around her head.

School

"During my early years," relates Katharine, "home, church, and school fitted together neatly. It was a way of life, as natural as breathing, to everyone in town, or at least I thought it was. We were surrounded by the fragrance of happy thoughts and sayings such as *There never was heard a discouraging word*, and *The thing that cost the least and means the most*. My learning was fun and I remember my father teaching me to count using the needles from the Christmas tree." Katharine attended the old Stanton Grade School at Fourth and Dock Streets. The school was located on the grounds of the present Steubenville High School and was across Dock Street from the home of Katharine's grandparents, the Donaldsons. She well remembers Stanton School, which had a playground of bricks. "Our gym equipment consisted of marbles, a volley ball net and ball, jump ropes, jacks and balls. The school pump was near the corner of the building, and a wide walk led to it from the corner. The walk had low, rounded cement curbing on either side which was supposed to protect the adjacent iris beds, and I think it did."

"My first grade teacher was Miss Holliday and my second grade teacher was Gracia Spencer. Our extra-curricular activities back in our early school years consisted of an art course once a week by Miss Shellart, who I later met quite by chance in the Louvre on a trip to Paris, and music once a week from Mrs. Munslow. It was a full, contented and happy time. I'm sure it never occurred to us that school life ever could or would, hold anything more, or that it could be more fun. When we were asked questions we were expected to answer yes or no. There was no uncertainty."

"One day after school a group of us fourth graders was walking home and one shy little boy pressed something into my hand and said, 'Get something nice for yourself.' It was a dime, his week's allowance, if he had an allowance. He melted away and I don't even remember his name - but thank you, wherever you are. The little things make a difference. Acts of kindness help so much. When people did unkind acts, my mother always said, 'They don't know any better.'"

Flying
In the teens, when flying was new, there was a rumor that an airplane actually was going to fly over Steubenville, at 2 o'clock one afternoon. The children brought excuses from their parents asking that they be excused to see the plane. Three times the rumor started and three times they were excused. When it finally came, teachers and students all poured out to see this new marvel. Later a plane actually landed in Steubenville. Mr. Swan, the pilot, crash landed on the golf course of the Riverview Country Club, near Pottery Addition. He hit a bunker and turned over the plane. Luckily he was not injured. However, he waited a few days for parts, and during that time Frank Sinclair gave a party one night for the stranded pioneer pilot. If he'd been the first man on the moon, he couldn't have been more of a hero in anyone's eyes.

Automobiles
When automobiles started to replace horses and buggies, they were always black because that was the fastest drying paint. Katharine vaguely remembers their electric first car. The car was an enclosed two-seater, and it was steered with a black horizontal rod. The car glided noiselessly along N. Fourth Street and was the only car Katharine's mother ever drove. The garage, for the electric car, was a two-story barn-like building with the horse stalls intact on the south side. The *stairway* was a ladder attached to the wall with an opening in the floor of the second story. One day Katharine's nurse, Nana, attempted to park the car in the garage. She stepped on the wrong pedal and the silent electric car crashed out the back of the stable!

The Sinclair family car was a seven-passenger Peerless, with brass trimmings. It boasted front and back seats, plus two folding seats in the back. When not in use the small seats folded against the sides of the car between the back seat and the doors. Katharine remembers, "Mother and Father could walk into the car standing up, almost. I will say this for the Peerless, it was built for human beings, not cave dwellers as seems to be the doctrine out of Detroit these days. It had a large running board, a generous number of shining brass lamps, and a temperamental crank. In inclement weather, six men could put the top up fairly easily on twenty-minutes notice. The top was anchored to either side of the engine hood by two stout leather straps, then the isinglass side curtains were snapped into place, and we were dry except for a dozen or so leaks from unsuspected sources. If we didn't get home before dark, we'd have to get out and light the carbide gas head lamps. The gasoline was kept in large metal drums in the garage."

The family was not always lucky to have one of these new motor cars. Late one October afternoon in 1912, word came to one of the family members that Dohrman Sinclair had been in an automobile accident. He was being driven up Washington Street to the Pennsylvania Railway Station to catch a train for Pittsburgh. The chauffeur of a white Packard car, believing himself late in meeting his employer at the train, roared out of Fifth Street much too fast and banged into the car in which D.J. Sinclair was a passenger. Sinclair was thrown out and his right shoulder took the full impact as he crashed into the curbstone. He was taken to the hospital in the Lacy Hotel, where he became patient number 41. There was no x-ray in Steubenville at the time to check for broken bones. At the hospital a massive doctor, believing the shoulder was just dislocated, had him lie down on the floor, and with his foot in the patient's armpit, pulled as hard as he could to put the shoulder back in place. Dohrman's whole torso soon turned black as coal.

While D.J. Sinclair lingered between life and death, he wrote the following letter October 25, 1912, to

> *My dear little Kath,*
>
> *Your Papa may be going away dear one. My Papa left me when I was four years and one half old, you are not quite so old. I can just remember my Papa. I hope, if I should leave, My dear little Kath will remember her Papa for I loved you so much my dear. Be kind, honest, truthful and good. When you grow up do not speak harshly or unkindly. I would like, if you love the hills and country as I do, to have you take a course in agriculture. Obey your Mama and your brothers and sisters, they will guide you right. Love God and mankind. May God bless you and keep you. Good night dear one. Papa*

Katharine kept this note in her lockbox and had a copy at her home. "Through this note to me, another intimate facet of my father's great life shows in his words and thoughts," says Katharine.

Dohrman's right shoulder was completely shattered and the smashed bones had been driven deep into his side, due largely to the terrific pressure of the doctor's foot. Dr. John M.T. Finney, chief surgeon of John Hopkins Clinical Dispensary, Baltimore, Maryland and Dr. George L. Hays, Pittsburgh, Pennsylvania arrived by train to perform a "complete complicated surgical operation on the comminuted fracture of the neck of the humerus with dislocated head," according to a Lacy Hotel Hospital report. At the time it was a very unique operation consisting of making an incision through the fibers of the deltoid muscle of the right shoulder, removing the head of the bone and the fragments, and trimming up the shaft of the humerus. Since the patient's condition was critical by this time, great care was taken not to injure the artery or the muscularspinal nerve.

When he was released from the hospital Dohrman, believing that his handicap could be overcome, had a small gym built in his office. With time and constant exercising he was able to strengthen his arm muscles to such an extent that the missing ball and the bone of his upper arm was almost unnoticeable. At work one day a bank employee came to Dohrman saying that a competitor had stated that he was angry enough to give Sinclair a beating. Sinclair's response was to show the employee that he could still throw a punch. He told the employee he was going to see the competitor to settle the matter and instructed him to call the Sheriff's office if he had not returned by 10 a.m. Just before 10, Dohrman called the bank to say he was fine. The two competitors were laughing after having ironed out the difficulties.

Sometimes the family was luckier with cars. One day Katharine was in the car with her brother Frank when they had car trouble. They called their cousin, Frank Dohrman, and asked him to come to tow them, which he did. Cousin Frank got to the Market Street train crossing pulling the car with Katharine and her brother and breezed across the railroad tracks. A train was coming. Luckily the rope broke and the train went between the two cars.

Katharine's Father

Dohrman found time to take his young daughter with him. "Once my father took me to the McCauslen-Huscroft Farm where McCauslen Manor is now located," recalled Katharine. "The McCauslens had twin daughters, Mary and Martha. While 'our fathers talked business' I was happily led around with a twin on each side. I felt I had arrived!" In 1997 Katharine and

Martha McCauslen Hunt Burgham were driven to a luncheon by the author when she heard this story. Katharine also related how she had gone to the twin's weddings early, so she could get a really good seat at the church, which was flooded with flowers. Martha was in an automobile accident a few days before the wedding and had a cut on her forehead.

Another time Katharine and her family went with Dohrman, who was a great advocate of river transportation, down to the dedication of the Steubenville River Lock. The family watched the formal presentation on a river steamer.

To Dohrman J. Sinclair, people were important. When the flood of 1913 came he loaned trucks and equipment to Wellsburg citizens, so they could dig themselves out of the mire. When there was a run on a county bank and the officials feared they would have to close the doors of the bank, Sinclair came to the rescue. He took a pile of money from his bank and drove up to the failing bank in a car. Together he and the bank officers stuffed the bank windows full of bills. It calmed the depositors' fears and saved the bank. He built a sidewalk to an Empire school when he saw the school children walking in the mud. He bought the hillside in West Virginia to guarantee people in Steubenville a pleasing view. He paid gas bills of those who could not afford to pay and provided turkeys to needy families at Thanksgiving and Christmas.

"My father," Katharine relates, "was always thinking of others and trying to be helpful. One evening he came home and mother was sitting on the swing on the front porch. The doctor's horse and buggy were parked across the street. Margaret Cook was in labor with her first child. Father immediately went over. The only medication for any pain at that time was aspirin! Shortly he hurried back and asked my mother if we had any whiskey in the house. A half-filled bottle was found in the back shelf of an upstairs closet. As he was about to hurry across the street my mother asked how Margaret was doing. Father replied, 'This isn't for Margaret. This is for Homer.' "

Father Powers

Father Powers was a great friend of Katharine's father, and she remembers many talks they had as the swing squeaked back and forth in the pergola in their back yard at 523 N. Fourth Street. Katharine guesses it was an early Ecumenical Movement in practice. Decades after D.J. Sinclair's death, one of the priests at the Roman Catholic church told Katharine that when he was a young man he served with Father Powers. One day her father had stopped to see Father Powers. When he left, the then young priest had gone to Father Powers' office very apologetic, saying he had turned away the first two *bums* but the third one refused to take "no" for an answer and had walked into the office past him. D.J. Sinclair had been there to discuss how to help someone who was having trouble.

In the January 30, 1993, *Herald-Star's Through the Century 100 Years Ago* listing, the following appears: "The shoot of the month took place this afternoon at the Steubenville Rifle Club's range on Upper Franklin Avenue. Some good records have been made during the month and several novices developed into experts including Father Powers who received the Rash Dohrman medal, he having made the best record for January." Rash (Horatio Garrett Dohrman) was a Commander in the Navy and was said to have been a national authority on gun powder. Both he and his son Frank Sinclair Dohrman served in World War I. Father Powers was the head priest of St. Peter's Roman Catholic Church at Fourth and Logan Streets from 1904-1939.

John Matheus

John Matheus, the Sinclair's houseman, was always a great help to the Sinclair family. Dohrman hired him to work at the bank which he served well for 50 years. He was a fine, honest responsible black person who occupied a very important place in the Sinclair family. The son of a slave, Matheus had a wife, Mary, six sons, and one daughter. The eldest son, Fred, who was very smart, had a college education, specializing in languages, and taught for many years at Booker T. Washington University. He represented the United States on important diplomatic missions to many of the African countries. This educated son, when he was home, would come to visit and sit in the living room with Katharine's mother, a rather unusual thing to have happen at this time.

Three Shots

John Matheus was present when Katharine's father was working one Saturday morning at the bank. He heard three shots ring out and rushed in to find Dohrman Sinclair had been shot by Charles Gilmore, who then committed suicide. In Wilma Sinclair's book *Father and His Town,* Wilma relates,

> One morning, about seven-thirty, when my husband and I were dressing, the phone rang in our bedroom, and a voice shouted "Your father has been shot. Come at once to the Bank." My husband and little son Garrett and I were living next door to the family home. We rushed outside, met my mother and brother Frank, and piled into somebody's car which took us down to the corner of Third and Market

Streets. We got there just in time to see them bringing Father down the steps of the Bank building on a stretcher. As they were placing the stretcher into a waiting ambulance, Father said to the little group of horrified and shocked townsmen huddled on the sidewalk, "Well, boys, he got me."

Father had a private office on the third floor of the Bank building, to which he retreated at times to work in quiet and escape the crowds of people always waiting in the Bank to see him. This tragic morning Father had gotten up as usual about six-thirty and had gone to this third-floor office to work. About an hour later, Charlie Gilmore appeared in the room and demanded $20,000. He scribbled the amount, $20,000, on a piece of scratch paper, and as he tossed it across the flattop desk toward Father, he pulled a revolver and shot Father twice through the abdomen. Father rose from his chair and tried to grapple with the insane man, but with his crippled right arm, and the awkward position of the desk which was between them, he could do little. Charlie Gilmore then turned the gun upon himself and died instantly. It was a horrible thing, but for the sake of Charlie Gilmore, who was simple minded, his family and all concerned, it was just as well he committed suicide. Feeling ran very high in the town that day, and with Charlie Gilmore alive, it is quite possible that there might have been a lynching north of the Mason and Dixon Line.

D.J. Sinclair was taken to the old Lacy Hotel, which Sinclair had given to the Ohio Valley Hospital rent free while the new hospital was being constructed on the hill west of the City. The hotel-hospital was at the foot of High and Market Streets. On several occasions Sinclair had sent for Dr. George L. Hays of Pittsburgh to come to Steubenville to operate on some worthy but poor soul who could not afford to pay the cost of expert surgery. Someone telephoned to him in Pittsburgh, and he was rushed to Steubenville by the Pennsylvania Railroad in a special car. He operated at once and stayed through that night, leaving for Pittsburgh the following afternoon. When D.J. asked the doctor what his chances were the doctor replied, "50-50." "Well," said Dohrman, "then I'll make it." During the twenty-four hours the doctor was in Steubenville, several local doctors brought their patients to the hospital, and Dr. Hays operated upon them, while watching over his friend, Dohrman Sinclair.

The family went through many days of anguish. The town was shocked, and prayers were said in Catholic and Protestant churches alike throughout the city. Finally his powerful physique and sound body asserted itself, and slowly Sinclair recovered.

Later, a letter addressed to D.J. Sinclair from Dr. Hays in Pittsburgh arrived. Mrs. Sinclair opened it and found a bill for $15,000! She could scarcely believe her eyes. Dohrman was still too weak and ill to be told of this exorbitant and startling amount. She returned the statement to Dr. Hays with a note, saying she had not told Dohrman of its receipt, as she felt sure Dr. Hays' secretary had made a mistake in typing. In due course, Dr. Hays replied that there was no mistake, that $15,000 was the amount owed.

In a couple of months Dohrman made an appointment with Dr. Hays in his office in Pittsburgh. When he arrived at the office there was another man present with Dr. Hays. D.J. Sinclair inquired what his business was, and when told that he was an attorney, said, "Very well. I will go back home, and come again and bring my own lawyer." A few days later he returned with his very dear friend and outstanding attorney, Mr. Addison C. Lewis. Dr. Hays' attorney was also present.

Sinclair said he felt the bill was grossly excessive. Dr. Hays replied that he had saved his life, and that people like him who had money were called upon to pay for doctors' services for poor people who were unable to pay anything. Sinclair said he had paid Dr. Hays many, many times for poor people, and still wanted to do his part, but he did not propose to pay the bills of all the poor of Allegheny County, Pennsylvania. He informed Dr. Hays he had a certified check for $5,000 with him, which Dr. Hays "could accept and give a receipt in full, or he could go to court and sue and be dammed." Dr. Hays accepted the check for $5,000. The amount of $15,000 then was about the equivalent of $248,000 today. Word of the exorbitant charge and settlement spread like wildfire, and never again did anyone in Steubenville dare run the risk of seeking Dr. Hays' service.

Everything was lovely after Katharine's father recovered. Life was perfect, Katharine thought, and it would go on this way forever. She had just turned seven and had had a wonderful birthday party. "Our parties were like icing on an already good cake. We had peanut hunts, with the children finding the silver and the gold peanuts getting a special prize. We pinned the tail on the donkey; we had three-legged races; we played ring-a-round-a-rosy, blind man's bluff, London Bridge is falling down, and drop the handkerchief. Life was wonderful."

Train Trouble

Two weeks after her birthday young Katharine was playing at Katharine Wickersham's home in the 500 block of N. Fifth Street. It was shortly after

6:30 when her father passed the office of the La Belle mill, where he joked with a couple of officers and then set out with a blue print to look over the site of a proposed bi-product coke oven for the mill.

"Then suddenly my world came apart at the seams," recalls Katharine. "In the early evening of August 6, 1915, my father was hit by a train and killed. He loved his town and its people. He had sparked the building of the Market Street bridge so that workmen could cross the river to both Weirton and Follansbee, both of which he brought to Steubenville. The only means of crossing the river until then was by ferry boat or the railroad bridge. The trolley lines, the many jobs he provided, the Ohio Valley Hospital, the Water Works and the Filtration Plant so Steubenville would have good drinking water when typhoid was prevalent, were all part of his dreams which became reality. He had built Steubenville's first sky-scraper, the Sinclair Building, which was ten stories high and towered above all other buildings in his town. It was the largest building between Pittsburgh and Cincinnati and was due to open the next day. He towered above his fellow men in outlook but always was part of the team. There were many who swore he was the best friend they ever had. He loved and helped his fellow men," relates Katharine.

Dohrman J. Sinclair died when he was just 55 years old. It was Friday. He went to work at the Union Savings Bank the day he died. The new bank building at Fourth and Market Street was completed, and the money was to be moved the next day. A gala opening was to be held. That day D.J. had talked with the editor of the newspaper in town for about half an hour. As an active member of the Steubenville community and the one who had bought the land for the LaBelle Iron Works, he was knowledgeable about the area of land where the LaBelle steel mill was located. That afternoon he was asked by the president of LaBelle Iron Works to help find the water springs located there but covered for years.

As the story was told by the men who watched, Train Number 399 heading south was a little behind schedule, and as it gained speed in order to make up the time, it passed through the mesh of sidings and switches in the LaBelle Iron Works yards. Dohrman Sinclair was standing among the tracks pouring over the blue print in his hands. When the engineer spotted him he sounded the whistle. A startled Dohrman looked up and tried to step aside. Whether he had pain from the bullets in his abdomen catch him off guard or whether he was unable to respond to such an unexpected situation because he was still absorbed in looking for the spring, no one will ever know. Instead he was hit and his body was flung through the air. He was still alive when he was lifted to the train but died before the ambulance arrived. Katharine's nana came and took her home from her friend's party. Life was never quite the same for her after that.

Dohrman J. Sinclair

Front pages of papers covered Sinclair's death in many columns. His biography appeared as his obituary among the accolades:

Dohrman J. Sinclair, one of the leading citizens of Steubenville, Ohio, who is cashier of the Union Deposit Bank and is identified with other institutions and enterprises in this section. He was born at Erie, Pennsylvania in 1860, and was the son of Thomas and Kate Dohrman Sinclair. The latter a member of an old and prominent Steubenville family. Coming to Steubenville when five years old, he was educated in the schools of this city. In 1873 he entered the Union Deposit Bank

in a subordinate capacity and has been continuously connected with this large financial institution ever since. He has been a most active and public spirited citizen and it is largely due to his untiring efforts that much of the material prosperity of Steubenville and vicinity is due. In advancing the interests of the community, he has been unsparing of his time, labor and means. Never an office seeker, he has been a force in local politics, which has always been exerted for the public good. As President of the City Council he instituted important reforms in municipal management, and as a member of the Board of

Water Works trustees, he inaugurated and carried out the present magnificent water system, conceded to be the best in the Ohio Valley. Practically he was a Board of Trade for a number of years, and it was chiefly due to his untiring efforts that the enlarged La Belle Iron Works were located here; also the Pope Tin Plate Works and the Follansbee and Weirton works, across the river, which, with the Jefferson Glass Works, have built up two thriving manufacturing suburbs with access to the city by the fine suspension bridge, also erected through his efforts. The electric line to Follansbee, with another projected to Weirton is also among the fruits of his efforts, as are the extensions to Toronto and a short line to Mingo, to say nothing of the magnificent brick boulevards from the city north and south on both sides of the river. He has been one of the most active members of the Ohio River Improvement Commission which is now making steady progress toward the canalizing of the river, and rendered material aid in the construction of the Wabash Railroad through Jefferson County, including the projected extension up the river from Steubenville. In most of the enterprises we have mentioned, he is a member of the Board of Directors, where his work and counsel are always sought. In fact, the mere enumeration of his numerous enterprises, of which the above are only a portion, would fill a volume.

In 1884, Mr. Sinclair was married to Miss Mary Donaldson, a daughter of William B. and Emelda Junkins Donaldson, and they have five children: Marie, wife of Harry F. Grant, of Franklin, Pennsylvania; Wilma, who is the wife of Garry B. LeVan, of Steubenville; Frank D., who is associated with his father; Dohrman J., Jr., and Katharine at home. H.G. Dohrman of this city is also a half brother.

Mr. Sinclair was a member of the Chamber of Commerce and the Board of Trustees of the Union Cemetery Association. Mr. Sinclair's business interests reached out for many miles from Steubenville. While in some instances he was not connected with the firms in recent years his associations and activities marked their advancement in the business world. He was President of the Union Clay Company, Empire, and in recent years had been connected with the LaBelle Iron Works, The Follansbee Brothers Company, The Jefferson Glass Company, The Pope Tin Plate Company, Tri-State Railway Company, Steubenville; Wellsburg and Weirton Railway Company,

Steubenville Bridge Company, Columbia Fire Brick Company, Canton; Stratton Fire Clay Company, Myers Fire Clay Company, and many other concerns of lesser importance. Mr. Sinclair was a member of the Congregational church and was a convert during the Billy Sunday meetings in 1913. He was a trustee of the Congregational, Finley Methodist Episcopal, St. John's Lutheran and Simpson Methodist Episcopal churches, of Steubenville, as well as having association with a number of other congregations in this vicinity. He was a member of the Steubenville Elks, Knights of Pythias, the Duquesne Club of Pittsburgh; the Spruce Creek Rod and Gun Club of Pennsylvania; Fort Henry Club of Wheeling; Ohio Society of New York; Cheat River Rod and Gun Club of Virginia; President of the Cemetery Association; member Wintersville Grange; Vice President of the Ohio Valley Improvement Association; and Vice President National Rivers and Harbors Commission. He was recently appointed by Governor Willis to represent the Rivers and Harbors Commission in San Francisco on September 17 to 21.

Dohrman J. Sinclair

Dohrman J. Sinclair gave so much to his city. One of Sinclair's employees described Sinclair's labor by saying, "He tore into everything, enveloping the project entirely. Nor did he delegate a job which he could not master himself." Dohrman moved Steubenville toward progress, and, as he stepped to a higher level of achievement or greater wealth, he brought the people along with him.

Saturday and Sunday, throngs moved through the Sinclair home past the body of Dohrman James Sinclair. On Sunday evening 1200 visited the Sinclair home. Many were from out of town who were there to attend the funeral the following day. Thousands turned out for Dohrman Sinclair's funeral. All the businesses in town were closed on Monday, so that people from all walks of life could attend the funeral or stand outside the packed Westminster Presbyterian Church. The funeral procession passed the bank that would have been open that day except for the funeral taking place and made its way up Market Street to the Union Cemetery. People bowed their heads and mourned.

At Thanksgiving and Christmas, many became aware of the identity of the anonymous donor who for years had given food and gifts, for none came that winter of 1915. Dohrman Sinclair had been a benefactor of the poor and needy. At the time of his death, the front page of *The Steubenville Weekly Gazette* stated, "His purse was never closed to a deserving man, woman or child. He was a cheerful giver and enjoyed doing a charitable act, not for the publicity it gave him, for he did most of his kind deeds unknown to the general public, but for the real good it did for others."

Nearly 80 years later in July, 1993 a letter by John Kundrat of Mingo Junction ran in the Steubenville paper:

> *This is a continuation of the achievements of Dohrman Sinclair, the man who built a city.*
>
> *He understood the need for commerce. He must have known that retailing only generated wealth for the individual but that manufacturing a multitude of different products that could be sold all over the country generated wealth for the entire community and that it was from this wealth that a city and the surrounding communities are able to flourish. When the ability to do this no longer exists or the community resorts to retailing to create jobs it will fall into decay over an extended period of time.*
>
> *Dohrman Sinclair understood the vitality in the Anglo-Saxon concept of the economics of Adam Smith combined with the resourcefulness of the British merchant princes who traded*

goods all over the world.

Steubenville was basically a steel producing city but it also manufactured many other products. It was not solely dependent on steel as it is today.

A system of parks and recreation areas are the crowning achievement of anyone who builds a city. Dohrman Sinclair's life long dream was to encircle Steubenville with parks. In a small city one park should be highly visible in the central area.

He began purchasing land on the north, south, and west ends of the city and in West Virginia on what is now Highland Hills. He did not live to fulfill this part of his life's work.

Dohrman Sinclair built the first steel frame high-rise office building in Steubenville known as the Sinclair Bank Building. One day in August of 1915 he was on the north end of what is now the Wheeling-Pittsburgh plant in Steubenville studying blueprints for a new battery of coke ovens. He was standing in the middle of one of the several railway tracks down along the river when he looked up to see a fast approaching train. Believing that he was in the track of the approaching train he moved over to another track and became totally engrossed in the blueprint. Unknowingly he stepped into the track of the approaching train and he was struck down. His tragic death occurred on the day before the formal dedication and opening of the Sinclair Bank Building. An era abruptly came to an end.

On the afternoon of the day of his funeral all of the business houses in Steubenville were closed and the people of the city lined the streets for many blocks to honor this great and benevolent man.

Within five years after his death the make-up of the city changed and it was out of control. Had Dohrman Sinclair lived the corruption and lawlessness of the 1920's would never have happened in the city of Steubenville.

Dohrman Sinclair was not an industrialist. He was a banker, a philanthropist, a humanitarian. He was a man of foresight who made dreams come true. He was a giant among men. He was unable to move mountains but he did move hillsides. All of his aspirations were noble and in the best interests of all the people in the entire community, not just Steubenville.

He was on the board of directors of no less than 20 local corporations. He survived two near fatal bullets to the abdomen by a crazed robber who then turned the gun on him-

self. He was the victim of a terrible automobile accident that
left him crippled in his right shoulder and he was struck down
by a fast moving train. His life reads like a script for a movie.
How could I possibly pay him the tribute and respect he
deserves in a short letter to the Readers Forum?

William B. Donaldson

Mary Sinclair grieved over her husband's loss. However, she was soon to experience more misfortune. Mary's father and Katharine's grandfather, William B. Donaldson, died on June 1, 1916, less than a year after Dohrman. William was born in 1837 and in 1861 was appointed Superintendent of the Transportation Department at Washington, D.C. Later, during the Civil War, the Government placed him in Boston in the post of Inspector of Horses with the Transportation Division. At the close of the war, he was the third highest ranking officer in this service. After the war he was sent to New York City. He, his wife Emelda, and daughter Mary lived for a number of years at Times Square in the Flat Iron building, which was an apartment house. In 1879 he had founded and become president of the Steubenville Pottery, but he was new at the business and still learning when an economic depression came along. The business was struggling and D. J. Sinclair bought out his father-in-law. With the money Donaldson built the row of four colonial brick houses on South Street between N. Fourth and Fifth Streets in 1893. The homes contained nine rooms and were mentioned in the Steubenville Centennial Souvenir of 1897. He used them as rental property, and this gave him a good income. He also built two red brick houses on Dock Street, one of which served as his home.

Marie Sinclair Grant

After her father's death, Katharine occasionally went on the train with her mother to Franklin, Pennsylvania to visit her sister, Marie Sinclair Grant. Marie's son, Dohrman Grant, was six years younger than Katharine and had a three-wheel plaything called *Dandy Dan*. When she was visiting Franklin for a week, one time she tried out *Dandy Dan*. Riding too close to the trellis covered with roses, Katharine tumbled down into the flowers and spent weeks picking thorns out of her body.

The year following her grandfather's death Katharine's sister, Marie, died on March 11 leaving a three-year-old son. From Marie's obituary the following is quoted.

As a child she took great interest in the Home for the Aged
and was one of the band of seven little girls who worked to
raise a fund for the establishment of a Home in this city. She

was a member of the former Second Presbyterian church, and a member of the choir and had a sweet soprano voice. She was also the teacher of a boys class in the Sabbath school and is still held in kindly remembrance by these boys who are many of them now occupying honorable places in life, her influence making an impression for time and eternity. She was beautiful in person and of a kind loving disposition that shed its fragrance in the home, and throughout the circle of young friends who today mourn for a beloved member of their circle. She was also a member of the Query Club and an active member until her marriage and still an honorary member of the roll. She was married to Harry Fay Grant, a prominent young business man of Franklin, Pennsylvania on June 20, 1907, at her home in Steubenville and was a beautiful bride, around whose memory there are many hallowed associations. She made her home in Franklin, Pennsylvania and became a leader in church and social circles and her home was an ideal one of the beauty of Christian living and a Mecca for the family circle and friends, her true womanliness shining out in a hospitality that made her a charming hostess. She was a devoted wife and a daughter who was ever solicitous for the welfare of her parents, and a sister who was beloved and adored in the family circle. Of those loved ones she leaves to mourn her presence her husband and one small son, Dohrman Sinclair Grant, at the bereaved home; her mother, Mrs. D.J. Sinclair, and sisters, Mrs. G.B. LeVan and Katharine, and two brothers, Frank Sinclair, cashier of the Union Deposit Bank and Trust Co. and Master D.J. Sinclair, Jr., at home. Also her grandmother, Mrs. W.B. Donaldson and her aunt, Mrs. H. H. Henderson, of Steubenville, who have been summoned to the stricken home where her mortal remains will be laid to rest on Tuesday after. In the closing of this beautiful life it may be said that the funeral anthem is a glad evangel, for the good die not, and while God calls our loved ones, we lose them not, for they live on earth in thought and deed, leaving an impress on a true faith and devoted life that time can not efface.

Marie's husband felt the loss greatly. In fact his mother worried so much about her son, Harry Grant, that she arranged for him to marry the girl he had broken his engagement to when he met Marie at the Chickering's family home in Oil City. The arrangements were all made, and

Harry was on his way to California when he got cold feet and returned after reaching Chicago. Mary Burnam's brothers came and made him come, saying he was not going to stand up their sister twice. The marriage never worked, and it is said that Mary didn't even open her wedding gifts. When they returned to Franklin, Harry didn't even introduce Mary to the servants. He died three years after Marie did, and both of them are buried in the Franklin, Pennsylvania cemetery. Dohrman Sinclair Grant then went to live with his grandmother Grant at the age of 6. He was nine when she died. He then came to Steubenville and lived with his aunt Wilma and her husband Garrett LeVan. He was three years younger than Wilma's son Garrett who had been born in 1911. Dohrman Grant eventually graduated from the Hill School and the Wharton School of Finance at the University of Pennsylvania in Philadelphia.

Mary Donaldson Sinclair

Marie's death brought to an end the terrible nineteen-month period for the Sinclairs, during which Katharine had lost her father, grandfather, and sister, and her mother had lost her husband, father, and oldest daughter. After a period of recovery, Mrs. Sinclair again reached out to the community. She was the organizer and first regent of the Steubenville Chapter of the Daughters of the American Revolution. Mary was active in the Steubenville Woman's Club, which her mother had founded and was also a member of the Query Club. Katharine remembers her mother starting the YWCA which her cook called "the Woman's YMCA" and becoming its first president in 1913, serving until 1916. When Katharine was eight she was the Queen of the Maypole for the YWCA. The YWCA first opened on N. Fifth Street with a cafeteria and living quarters then later moved to 320 N. Fourth Street. One of the YWCA programs was a class teaching young girls how to sew. Each girl worked on a pillow case. Katharine proudly went up to show the teacher her finished product and the teacher said, "You have done a very good job, now you can stitch it and take the basting stitches out." Years later she was well know for her needle work.

The Great War

"The First World War wove a pattern into our lives, although aside from my brother, Frank, and some of his friends leaving for camp, it seemed a long ways off to me," states Katharine. "There were the War songs: *It's A Long Way To Tipperary, Over There, Pack Up Your Troubles In Your Old Kit Bag, and How You Gonna Keep'em Down On the Farm, After They've Seen Paree,* and the romantic ones: *Smiles, It's Three O'clock in the Morning, There's A Long Long Trail,* and *I'm Forever Blowing Bubbles.* During the war we used a far corner of our yard for our *victory garden* which every patriotic American family cultivated. Its total production would not have saved one starving Armenian!" recalls Katharine.

In every parade there were large American flags, held on all four sides by the marchers, onto which people threw change to "help end the war." "From school we sold War Saving Stamps for 25 cents each," states Katharine. "These were pasted on a card and when the card was full it was exchanged for a War Savings Bond. As a bonus for each completed card, or equivalent that we sold, we were given a large stamp with a United States President's picture on it. My last stamp was Andrew Jackson showing that I'd sold $500 worth of War Saving Stamps."

"My brother Frank served in the 332nd division during the war. He decided he wanted to learn to fly and went to Buffalo from where the following telegram arrived one day. 'Been lying around all day.' It was not until later the family learned the telegraph man could not believe he had meant flying and had substituted lying instead. Anyone who knew Frank would have known he had not been lying <u>all</u> day."

"On our street two fine young men, George, a civil engineering graduate of M.I.T., and his brother Kenyon Roper, who was a captain in the artillery, both lost their lives in plane crashes during the war. Kenyon had taught me to do hand springs over his back. These boys were the only children of the Ropers and Mrs. Roper died soon after, which was assuredly of a broken heart."

During World War I Katharine's mother was Chairman of the Ladies' Executive Committee of the Jefferson County War Board. As a member of the Mothers of Soldiers Club, Mary Sinclair's heartbreaking task was to write to each new Gold Star mother in Jefferson County who lost a son while in the service of his country. Mrs. Sinclair said that some very sad letters were received from the bereaved mothers in reply to the ones she wrote. She kept a record and 71 letters were sent out, plus some written after the war.

As part of the Red Cross effort, Katharine's mother was placed in charge of the yarn and knitting with Miss Rose and Miss Elizabeth Hill to assist, and Miss Emma Grimes was placed in charge of the sewing. Tuesdays were Red Cross Days. Jefferson County knitting and sewing headquarters was in the basement of Westminster Church. On their heads the ladies wore white squares that had a red cross front and center on their foreheads and was pinned in back. They knitted khaki-colored sweaters, mufflers, sox and helmets, white wash cloths, and multi-colored blankets to be sent overseas. Yarn was distributed and instructions given. "Women came and brought their lunches and spent the day, and a noisier place I can't remember!" relates Katharine. " I usually went down after school with other girls and we played hide and seek in the quieter upstairs." Mary Sinclair's records report that they "distributed thousands of dollars worth of yarn to the women of Steubenville and Jefferson County which was made up into sweaters, sox, scarfs, helmets and wristlets and sent to the soldier boys. About nine thousand pairs of sox, three thousand sweaters, eight-hundred twenty-six scarfs, four hundred helmets, and one thousand fifty-two pairs of wristlets in addition to knitted ambulance robes, wash cloths, bed sox, etc." were made. Mrs. Sinclair wrote to the Red Cross Headquarters in Cleveland and secured permission to outfit the Jefferson County boys as they started for camp. This was a great convenience and benefit for them as letters from boys overseas and in training stated that knitted garments were given to them, which in many cases did not fit. Katharine's grandmother Donaldson gave a Bible to every soldier who left Jefferson County. Katharine's sister, Wilma, was active in the Red Cross and organized the Jefferson County Canteen.

"We survived the flu epidemic of 1917-1918 and celebrated *Home Coming* in 1919 with a magnificent flourish," remembers Katharine. "A huge canvas covered Fifth Street from Washington Street to North Street. There were parades and dancing in the streets. Meals were served to all our hero soldiers, who resented the passage in 1919 of the Volsted Act when they were overseas and couldn't vote against a law which prohibited the sale, manufacture, and transportation of alcoholic beverages. The 18th Amendment took effect at the stroke of midnight, January 15, 1920. I remember lying on the floor reading the Republican *Herald-Star* and the Democratic *Gazette,* and wondering what they would find to print after the war was over, except the comics like Maggie and Jigs, Mutt and Jeff and the Katzenjammer Kids."

California

On November 10, 1919, Katharine's mother, brother Dohrman, Grand-mother Donaldson with a broken arm, Miss Agnes Wells and Katharine took off on the train for La Jolla, California. Miss Wells was the grand-daughter of Bazaleel Wells, the founder of Steubenville. Mary Sinclair had friends in La Jolla and had rented a house there before they left. The five of them spent that winter at 7626 Draper Avenue in a two-story house. Later, the house was moved across the street to make it possible to build tennis courts on the original spot. The playground and Community House were practically in the back yard of their house, and the Presbyterian Church was just a short way down the street. Katharine started at the grade school and then switched to the Bishop School, Dohrman went to San Diego High because there was no high school in La Jolla. When it rained, the unpaved roads could get very muddy.

One day Katharine was home when Miss Wells fixed waffles. As she was about to eat, Katharine realized the syrup was full of dead black ants. She wondered if she should be polite and eat what Miss Wells had fixed or push it away. She was polite. The group returned to Steubenville in June.

"Steubenville was a good town. People emphasized the positive and the good and when someone did something well he was told that it was a job well done. If something needed to be done, a man didn't pass the buck to someone else, or the government, he did what had to be done, whether it was watering trees in front of his store or building a water works for his town. Steubenville was the best home town in the whole wide world in the second decade, at least to one little girl, who was about to leave a little bit of heaven behind her, to become a teenager in *The Roaring Twenties*," stated Katharine.

❦

Katharine E. Sinclair

The 1920-1929 Era

The twenties in the United States began with prohibition, and American women winning the right to vote. Harding died in office and Coolidge was elected president in the following election. Hoover became president in 1928. New York was the largest city. Railroad shop-men and coal miners both ended strikes. Tennessee banned the teaching of evolution and the Scopes trial followed. Seven gangsters died in the St. Valentine's Day massacre. Southern Ireland became a free state and in 1922 Britain took over ruling Palestine. Hirohito became Emperor of Japan. King Tut's tomb was located in Egypt. Amelia Earhart flew the Atlantic.

Joyce's *Ulysses*, T.S. Elliot's *The Waste Land*, Fitzgerald's *The Great Gatsby*, *Hitler's Mein Kampf, and* Hemingway's *A Farewell to Arms* were published. Dancing till you dropped was the rage and the Charleston was the newest dance craze. Cosmetics, head decorations, fans, jewelry and silk stockings were popular and the flapper dress with barely discernible bosom and a drop waist was fashionable. Art deco gained popularity. Al Jolson starred in the first talkie, *The Jazz Singer*. *Wings* won the first Academy Award best picture. Flagpole-sitting was popular.

General Mills created Betty Crocker and eight million American women held jobs. Chrysler Motor Company was founded and America had one car for every six people in 1927. Black Thursday, October 24, 1929, witnessed the stock market crash.

Walter Hagen and Bobby Jones both won the British Open. Babe Ruth hit his record 60th home run. Bill Tilden won at Wimbledon, Gertrude Ederle swam the English channel and Johnny Weismuller set three freestyle swimming records.

III.

Maturing In The Roaring Twenties

Katharine began her teens at the beginning of the 1920's. It was a time of learning. Her education took her from the public schools of Steubenville, Ohio to finishing schools in the east and to Europe with her family. She developed friendships away from her home. Her love of athletics became strong as she participated in school sports and summer fun. The Depression hit her family very hard at the close of the decade.

Smoke Hole

Back from California in 1920, Katharine went with her sister Wilma and young nephew Garrett for a week's outing. Her aunt and uncle Florence and Harry Henderson with their children Catherine and Harriet and their maid Lizzy joined them in their trip to Smoke Hole. They were driven to Wheeling, West Virginia, where they caught the train to the nearest train station to Smoke Hole at Charleston. If they had taken the train from Steubenville to Wheeling, they would have changed trains at Holiday's Cove, which is now Weirton. From Charleston they went by horse to their destination. Wilma's husband along with some other men from the mill had bought a house at Smoke Hole and this group was going to enjoy it. The house had no inside plumbing, faced a stream and was very plain. Food was kept cold in the turbulent stream since there was no refrigeration. At a nearby farm there were four hogs which soon discovered everything being kept in the water and, of course, ate it all. The group also had to deal with an unbalanced neighbor across the stream who would later shoot his wife.

The entertainment was very plain. The children had a wonderful time one evening roasting marshmallows over an outdoor fire. Another night there was a lot of commotion and Wilma found a snake crawling across the floor. Finding a broom, she managed to kill it. She carried it outside and threw it in the yard. Later the snake's partner came to rescue it.

Harry Henderson's arthritis worsened while they were at Smoke Hole and he spent most of his time in a rocking chair. On their return trip he was too crippled to ride a horse, so the only wagon around was brought for him. Harry sat atop it, rocking in the chair. The rest of the group were on horses as they started back to civilization over the hills in this strange procession. There were no real roads. On the hills, the cart had to be held up on the lower end by a couple of men so Harry wouldn't roll off the wagon. Just before they reached the farm house where they would leave the horses, the horse which Katharine was riding was stung by a bee. He bolted, throwing his young passenger over his head to the ground, then stepping on her head. The damage was a very bloody head, a broken nose, a black eye and an arm that needed bandages. She was taken to the doctor, who gave her the needed attention. That night the group stayed in town at a hotel near the train station.

Wilma, young Garrett and Katharine stayed in one bedroom. All were on the second floor with a porch around the outside which connected to all the rooms. Since there was only one bathroom and everyone had to go past their bedroom to get there, the night started with a steady stream of people silhouetted against their curtains. As the night progressed, Katharine found she was getting eaten alive by bed bugs besides all her other aches. When Wilma turned the lights on the bed bugs scattered and there was blood everywhere. For some reason the bed bugs did not bother either Wilma or Garrett. Wilma left the light on in the room and took Katharine to another room. Wilma then decided to sleep in the room with Florence. Garrett had a start when he awoke with the light on, no mother or aunt and blood on the sheets. The next morning the conductor was very reluctant to let this motley group board the train because he was sure they did not have enough money to ride the train. Harry had to be lifted, rocking chair and all, on to the train. In Wheeling they were met by Frank Sinclair and Garry LeVan and driven home in two cars. Katharine went with her brother Frank, who managed to get lost on the way home. When she finally got home the doctor bandaged her up again. In time she healed, but for the rest of her life she always had trouble breathing through one of her nostrils.

Election Nights

Presidential election nights were exciting. Wilma, who was active in the Republican party, would phone the election board and the newspaper to obtain results. Katharine remembered that the phone Wilma used was in the diningroom at their 525 N. Fourth Street home and that the guests always seemed very noisy. In Steubenville the returns were posted on the plate glass front of the *Herald-Star* newspaper located on the east side of the 100 block of N. Fourth Street next to the Ft. Steuben Hotel, today an apartment complex. The Herald Publishing Co. had been established in 1806 and was the pioneer paper in Ohio. In 1896 J. J. Gill purchased the *Herald*, having previously purchased the *Evening Star* March 1, 1896. On February 8, 1897 the papers were combined. The *Herald* offices were moved from Market Street to the *Star* office in the Odd Fellows' Block, on Fourth Street, according to the Steubenville Centennial Souvenir book. Crowds gathered and filled the sidewalk and half of the street when election returns began to be posted. The signs changed frequently. There was great excitement when the women finally got the right to vote August 26, 1920 after 81 years of trying. At that time there were no radios nor televisions.

Westminster Presbyterian Church

Church and Volunteer Help

In her early teens Katharine became a member of Westminster Presbyterian Church. The First and Second Presbyterian Churches merged in 1911 to become Westminster Presbyterian Church. The First Presbyterian Church was organized in 1800 and was originally located on the west side of S. Fourth Street in the 200 block. In 1872 the church moved to the present site of Westminster Church at 235 N. Fourth Street. The Second Presbyterian Church was founded in 1838 and was located where the Fort Steuben Hotel was built in 1920. Billy Sunday gave a stirring address at the laying of the corner stone of the new church on September 30, 1913. The sanctuary was built to hold 750. The dedication service for the completed church was held November 22, 1914. Everyone was well pleased except one man who said the edifice would be improved if they had five funerals right soon, and he knew whose they should be! The women of the church presented the beautiful German-made stained glass window on the east side at the entrance. Katharine usually attended the Wednesday evening prayer meetings. She taught Sunday school there for six years and remained a strong member of the church all her life.

About this time Katharine and her sister Wilma organized the Junior King's Daughters Circle, which was later called the Willing Workers. The members did volunteer work and helped the King's Daughters give lawn fetes for Martha Manor. Katharine remembered Mrs. Erskine, who lived a few houses away from the Sinclair home, giving them $15, which was their biggest donation. Katharine later became president of the Willing Workers Circle of the King's Daughters.

Wilma had learned to read palms, and at a lawn fete or church benefit, Wilma was usually the official fortune teller. Katharine did some reading on this subject, and it proved to be a very interesting asset. Often at parties or at social gatherings if things began to get dull, Katharine would volunteer to read palms. There was usually a waiting line of interested subjects. On one occasion at the Dartmouth Carnival she told one of the boys that according to his palm, he had died when he was five years old. He grinned and said that the doctor had pronounced him dead during a serious illness when he was five.

Emelda Junkin Donaldson

Family played an important part in Katharine's life. Her last remaining grandparent died at the age of 82. To capture some of Katharine's past, her grandmother, Emelda B. Junkin Donaldson's obituary, which appeared on the first page of the Steubenville *Herald-Star* March 7, 1922 follows:

> *Prominent Citizen is Summoned - Mrs. W. B. Donaldson dies today after brief illness - City Mourns Passing of Woman Who Devoted Life to Useful Service - Leader in Church, Clubs and Social Life of Community. Death early today claimed one of Steubenville's oldest and most highly*

esteemed citizens. Mrs. Emelda Junkin Donaldson, widow of the late William B. Donaldson, entering into rest at her residence, Fourth and Dock Streets, at 3 a.m. Tuesday March 7, 1922 following a brief illness.

She was in the 82nd year and her death brought to a close a long and useful life, one that was devoted to helpful, unselfish service in the religious, educational and patriotic work of the community. She was prominent in church, club and social circles of the city and actively associated with numerous societies and serviceable organizations until her last illness.

Mrs. Donaldson was taken ill about ten days ago but her condition was not regarded as serious until Saturday and she grew weaker daily and early this mourning slept peacefully away. Her death is attributed to a physical breakdown, incident to her advanced age.

Deceased was born in Steubenville on the nineteenth day November 1840, the daughter of Matthew Oliver and Rebecca Buchannan Junkin, pioneer resident of this section. She was a descendant of Revolutionary stock, being a real granddaughter of the American Revolution on both her father's and mother's side. She received her education at the Steubenville schools and with the exception of seven years resident in New York City after her marriage a life long resident here.

Christmas night of 1861 she was united in marriage with William. B. Donaldson, being one of the war brides of that period. The ceremony was performed in the Old United Presbyterian church at Fifth and North Streets. The marriage shortly proceeded the entrance of her husband into military service with the Union forces and befitting the wife of a soldier, she became actively engaged with the Soldiers' Aid Society which performed a noble service during the conflict and which was later merged with the Women's Relief Corps, the local organization of which she was a driving spirit and one of the charter members.

Having united early in life with the United Presbyterian Church, Mrs. Donaldson became associated with religious activities and throughout her life devoted herself faithfully to the advancement of Christ's Kingdom. She later united with the old Second Presbyterian church, now the

Westminster and at the time of her death she was a Deaconess; superintendent of the Sunday School Cradle Roll in which capacity she had served for many years and also honorary treasurer of the Home and Foreign Missionary societies, she had been treasurer for a period of thirty five years. She was familiar in all branches of church work and her influence and guidance in these circles will be sadly missed.

She was a member of the Daughters of the American Revolution and Chaplain of the Steubenville Chapter which was organized here recently, she being one of the organizing members. She was also president of the Alumni Association of the Steubenville Seminary and in that capacity presided over many happy reunions of the students of this popular school of early days. At the time of her death she was planning for another meeting of the association which was to have been held here.

As president of the Steubenville Bible Society, Mrs. Donaldson performed a noteworthy service, the function of this organization being to supply the public schools, various fraternal organizations and hotels with Bibles. During the World War she became acquainted and endeared herself to hundreds of the young men of the city and county who were called into military service, presenting personally, as far as possible, every soldier and sailor from this community with an autographed Bible.

Mrs. Donaldson was one of the organizers and had the honor of being the first president of the Woman's Club which was formed here about twenty years ago. She was a woman of keen intellect and remarkable memory, a speaker and writer of ability and was the author of many papers, not often appeared, but of great educational and historical value. Her praiseworthy skill in the literary field was exemplified in her history of the Woman's Club written and published in recent years. Mrs. Donaldson rarely missed a meeting of the society and was active in its affairs, despite her advanced years, until stricken with her last illness.

Deceased was also a member of the W.C.T.U. and a faithful steadfast soldier in the campaigns waged by that organization covering a period of many years.

While best known and esteemed for the service she

rendered through the channels of various organizations, many of them charitable and philanthropic, Mrs. Donaldson enjoyed a beautiful home life. Blessed with a charming personality and kindly grace of the old school, she was an admirable hostess, radiating hospitality to all who sought the shelter of her home. She was a successful wife and mother and the many years of happiness with William B. Donaldson were broken only six years ago when he preceded her to the Great Beyond.

Of her immediate family she is survived by two daughters, Mrs. D.J. Sinclair and Mrs. H.H. Henderson. She is also survived by the following grandchildren, Mrs. G. B. LeVan, who is now in France; Frank, Dohrman, Jr., and Katharine Sinclair, Catherine and Harriet Henderson, also two great-grandchildren, Garret B. LeVan, Jr., of this city and Dohrman Sinclair Grant of Franklin, Pa.

Beloved by all with whom she came in contact, admired and respected in all walks of life, Mrs. Donaldson's memory will long be cherished in the community in which she lived and labored for the best for all, for so many years.

Overseas Travel

People traveled by ship and it was not uncommon for them to have steamer trunks which had rounded tops and trays with compartments, some of which were covered. Later, wardrobe trunks were used. They stood on end and had one side for hanging clothes and the other side with compartments which pulled out as drawers would. Katharine remembered Mrs. Castner's new house on N. Fourth Street in Steubenville had no closets and she used wardrobe trunks. This certainly limited what she could collect and was probably a poor choice for the house, or perhaps a continual reminder of travel.

Katharine made her first trip to Europe with her family in 1924. That summer Katharine, her mother and brother Dohrman took a conducted European tour through England, Belgium, France, Switzerland, and Italy. They sailed on the Cunard liner *Ausonia* from Montreal. Her brother Frank traveled with them as far as Plymouth, England and from there he went to Paris for the Olympic Games. In London they had tea with a Sinclair family who at the time had relatives visiting from Ireland. Today Katharine's daughter, Mary, has developed a fine relationship with their descendants, John and Kate Martin. The group traveled to many places in England including London, the Cotswolds and Coventry.

As the tour traveled through Europe, Katharine was able to celebrate her 16th birthday at the 13,642 foot high Jungfrau in Switzerland. On August 15, 1924 the group went to the Casino de Monte Carlo. Katharine presented her pass to get in and at first was rejected because she was too young to be admitted. Only because she was traveling in a group of seventeen was she permitted to enter. Katharine's memory book is adorned with material from London, Milan, Rome, Pisa, Naples, Monte Carlo, Nice, and Paris. There were four young people on the trip who Katharine wrote about in her diary. She became good friends with Lucille who was practically engaged to George at the beginning of the trip. However, George and Lucille had arguments during the traveling. In Naples the two girls met American sailors who took them up Vesuvius one evening to enjoy the view and dine.

The summer trip lasted for three months and cost $1,200 each. The return trip from Europe was on the Sufferin (The French Line) which left Le Havre on August 26 arriving September 4 in New York. Included among Katharine's remembrances is the booklet showing all the passengers who accompanied her on her return to the United States.

Summer Fun

In the summer Katharine played golf and would go swimming. Her friend, Josephine Myers of Toronto, had a simple wooden beach house for changing into swimming suits so people could swim in the Ohio River during the summer. Josephine's house overlooked the river and the lawn sloped down to the river with a brick walk used to get into the water. When Katharine was about twelve she swam across the Ohio River from here. As she said, "It was probably without permission but I knew I could do it." Years later she swam across Lake Mendota when she was at the University of Wisconsin for summer school.

Stanton Park was always a great place to go. It was just north of Alikanna on the west side of old Route 7. It had a wonderful merry-go-round with small wooden horses that moved gayly up and down, accompanied by the sound of lively music. There was also a sliding board and a Ferris wheel with box seats that held four happy children. When the boxes swung back and forth however, it was not uncommon for someone to get sick. Nearby was a delightful swimming pool. John Dawson dove in the shallow end of the pool once and scraped his nose. It taught Katharine and the rest of her friends a good lesson. Across the road overlooking the river was the Casino. Dances were held there and the building was filled with happy memories. Often on a hot night the cool breeze from the river delighted the dancers.

Group dates were popular and frequently friends would meet at different people's home where they danced to 78 speed records and had refreshments. The music room with its Victrola to play the records was the dance area when the Friday night parties were held at the Sinclair's home. The girls who always attended were Eleanor Giles, Mary Peterson, Virginia Pearce, and Katharine. Margaret Arms was part of the group when her father was the minister of Westminster Church. Virginia remembers Dohrman dancing with each girl. Some of the boys who came to these gatherings were Jimmy Montfort, Johnny Dawson, Ed Cline, Harry Mueller, Herb Swickard, and future husband, Howard Minor who moved in across the street about 1921. As Katharine said, "My mother strongly suggested that it would be a good thing to invite him since he didn't know anyone." Katharine was reluctant because he was older than her crowd.

House Parties

Katharine had many good times at house parties which were fun and numerous in the 20's. When a house guest came to visit there were parties every night mostly at nearby homes. There were also luncheons where such things as chicken salad was served in patty shells or in tomatoes. There would be lots of side dishes and home-made pies or ice cream for dessert. One such house party was in Uniontown, Pennsylvania. Virginia Hennings, who first lived on Fifth Street, then later moved to N. Fourth Street into the home which today is McClaves Funeral home, would go to these house parties. Mrs. Hennings drove Virginia, Katharine and Martha Burt to the party. Martha was from Beach Bottom which was located on the Ohio River south of Steubenville. Martha gave a party, but instead of doing it at Beach Bottom, the Burts rented a house near Philadelphia, where all the girls were their house guests. They would go to the hotel for meals. At some of the house parties in Steubenville, the group would have a treasure hunt or even a scavenger hunt. In the one you went looking for something you wanted and in the other for something no one wanted.

Ann Slingluff, who lived in Maryland, was a good friend of Katharine's. Ann met her husband-to-be, Jimmy Montfort, at a house party given by Katharine in Steubenville. At a party Ann gave in Maryland one weekend, Katharine and Virginia Peters were house guests along with others. All were surprised to see Virginia's older brother drive up in a new car. He had come from Arizona to see his sister at school, and when he learned that she had gone to the Slingluff's party, he bought a car to get there. Over sixty years later Katharine met Virginia Peters Hagner at a D.A.R. convention in Washington, D.C.

Katharine E. Sinclair

Dances

During her teens the brunette five-foot-two-inch hazel-eyed girl attended a number of dances at the Academy Club, Fort Steuben Hotel Ballroom, fraternity dances, and some coming-out parties such as one for Miss Mary Kathryn Campbell. Katharine attended prep school and college proms including Lawrenceville, Dartmouth, Lafayette, West Point in Anapolis, Antioch, Princeton, Gambier College, Ohio State and others. Katharine was an excellent dancer and before her marriage was never at a loss for suitors. Her two-inch by three-inch dance cards were always filled with the names of a number of different fellows. One for the 1927 spring dance at Emma Willard school listed 12 dances. First the type of dance was listed, i.e., Fox Trot or Waltz, then there was a space for the man's name and on this card all different fellow's names were listed on all the lines. Under the names the music was written. That night *Rio Rita, The Same Old Moon, Je T'Aime - Means I Love You, In a Little Spanish Town, One Flower Grows Alone in Your Garden, The Desert Song, When the Bo-Tree Blossoms Again, What Does it Matter?, Blue Skies,* and *I Know That You Know* all appeared on the card. Katharine had an array of beautiful formal dresses. She could be seen whirling around the dance floor wearing a lovely long blue velvet dress or perhaps the black silk velvet dress with rows of silver beads for the shoulders. Flapper dresses were also in her wardrobe.

Both Katharine and her brother Dohrman loved to dance the Charleston. Katharine's daughter, Mary, learned the basics of the Charleston from her mother and picked up a few specialty steps from her uncle Dohrman. He had toured with his Dartmouth college music group as the speciality dancer. On June 1924 Katharine went to Dohrman's graduation from Lawrenceville Preparatory School where he had been a member of the Mandolin and Banjo clubs. At Dartmouth he had a friend whose father's owned a ship line that went to South America. Dohrman majored in Spanish with the thought of getting a job in the company, but alas, the company failed. Music, however, always stayed with him. He played the piano by ear. One of his favorites was "Kitten on the Keys." In his yearly trips to Europe after he retired, it was not uncommon to find him playing a piano on a boat or at a party gathering.

When Katharine was home from school on school vacations there would be dances at the Ft. Steuben Hotel. Dances were held there every night during the Christmas vacation and often there were afternoon dances too. The live bands played until midnight and there was a great exchange of dancing partners as the fellows signed their names to the beautiful dressed female attendants' cards. Katharine went with different dates each night, and afterwards they would walk the few blocks to her home.

One evening Katharine returned with a date to find her mother talking with a man. Earlier the man had come to the door and asked for some food. She was so generous that he decided not to steal from her. He was leaving as Katharine approached. Her date's remark was, "He certainly had a better appearance than the man lurking under the tree." At a different time Katharine went down to stoke the coal furnace after a date and had a strange feeling that someone was present. She looked straight ahead and went back upstairs. The next morning it was discovered that three fur coats had been stolen.

Katharine started a Memory Book May 27, 1924 which captured interests of this teenager. Quips cut out of magazines included **BE SLENDER,** *Reduce Quickly - Easily - without Drugs, Diet or Exercise, My Method Discovered In The Orient by a Prominent Opera Star.* Another saying was *She found a pleasant way to reduce her fat.* Improvement has often been publicized in papers and magazines so seeing a message in the book which read *We Guarantee - Your Voice Can Be Improved 100%* showed its timelessness. Romance stirs the hearts of teenagers and Katharine included the following quote in her memory book. *"All right, " he said, "Forget it; it wasn't real"; and he drew her to his level; and he continued the motion of his arms and brought her to his heart; and she caught her breath; and she said, "Oh, is this real?" and she was enfolded to his heart and he said, "Real, real, forever!"*

There were also notes and a number of telegrams. "Don't forget your

Katharine E. Sinclair

promise." was an August 21, 1925 telegram from a friend. Other items included playbills from plays and films at Poli's Theater in Washington. Many of the films had programs giving a synopsis and the cast of such films as *The Covered Wagon*. Katharine's book contained a program for the play *Wildflower* by Oscar Hammerstein which starred Edith Day. On February 19, 1924 she attended a concert there with Bruno Walter conducting the New York Symphony and Pablo Casals as the guest cellist. On another night she heard Rachmaninoff playing the piano. From the Shubert Belasco Theater there were programs from *Scarmouche*, Victor Herbert's *The Dream Girl* with Fay Bainter and Walter Woolf, *Pelleas and Melisande* with Jane Cowl, ballet with Anna Pavlowa and such singers as Elena Gerhardt and Toti Dal Monte. Katharine also attended the opera *The Bat* there. At the National Theater in Washington Katharine saw *Sancho Panza* with Otis Skinner and *Sally* with Marilyn Miller.

Education

Katharine's early education was in Steubenville. She was athletic and for a class extravaganza held at Wells Jr. High School she boldly stood on her head at the end of the program while the band played. First, though, she had carefully tied her dress at the knees so it did not come down, or up too high!

Katharine attended Mrs. Dow's School at Briarcliff Manor, New York when she was thirteen. She was only there for a year, then went to the Misses Eastman School at 1305 Seventeenth Street N. W., Washington, D.C. for two years. One afternoon the Misses Eastman School class of about 30 went to the White House and was ushered in to see the president. Each in turn shook President Coolidge's hand and said, "Good afternoon, Mr. President." One of her classmates was the cousin of Mrs. Wallace Simpson, who married King Edward VIII of England. When Katharine attended the Misses Eastman School, she played field hockey down at the Ellipse, which was beautiful in the spring with the cherry blossoms. She also captained the basketball team, or the cage team as it was called at the time. Once a week her class would go to a Washington art gallery. On December 8, 1924 Katharine went to the Ohio Society of Washington D. C. where Chief Justice Taft give a welcome. Katharine was sixteen when she attended Calvin Coolidge's Charity Inaugural Ball March 4, 1925.

"Boarding school was elegantly called *Finishing School*," recalled Katharine. "We were taught to become *ladies*. In school etiquette and elocution were always part of the courses taught. Our dining room was in the same building as our dorm rooms. We lined up at breakfast and as we entered the spacious and very formal room, each one of us was greeted by the principal while we curtsied. We then proceeded to our assigned table where the well groomed black-dressed waitresses with their white starched aprons awaited us. We wore uniforms and always dressed for dinner. We were permitted five or six dresses to wear for dinner and one Sunday church dress at school. Spiked heeled shoes were prohibited. The heel had to be at least large enough to be covered by a postage stamp. At four o'clock, frivolous things like bowling and basketball ceased and tea was served. We descended the semicircular staircase to enjoy tea and cake served by a gracious hostess. A senior student was chosen to preside at the tea table set elaborately with sparkling silver, flowers, and linen tea napkins."

Katharine usually came home from school in Washington on the train but in the early 1920's she took her first plane ride from Washington, D.C. to Pittsburgh. The day was drizzly enough that the two or three other passengers canceled, but not her. She and the pilot boarded a two-seater open cockpit plane that she said looked like it was held together with tape, and off they flew. Night flights began about this time and Lindbergh's famous flight across the Atlantic took place in 1927 some years later.

Katharine completed her high school years at the Emma Willard School in Troy, New York, where she graduated in 1927 after attending for two years. There she was the captain of the basketball team. During her high school years she was President of her Class, Secretary, and on the Student Council. She won her letters in gym, tennis, swimming and basketball. Her acting career didn't reach great heights, climbing no higher than a role as a tree in the school play.

In 1929 Katharine went to New York City to attend Columbia University. She, her mother and cousin Catherine Henderson took an apartment at Butler Hall on Morningside Drive near the campus. Her mother, Mary Sinclair, had lived in New York City with her parents for her first seven years. That fall the stock market crashed in October. Katharine remembered seeing a man committing suicide. She only caught a glimpse of him as he shot past the window of the apartment during this time when the market crash was affecting many.

In the 1920's many girls smoked and when Katharine's mother returned to the apartment one very cold day she saw the two girls leaning out the window many floors up smoking cigarettes. On arriving in the apartment she told the girls she definitely did not advocate smoking, but since they did smoke she suggested they buy an ash tray and not smoke out the window. They enjoyed the New York life seeing plays and going out to eat. There was a good restaurant on the top floor of Butler Hall where they often ate.

Katharine only went to Columbia University for a year and the University of Wisconsin for a summer. The Depression cut short her further formal education but she continued to learn throughout her life.

Underwriter

After high school and during the Depression Katharine had a position as Life Underwriter of The Equitable Life Assurance Society. This venture with the Equitable Company was fortuitous in its origin. Katharine and her sister Wilma were spending the day in Pittsburgh and had lunch with Mr. Woods, an old friend of Katharine's father, the head of the Equitable for that district. He jokingly suggested to Katharine that she join the forces of the Equitable as a Life Underwriter, not expecting for a moment that she would take him seriously. She did, however, hold him to his offer, commuting to Pittsburgh for several life insurance courses. She was very successful in the work and continued it until her marriage. She was making more money than the rest of the family combined during those hard Depression times. When she began the job she was the youngest Underwriter in the history of the Equitable.

Florida

Katharine made many trips to Florida during the winters to enjoy warmer weather. On one such trip in 1928 she and her mother were driving and Mrs. Nellie Wells and daughter Helen were in another car. Mrs. Wells lost control when passing and turned over landing in the ditch. No one was hurt and the Sinclairs and the Wells reached Wilma's house in Coral Gables the next day. Katharine and her friend Helen enjoyed their times in Florida, and made trips to some of the Carribean Islands. In 1930 they visited Cuba and brought back a postcard of Sloppy Joe's Club where they had been. She enjoyed the sun, sand, sea, and Florida sunsets.

One morning there was a knock on the door and it turned out to be Governor Myers J. Cooper of Ohio. He was there to see Wilma Sinclair Le Van who was very active in Ohio politics. Wilma was a member of the Republican State Central Committee in 1922, and served as a member of that committee until 1940, except when she held the office of Republican National Committeewoman for Ohio, which was during the terms of Coolidge and Hoover. She managed the Women's Campaign in Ohio for the Coolidge pre-primary in 1924, and also organized the Republican women of the state for the succeeding fall campaigns in 1924, 1926, 1928 and 1930. She was an Alternate Delegate-at-Large to the Cleveland Convention in 1924, and a Delegate-at- Large to the Chicago Convention in 1932. She was the Ohio member of the Notification Committee to notify President Coolidge of his nomination in 1924, and was a member of the Arrangements Committee for the Kansas City Convention in 1928.

Driving Miss Arms

One day while Katharine was in Grand Central Station in New York City she called her friend Margaret Arms whom she had first met in Steubenville when Margaret's father had been the minister at Westminster Presbyterian Church. Margaret came to the station and they had a nice visit and talked of many things including taking a trip out west. Katharine thought it was a nice idea but didn't think too much about it until she received a letter from Margaret saying she was arriving on such and such a date for the trip they were taking. As can be imagined, Katherine had said nothing to her mother and was a bit leery of doing so. However, it had to be done and she told her mother she was going. Katharine had an Essex car at the time which she took on the five-week automobile trip with Margaret Arms (now Mrs. Mason) through the west to include Mount Rushmore which only had Washington's face completely done, Yellowstone, Teton, Zion and Bryce national parks, Denver, Estes Park and the Grand Canyon, etc. It wasn't until the trip started that Katharine learned that Margaret didn't drive so Katharine did all the driving.

Genealogy Research

When Katharine's mother was gathering data from gravestones and compiling a listing of the names and dates recorded in 68 old graveyards, Katharine would often chauffeur her, since her mother had only driven their old electric car. Mary Sinclair's son, Dohrman and nephew, Dohrman Grant also drove her on different occasions. Mary Sinclair did a fine job of gathering data that could easily have been lost. However, she received a lot of kidding from her children about her many trips to the cemeteries. Over 10,000 references were compiled by Mrs. Sinclair for the Jefferson County section of Caldwell's *History of Belmont and Jefferson Counties*, published in 1880. A copy was sent to the Daughters of the American Revolution and she received recognition for it from the D.A.R. She also retrieved and alphabetized hundreds of marriages, baptisms and deaths of the early pioneer settlers of Pennsylvania listed in Dr. Cuthbertson's diary while he was a circuit rider, and the only minister from 1750 to 1780 in that part of Pennsylvania. Later in the 1930's she wrote a series of articles for the Steubenville *Herald Star* under the name of *Pioneer Days* which were later made into a book.

Ohio Valley Hospital Woman's Board

In the 1920's Katharine's mother helped Mrs. Emma Zeis with the Ohio Valley Hospital Woman's Board. Mary Sinclair became the first vice chairman for this organization which had the purpose of providing linen for the hospital and acting in an advisory capacity. The Women's Board worked to make the Ohio Valley Hospital the best in hospital services for the people of Steubenville and the surrounding district. On wash day these women often would check the clothes lines of hospital workers for O.V.H. marked linen which belonged to the hospital and needed to be returned. Katharine's aunt, Mrs. Carrie P. Dohrman, helped to set up the organization of Twigs. Later, in 1936 Katharine joined the Blossom Twig.

❦

Katharine E. Sinclair

The 1930-1939 Era

As Katharine lived through the 1930's, the following events took place. The depression became worldwide and all the German banks were closed. In 1933 Hilter was named German Chancellor. When Hindenburg died Hitler became President of Germany. In 1935 the storm clouds were gathering over Europe. Mussolini's armies invaded Ethiopia. 1936 began with George V dying in England, Edward VIII succeeding him, abdicating to marry Wallis Warfield Simpson and George VI becoming king. Unrest was growing as the Nazis marched into the Rhineland and the Rightist forces started war against Republican Spain. Japan bombed Shanghai. Hitler promoted himself to military chief and took Austria then the Sudetenland. Franco was recognized as Spain's leader. Pope Pius XI died. Germany took Prague, made a treaty with Russia then invaded and divided Poland with Russia. Britain and France who had guaranteed Polish independence declared war on Germany September 30 and the Soviets attacked Finland.

Babe Ruth of the New York Yankees accepted a two-year contract worth $160,000 for 1931-32, which was more than President Hoover was making. Bobby Jones retired in 1930 after winning the United States and British Opens and the British and United States Amateurs. The 1932 winter Olympics were held at Lake Placid, and Sonja Henie skated to a gold medal. Omaha became the third Triple Crown winner. Joe Louis floored Max in the first round, and Helen Wills Moody won her 8th Wimbledon singles title.

In 1931 the Empire State Building opened. Jane Addams received the Nobel Peace Prize. FDR took the United States off the gold standard and created the Civilian Conservation Corps. The infant son of Charles Lindbergh was kidnaped. Prohibition ended in 1933. The United States was hit by dust storms. Social Security was enacted. The Hindenburg dirigible blew up. Between 1930 and 1934 TWA had cut their flying time from coast to coast in half to 18 hours.

The movies offered an escape from hard times. *Grand Hotel* received the best picture award in 1932. Walt Disney's *Snow White and the Seven Dwarfs* was released at the movie theaters and the decade ended with *Gone With the Wind*. Thornton Wilder's play *Our Town* opened in New York. Americans panicked over the scary radio show of H.G. Wells' *The War of the Worlds* and the hero *Superman* was created. Benny Goodman's band took the country by storm.

At the end of 1930, it was estimated, 4.8 million Americans were unemployed. By 1938 nearly 8 million were jobless, and the minimum wage was set at 40 cents an hour. Du Pont patented a new thread called nylon in 1937. Strikers won a wage hike and ended the General Motors sit-down. Hydrogen atoms were split into helium atoms.

IV.

Marriage In The Thirties

Depression Ramifications

"The third and fourth decades were the best of times and the worst of times, to quote Charles Dickens," recalls Katharine. "These were the years that covered my marriage to the kindest, most thoughtful man, the birth of our four wonderful children, and the tragic World War II years. It was the time when I could be with my husband and children, my mother died, and many homes were broken when sons died on the battle field."

The Depression was devastating. It affected many people in different ways. Katharine remembers a woman sitting in a doorway near Market and Fourth Streets with a needle and thread. She would sew up a run in a stocking for five cents a run. Another woman, who lived on Fifth Street, tried to sell her own jewelry to buy food for her family, but no one would buy the jewelry. Day help was a dollar a day. One day Katharine's brother Frank, received a call from some friends who were at the hotel having breakfast and wanted Frank to join them. Frank asked Kath for some money and she replied that they would pay for their own breakfast. Frank said, "I just want to have some change in my pocket." Katharine says, "You had to live through the Depression to fully understand it."

Union Savings Bank & Trust Company

The Union Savings Bank & Trust Company of Steubenville, Ohio celebrated its 75th anniversary in 1929. Katharine, dressed in a costume of the 1859's, was one of the hostesses. In the fall of 1931 the Union Savings Bank & Trust Company of Steubenville closed its doors due to fear and panic. This bank had been founded by Katharine's great great-uncle, Horatio G. Garrett, Jr., and her father had been President of its forerunner, the Union Deposit Bank, until his untimely death in 1915. Wilma Sinclair

Katharine Emelda Sinclair at her great-grandmother's spinning wheel. (1929)

LeVan, Katharine's sister, was made Chairman of the Reorganization Committee of the Bank, and was largely responsible for its reopening in 1933. Wilma had neither been an employee or an officer when the bank closed. She was elected president of the bank on January 3 of that year. She remained president until January 14, 1941. Katharine's brother, Dohrman, worked for the bank. He made a trip to seal a deal and sent a Christmas telegram to convey the good settlement. It was the middle of July and the telegraph company was sure there had been some mistake. Therefore, the Western Union people did not deliver the telegram. In 1936 Dr. Howard H. Minor became a member of the board on which he served for forty years. The Union Bank had another Sinclair become president when Frank Sinclair's son Frank served as president years later.

Sports

Tennis was popular and courts were constructed on the Ohio Valley Hospital grounds in the 1920's. Katharine and her sister Wilma won the Women's Doubles Tennis Championship at the Steubenville Tennis Association. Katharine twice won the Steubenville Women's Golf Championship, in 1930 and 1931, at the Steubenville Country Club, which was organized the year Katharine was born. When she decided to learn the game of golf, she arranged to take instruction from the pro at the Riverview Country Club in what is now the Pottery Addition. The pro later reported, "On her first lesson she connected with the ball only once, but on her one good shot she drove the ball 250 yards." The club house burned down in the early 20's. In 1934 Katharine and John Sherrard were the winners of the Scotch foursome tourney. Katharine played a lot of golf and was a great person to find four leaf clovers. She would be walking along the fairway and lean down to pick one. The family was never sure whether her golf game was one of just skill or lots of luck. Chances are, it was a bit of both. When Katharine was teaching the game of golf to her daughter, Mary, she would remind her to forget the bad holes and play the next hole with a fresh start.

Katharine's nephew, Dohrman Grant, arranged to teach his aunt how to shoot. One day Dohrman and Henry 'Rudy' Rudolf took her hunting. When a squirrel arrived on the scene she took aim and with a steady hand was right on the mark. The others were impressed. Katharine went over to the squirrel and picked it up. It had not quite died, so she carried it to the car and held it. When the others returned they found her asleep holding the dead squirrel on her lap. She decided never to go hunting again.

Moving in with Family

For a few years during the Depression, Katharine and her mother closed the large home on N. Fourth Street and moved in with Wilma and Garry LeVan at 3153 Sunset Boulevard on the corner of Homestead, to save money while people were away. Both households had shrunk. Marie's son, Dohrman Grant, was away at the Hill school and Wilma's son, Garrett B. (Gary) LeVan, who had starred for Steubenville's Big Red football teams during his high school days was at Princeton University. Katharine's brother Dohrman was in California, and brother Frank was in West Virginia at Lost Creek at the time. Living with the LeVans proved interesting. Garry LeVan, Sr. had a very short temper and swore. One day he pulled on the livingroom table drawer which was always stuck, and suddenly it became unstuck. Everyone could hear him yell, "Any damn person knows that this drawer doesn't open, why did it this time?"

Dates with Doc

Kay dated Doc Minor quite a bit during the Depression. Late one evening while Katharine was living with the Le Vans, she was out on a date with Howard Minor, who had been called Doc since he was a kid. Katharine had forgotten her key to the house. Doc climbed up on the roof and through the window to get to the door and let them in. Garry was there with a gun and Doc kept saying, "Don't shoot Garry, it's Doc, it's Doc," recalled Katharine.

Doc invited Kay over to Philadelphia when he was at medical school at the University of Pennsylvania. They both enjoyed going to football games and attended many during the early thirties. Graduating in 1931 Doc returned to the area and interned at Allegheny General Hospital in Pittsburgh. His dad died May 9, 1932. Howard Clarence Minor was born July 21, 1869 in New Cumberland, West Virginia to Samuel and Hannah Mary Garlick Minor. He originally practiced medicine in Toronto, Ohio before moving to Steubenville to continue his medical practice in 1918 at 117 N. Fourth Street. The Minors lived near the Sinclairs at 504 N. Fourth Street. Katharine remembered going to Dr. Minor on one occasion for treatment after a fall. Both families attended Westminster Presbyterian Church. The Minors sat in the pew in front of the Sinclairs. When Doc needed a haircut Kay knew it.

Howard Minor had gone to Wells Grammar school and graduated from Steubenville High School. He was co-editor with Clyde Chalfant of *The Hornet's Nest* and associate editor of the 1923 year book, *The Bulletin,* which mentioned him wearing out two pairs of shoes in East Liverpool. Doc also was an associate editor for the *Bulletin Weekly* which was in its third year in 1923 and had grown from a four to a five column weekly. He was the chief torch bearer of the *Hi Y Club* and was Molyneux in the senior class play, *M. Beaucaire* by Booth Tarkington. He was president of the French Club, in the Science Club and a member of the Philomaetheon Literary Society which met for the purpose of gaining knowledge and enjoying literature, parliamentary law, social and athletic activities. Doc

HOWARD HOLLAND MINOR
"Doc"
Steubenville, Ohio
Washington and Jefferson University, B.S.
Phi Gamma Delta.
Alpha Mu Pi Omega.
Allegheny General Hospital, Pittsburgh, Pa.

*From the University of Pennsylvania Medical School
1931 Year Book*

Howard Holland Minor

served as both Treasurer and Vice President of the Senate Literary Club in high school. He furthered his education at Washington and Jefferson College and the University of Pennsylvania Medical School.

As an intern, Doc would drive down to Steubenville from Pittsburgh to take Kay out in the evenings. One night he was late because he had given blood first to get some money for the movies. Kay and Doc decided to set up a double date with their close friends. Katharine's good friend, Helen Wells, lived on the Wells farm in Colliers, West Virginia. The night set for the date, Doc drove down to Steubenville and picked up Kay, then back to pick up John Hamilton at the hospital. By the time they arrived at the Wells farm Helen had gone to bed. When Kay called up the stairs for Helen, her mother answered, covering for her daughter. The pair did meet that night and the four often double-dated after that. Another pair who would often go out with them was Henry Kirk and Betty Zane, who were both from

Allegheny General Hospital where Howard interned and
three Minor children were born.

1932
Katharine Sinclair, Howard Minor, Betty Zane, Henry
Kirk, Helen Wells and John Hamilton.

1974
Minors, Kirks, Hamiltons

July 1998
Mary Minor Evans, Brock Hamilton, Howard Minor, Keekee Minor, Zane Kirk, Margaret Minor, John Hamilton

Steubenville. Katharine kept a picture of this group of six taken in 1932 before any of them were married and a picture with the same six, all married, taken in 1974 in her living room.

When Doc took up his residency at the Ohio Valley Hospital in 1932, Kay and Doc would drive north up the river to Toronto, Ohio for a cup of coffee or lunch. There was never a lot of money spent on a date. It was during the Depression and Doc was not making much money. It was a relaxed life and Doc and Kay dated when they could. Listening to phonograph music or the radio, which was just coming into homes, were common activities for dates. In Steubenville, Bill Robinson's father owned a music store. Bill would take some of the records up to the top floor of the Sinclair Building where he would play the records over the air with his transmitter. There were no advertisements. Steubenville acquired its own official radio station in October 1940 and has continued to broadcast with the call letters WSTV.

Marriage
Katharine had a busy social life and was making good money in her job. She enjoyed golf and bridge with friends, and dated. She was a modern woman in her freedom but an old-fashioned lady when it came to dedica-

Katharine Sinclair Minor

tion to her husband when she married. In an August 18, 1934 letter from Doc, he wrote, "My life would be over if anything happened to you. It is a constant source of happiness to me that you have pledged your love to me for always and that you are going to marry me. My only hope in life is that I will be able to make you perfectly happy." Kay's diary shows many lunches and evenings with Doc. The two of them played bridge with her brother and mother or friends, went to dances including the nurses' dance at the Masonic Temple, saw movies and visited with friends. He often stopped by late in the evening if he had been out delivering babies or seeing patients.

Katharine was wed April 27, 1935 to Dr. Howard Holland Minor at the Sinclair homestead at 523 N. Fourth Street. It was a lovely wedding with family and close friends. Attending were Katharine's mother, Mary D. Sinclair, and both brothers Frank and Dohrman, Howard's mother, Carrie Holland Minor, and only sister Evelyn, her husband Earle Drake and two of their daughters Carolyn and Diane Drake, nephew Dohrman Grant, her aunt Florence and uncle Harry Henderson and daughters Harriet and Catherine with her husband Stanley Miles and daughter Patricia; Mr. & Mrs. Harry D. Wintringer, Dr. John and Helen Hamilton; Dr. Fred Slaughter, Miss Margaret Cook; Clyde Chalfant, Miss Mary Peterson, Henie Kirk, Miss Betty Zane and Mead and Gertrude Patterson.

After the elegant wedding in the music room with candles and beautiful flowers, a lovely luncheon was served at the home. Katharine remem-

Doc   Kay

805 Lawson Avenue, Steubenville, Ohio

bered that in addition to the wedding cake, individual ice cream forms were served. Their wedding night was spent in Columbus, Ohio, and much to their surprise, they found flowers from the hotel in their room. Dr. Minor was the doctor for the Ft. Steuben Hotel in Steubenville and the hotel had sent word to the Columbus hotel that the bridal party was coming. Kay and Doc proceeded on their honeymoon to California stopping on their way in Albuquerque to see Katharine's sister Wilma and husband Garry. Wilma was recovering from appendicitis at the time and had not been able to attend the wedding. It was the Depression, and at one filling station where they stopped, the attendant found their can of baked beans heating next to the engine when he lifted the hood of the car.

When they returned to Steubenville they lived at 805 Lawson Avenue with Doc's mother. The bridal couple was alone at first, since Doc's mother had gone to visit her daughter in Cleveland, Ohio.

Kay and Doc occasionally drove over from Steubenville together with friends to see Katharine's nephew, Garrett LeVan play football for Princeton on fall weekends after they were married. Once on the way over to New Jersey, as Kay tells the story, "The car was getting cold and Doc offered me a sip of wine to keep warm. I said the wine was strong. And so it was. It was whiskey."

Community Organizations

Both Kay and Doc were active in the community and continued to be so. Katharine followed her father and sister in being a Republican and belonging to the party that freed the slaves. Katharine and Bob Quinn had started the Young Republican Club of Jefferson County in Steubenville. She served as president of the Young Republicans and also attended the 1931 Congress of Young Republicans on June 11 and 12 at the New Willard

Hotel in Washington, D.C. as one of two Ohio delegates to the First Congress of Young Republican Voters. She was a Republican all her life, going to the inauguration of Calvin Coolidge and Richard Nixon's first inauguration. However, she did receive an invitation from Mrs. Roosevelt to attend a luncheon in 1935.

In 1930 she followed her grandmother Emelda Junkin Donaldson, her mother Mary Donaldson Sinclair, and her sister Wilma Sinclair LeVan by becoming a member of the Daughters of the American Revolution. She became the Registrar for the Steubenville chapter of the D.A.R. in 1934 and also served as a Page from Ohio at the Congress of the D.A.R. in Washington, D.C. Today her daughters Margaret and Mary are members keeping up the tradition started three generations earlier.

In 1933 Katharine was invited to a luncheon at the Ft. Steuben Hotel where the head of the Junior Women's Club in Columbus wanted to talk about starting a Junior Women's Club for those who were too young for the Woman's Club in Steubenville. Mrs. Brooks, who was a member of the Woman's Club of Steubenville and who Katharine did not know well at the time, was also there. Katharine heard the expectations of the Junior Women's Club and said she would give it a try. She, along with twelve others, started inviting women to join, and soon women were flocking to enroll. Finally a maximum was set at 100. Katharine became the first president. The organization is still active today.

Shortly after she was married Katharine took the train to Chicago to attend the National Women's Club Convention in Detroit as the Junior Representative of Ohio. There she met Helen Chapman, who became a life long friend and later national president of the General Federation of Women's Clubs. They were both in the Jr. Woman's Club at the time.

Steubenville and Katharine made a good fit. She enjoyed taking part in the community and joined the Query Club. It was an organization where joining members had to be related to the original founders. The club had been named after the practice of drawing from a collection of questions at one meeting and discussing the query at the next meeting. She was later to serve as president of this organization.

Kay was a member of the Laura E. McGowan Circle of the International Order of King's Daughters and Sons, which had been organized October 26, 1893. In the organization's desire to help, the Circle became known as the *Nursing Circle* and helped the sick and disabled, young and old. In 1901 the King's Daughters' Circle took over the administration of the private Gill Hospital and continued until St. John's Hospital was built in 1950. They supported local organizations such as Family Service, Martha Manor, YMCA and YWCA camp programs and helped the North

American Indians in education and encouragement. Later they provided student scholarships to study in Chautauqua, New York in the summer. Katharine was also a leader of the Girl Reserves, now known as the Y-Teens, of the YWCA. In 1930 Katharine became president of the Jefferson County Tuberculosis and Health Association.

When Dr. Howard H. Minor had gone into practice in Steubenville he had his office at 301-302 in the Steubenville Sinclair Building. His office phone was 122 and his residence phone was 123. Office calls were $2, and if he made a house call he charged $3. There were times when the bill was paid in eggs or other items. In December of 1935 Dr. Minor was re-elected president of the Jefferson County Medical Society. He also became a member of Rotary International in October 1936.

1936 Flood

In March the Ohio River began to rise to the flood stage. As a diversion from all his work, Doc went to the YMCA to play a little basketball and sprained his ankle. The next morning he received a call at 4 a.m. that people in Empire, Ohio needed medical help. Since he could not walk on his ankle, he made his house calls in the perfect way for a flood, in a boat. The flood was a terrible experience with houses, people, and cattle being washed away. The radio stations in Pittsburgh and Wheeling were broadcasting 24-hour flood news. Kay worked at the Red Cross Clothing Center for the next few days and described the atmosphere as a regular war time environment.

The history making flood on March 19, 1936, swept through the Steubenville district imperiling thousands and causing millions of dollars damage, according to an article in the *Herald-Star*. At noon the stage stood at 52.6 feet. This was three and five tenths feet higher than the waters of the 1884 flood, theretofore used as a measuring stick. The old record of 49.1 was passed at 11 p.m. An appeal was issued to conserve water since the Alikanna pumping station would be flooded at 50 feet. After that, the city's only water supply would be the water that was already in the reservoir. All the houses on Wells Street and the lower end of S. Third Street were evacuated as the water covered the lower Lincoln Avenue sector. Hundreds of residents in lowlands were forced to move out; others carried house furnishings to the safety of second floors. The mills stopped. Roads were impassable and bus and trolley service was cut off. Telephone lines were either severed or overloaded. In some instances, drinking water and food shortages were feared. The blocking of Lincoln Avenue stopped delivery trucks and at least three families suffered from fuel shortage. Gas and electric company emergency crews traveled over the flooded areas for special services. The river broke its banks on the north end of Steubenville and inundated LaBelle Avenue cutting off traffic, covering that portion of Route 7 to the Fort Steuben bridge and forcing the removal of several families from dwellings in that section. Water climbed quickly over the C & P tracks and soon poured out over Water Street and lower Market, Washington, Adams and South streets and practically isolated the municipal disposal plant and the River Sand Company along the river bank at the foot of Adams Street. Six-foot highway route markers were submerged in the Wells Street area and heavy traffic over Third and Bates Streets had to be rerouted. The River Sand Company building was half under water and some of the smaller buildings standing on Water Street were far beneath the river's surface. Piles of driftwood littered waterfront houses that were submerged to the eaves. Wallpaper and plaster fell off the walls. Furniture was lifted by the water and smashed to kindling wood against the ceiling.

First Child

When Katharine was expecting her first child, she described Doc to her friend Margaret Arms Mason, as being so happy he was "just like a little boy waiting for the circus." Just after her 28th birthday she finished an afghan she had been working on in her pregnancy. Her doctor was in Pittsburgh and after one office visit she went shopping for a crib at Horne's and Kaufmann's. During the last month of pregnancy the delighted couple would stop by friends in the evening to visit and go to movies such as *Swing Time* with Fred Astaire and Ginger Rogers. They would take drives which regularly included ice cream on a hot summer evening. Katharine's diary entry on September 26 read, *The Blessed Event Arrived.* Doc and Kay's first child, Mary Carolyn was born in Pittsburgh in what is today the old part of the Allegheny General Hospital. Fred Slaughter, Chester F. Beall, John Hamilton and Howard had interned in the very old part together. Dr. Gilmour, head of Obstetrics and Gynecology had a baby boy the same day. On Saturday, Kay was listening to a Pirates' baseball game on KDKA radio before the delivery. During the delivery, Dr. Beall, the delivering doctor, took Howard into the hall and talked about a small complication and decided to hurry up the birth. Back in her hospital room Kay picked up the last part of the Pirates' baseball game. Doc came up to Pittsburgh every day during the two weeks his girls were in the hospital. Katharine remembers about 25 bouquets of flowers and lots of baby presents. An old 16 mm movie still exists of Mary Carolyn and a happy, laughing new mother. Kay never quite became accustomed to the doctor's rounds at untimely hours in the hospital. In October the new daughter and mother came home to 805 Lawson Avenue in Steubenville.

Times were busy with a new baby. As the youngest in her family Katharine had had little experience around babies. Her mother-in-law helped her learn, and of course she had good medical service from her husband. The four people adjusted well in the three-bedroom home. The dog, Rascal, also seemed to respond well with the new baby. There were splash baths in the wading pool in the summer and bundled-up walks in the winter. In 1938 Doc, Kay, and Mary Carolyn traveled to Florida to visit Wilma and Garry LeVan. It was a great vacation with lots of swimming. The trip was the beginning of many trips these two would take with their children.

Another Child

With another child on the way in 1939, the Minors decided to move to a new house at 915 N. Fifth Street. It would be the first of many moves in the next ten years. Their second child, Katharine, or Keekee as she became known, was also born in Pittsburgh at the Allegheny General Hospital. When Katharine went into labor at the end of November, she and Doc drove to Pittsburgh to the hospital. Katharine stayed overnight and part of the next day when her labor stopped. Deciding that she still needed to do some Christmas shopping, Katharine went to Boggs & Bule to get a few last minute gifts, knowing full well that she would have little chance later. However, when her labor did not start again, she went to stay with Doc's sister, Evelyn Minor Drake, who lived in Mt. Lebanon, a suburb of Pittsburgh. Katharine stayed there for three or four days. Doc stayed overnight, traveling back to Steubenville for his medical practice during the day. At 2 a.m. on December 7 the labor began again and this time Kay and Doc drove through the Pittsburgh tunnel at break neck speed to the hospital. Katharine Evelyn was the largest of the Minor children at birth at 8 pounds 8 ounces.

From the hospital Katharine wrote her friend Gertrude Patterson after she had managed to get the hospital to cook a squab Gertrude had brought to her.

> *Mother like daughter or daughter like mother - at any rate you should see little Katharine eat squab (or its equivalent). She thinks it is wonderful. I had it the night you brought it and I wish you could have stayed to see and smell how good it was. Everyone on the floor was quite envious, and rightly so. It was delicious, both Katharines thought so.*
>
> *It was so good to see you and your husband. Knowing how busy everyone is just now, and particularly you, I especially appreciated the effort you made in coming. Somehow,*

Gertrude, you <u>never</u> disappoint. You always go the extra mile.

You were awfully sweet to phone, too. But my oh my, where are your Scot ancestors? They'll turn over in their graves if they knew you had called 'person to person' from New Castle, when you knew I'd be here. Better mend your ways.

I sat up in a chair today! I feel so proud of myself. It was really a red letter day. Guess I've loafed long enough and they'll soon send me home. I hope the bassinet is still covered with tissue paper awaiting our arrival! In that connection, do you still have its mattress? Are you using it? If not may we borrow it too? I'm not sure whether I had it last time or used a pillow. I can use a pillow this time very easily if you are using it.

I'm still not sure when I'll be home. The doctor says Wednesday (or possibly Tuesday) so I'm counting on Thursday. It will be awfully good to get home whichever it is - I've been away three weeks this Sunday.

Time for the little love coupon to be brought in so must sign off. Again we thank you for the squab, your visit, your phone calls, your bassinet and everything.

Both Katharines went home to the N. Fifth Street home for a wonderful Christmas. Mary Carolyn wanted to make sure her new sister enjoyed the things she liked. One day she was feeding young Katharine who was lying on her back. Luckily, it did not have disastrous consequences.

❦

Katharine with her first daughter, Mary Carolyn Minor.

The 1940-1949 Era

The 1940's saw war spread. Russia, in the Nazi-Soviet nonaggression pact, took East Poland, attacked Finland and took the Baltic states. Germany went on to take Denmark, Norway, the Netherlands, Belgium, and France while 350,000 British and French troops were evacuated at Dunkirk. The Italian and German campaigns took the Balkans in 1941, and invaded Russia in June marching to Moscow and Leningrad. In the next two years Russia drove the Axis out of Eastern Europe and the Balkans with the help of the British and U.S. Lend-Lease aid. The United States, Britain, and free France combined to fight Germany in North Africa in 1942, Italy in 1943, and invaded Normandy on D-Day, June 6, 1944 before reaching Germany and bringing about the German surrender May 7, 1945. In the Pacific the Japanese occupied Indochina in 1940, Thailand in 1941 and attacked Hawaii December 7, 1941 as well as the Philippines, Hong Kong, and Malaya. Indonesia and Burma were attacked in 1942. The Battle of Midway on June 1942 stopped the Japanese advances. The islands of Guadalcanal, Leyte Gulf, Iwo Jima, Okinawa all saw battles. In 1945 massive bombing raids on Japan culminating with the United States dropping atomic bombs on August 6 and 9 on Hiroshima and Nagasaki led to Japan agreeing to surrender August 14, 1945. An estimated 5-6 million Jews were killed by the Nazi regime, 70,000 British civilian lost their lives from German bombs, 100,000 Chinese civilians died from Japanese bombs, 80,000 - 200,000 Japanese civilians lost their lives and 45 million military personnel died in the war. The United Nations charter was signed in San Francisco June 26, 1945. The Nuremberg Tribunal convicted twenty-two German leaders in 1946 and in 1948 Japanese leaders were convicted. Berlin was divided. Japan adopted a constitution and West Germany set up a basic law. The Marshall Plan sent $12 billion in aid to western Europe.

In 1946 the British Labor Party set up a national health program and nationalized basic industries. In 1948 Czechoslovakia fell to the Soviets. From April 1948-September 1949 the Berlin blockade existed. NATO and the Organization of American States were formed. Israel was proclaimed a state in May, 1948 and Korea was divided into two republics. The Philippines became independent in 1946, India and Pakistan in 1948 and Indonesia in 1949. The People's Republic was proclaimed in China.

During the war Roosevelt was elected to a fourth term in the United States and died shortly thereafter. Truman became president and then defeated Dewey in his own run for the presidency. Veterans returned home after the war and tried to find work. Many women gave up jobs and returned to home life. In the art world abstract expressionism became popular, existentialism captured literature and philosophy, and the radio and phonograph records spread American popular music around the world.

V.

The War Years In The Forties

Mother's Death

*A*t the beginning of the nineteen forties, the four Minors were living on N. Fifth Street in Steubenville. Although the war was raging in Europe, the United States was in an isolationist mood and most lived their regular lives. At thirty one, Katharine was active in family life. She was to lose her second parent shortly after 1940 began. Speaking of her mother's death Katharine relates, "My mother and her sister Florence had gone to Florida to escape the northern winter. She was not well when I met her at the train station upon her return. She stayed at her home on N. Fourth Street with the house staff and a nurse. On April 1, 1940 she died with my brother Frank, Doc, and me by her side. She lived a full and useful life."

From her obituary in the *Steubenville Herald-Star* the following is taken:

> *Mrs. Mary Donaldson Sinclair, socially prominent and active in numerous lines of public welfare here for many years, died at her home, 523 N. Fourth Street, at 4:45 a.m. today.*
>
> *She was the widow of Dohrman James Sinclair, banker and philanthropist, of this city to whom she was married November 19, 1884, and who preceded her in death August 6, 1915.*
>
> *Mrs. Sinclair returned ten days ago from St. Petersburg, Florida, where she had spent ten weeks at the Hotel Deermont. She was ill when she came home and her heart condition became aggravated to such an extent that her condition became critical two days ago. News of her death was received with regret by the entire community.*

Mrs. Sinclair was born in Steubenville, the daughter of William B. and Emelda Junkin Donaldson, pioneer and influential early residents of this city. She was educated at Steubenville Female Seminary and Washington, Pennsylvania Seminary. She was a member of the Steubenville Seminary Alumnae.

Mrs. Sinclair had the ability, education and refining personality that endeared her to others and made her a born leader in public endeavor. She was ever a gentlewoman with queenly physical appearance. She was always prominently active in church work, first in the Second Presbyterian and later in Westminster Presbyterian Church.

Mary (Donaldson) Sinclair

She was an organizer and was first president of the YWCA. She was head of the Red Cross knitting for Jefferson County during the world war. She was organizing Regent of the Steubenville Chapter of Daughters of the American Revolution, and a member of the Daughters of the American Colonists.

In recent years Mrs. Sinclair became an acknowledged authority on American genealogy and was a member of the Institute of American Genealogy. She was awarded a certificate of merit by the council of the Institute in recognition of original research and a meritorious contribution to the archives of American genealogy.

Her most recent accomplishment was the compiling and indexing of the first fifty years of marriage licenses of Jefferson County, which is the official record used by the D.A.R. headquarters at Washington, D.C.

Her death closes a life of unbounded activity, one of cheerful industry for others in seeking out information about ancestors when it was difficult to obtain. She had spent days and driven over many miles seeking such information for which there was no reward beyond a letter of thankful appreciation. Mrs. Sinclair delighted in helping others, doing so unselfishly, the very acme of public service.

Five children were born to the union with Mr. Sinclair. One, Marie, wife of Henry Fay Grant, died in March, 1917. These children survive: Wilma, wife of Garrett B. LeVan; Katharine Emelda, wife of Dr. Howard H. Minor; Frank Dohrman Sinclair and Dohrman James Sinclair (II) at home.

These grandchildren survive: Garrett B. LeVan, Jr., Dohrman Sinclair Grant, Mary Carolyn Minor and Katharine Evelyn Minor; also three great-grandchildren: Garrett Julian LeVan, Katharine Wilma LeVan and James Denison Grant; also one sister, Mrs. H.H. Henderson.

Life during the early 1940's has been captured through Katharine's notes to her friend Gertrude Lippencott Patterson.

That hour I was waiting for, to write you a long letter seems more distant every day so - Thank you so much for loaning me your book, for writing such a beautiful, consoling letter for being there when I needed you.

Miss Katharine has out grown the bassinet (with her 18 lbs.) but I'll keep it in case I need it again before you do - if that's all right with you. Little Katharine can sit up alone - just holding on to a couple of mama's fingers, and she thinks she's wonderful.

In an April 20, 1940 letter Katharine wrote,

> *Doc and I do so appreciate your generous and hospitable invitation to come up next weekend on our anniversary, but our romantic souls feel the urge of going to Columbus - just as we did five years ago on our honeymoon.*

Mexico

As a testament to their sense of adventure, Kay and Doc decided to drive to Mexico. They went with good friends, Fred and Marney Cook Slaughter. In New Orleans they ate oysters Rockefeller at a fine restaurant. Afterwards, when they were outside, Fred looked up and down the street. He was asked if he was looking for the car and his reply was, "No, for a good hamburger." Marney, never having been west of Ohio, was very excited about driving to see all the capitols of the states on their trips. They had a great time, but Katharine remembers that on the way home she found out that young Katharine was sick. Detouring to see the capitols of Mississippi, Alabama, and other states they visited on the way back was not really what she wanted to do but the die was cast.

Another Child on the Way

When Katharine went in for her postnatal exam after young Katharine's birth she learned she was pregnant. In July 1940, Katharine wrote,

> *The most important news first: Dr. & Mrs. Minor announce that their younger daughter can first crawl; 2nd can say "dada", and 3rd has one tooth. We can't see the tooth yet but when her lower 'ridge' is hit with a spoon we can 'hear' said tooth. So you see we really will have to put in our order on a new 1940 model.*
>
> *All of Dr. Minor's girls had such a good time in Cadiz with you and your family.* (Gertrude's parents lived in Cadiz and Dr. Lippencott, Gertrude's father, was the minister of the Presbyterian Church there.) *It is a shame we don't have more frequent reunions - and wasn't it fun on our steak roast or fry? We had a grand time. In fact it was such an inspiration Doc and Marilyn* (Mary Carolyn) *and I have had a couple since then - one with the addition of the two neighbor girls and young Katharine. Doc thinks four girls are nice. I don't know when we can drive up New Castle way - Thursday and Sunday of this week are out and next*

Thursday is also out but we'll try one of these days and let you know ahead of time if possible.

News flash - we've "given notice" and after September 1st please address all correspondence to 523 N. Fourth Street, Steubenville.

Thanks so much for your wire. Believe it or not I had a surprise birthday party - arranged by Miss Wanda! and Doc. The guest list consisted of Mr. D. Sinclair and Mrs. Harriet Henderson Watt, Doc and Marilyn and it was loads of fun. Miss Marilyn kept reporting progress in her usual way; 'You're to stay upstairs here mommee. You're not to go to the kitchen to see any of the 'sprizes, not the cake or anything.' She was quite perturbed when Uncle Dohrman arrived and before she ever came upstairs to tell me, 'He's a 'sprize' and you're not to know he's here,' she rushed to the kitchen to ask Wanda if there was 'enough' and to set an extra place at the table. We really had a grand time.

Just finished feeding Katharine and I find I'm mistaken about the tooth, there are two instead of one. They must have both arrived yesterday.

New Sister-in-law, House, and Son

Katharine's brother Frank married Dot Smith in September. Always the prankster, he would show his friends two pictures of two gaunt women with stringy hair, skirts down to their ankles, unwashed, and looking very woebegone. Then he would say, "The woman on the right is my new wife and the other is her sister."

In September Katharine wrote,

We are getting settled at 523 N. Fourth Street here in Steubenville and hibernating for the winter. Margaret Arms and her husband were here for five days soon after we moved - she expects the stork in December. Florence Brettell expects the stork 'most any time. (I'm still expecting the other half of my set of twins within the next three months.)

Katharine now weighs over 20 lbs. and has decided, herself, that three meals a day is what she should have, baked potatoes and all. She's walking around her play pen and crib, and is still as good as ever. She fell out of her buggy, upset the buggy, and rammed her two lower teeth thru her upper gum last Saturday. Miss Marilyn was a very

*placid child by comparison. Doc is very fine but needs a
vacation. He also declined being a deacon at church.*

Less than a year after their second daughter was born, Howard Sinclair
Minor arrived. His birth on November 26 was also at Allegheny General
Hospital in Pittsburgh, where his two sisters had been born. With three
children it was a very merry Christmas even though war was raging in
Europe.

War Heats Up
Early in 1941 Katharine wrote her friend,

> *How the time does flit by and carries changes with it. To
> begin at the present and work back: "We're in the army
> now!' Doc was called for two weeks active duty in the med-
> ical reserves on January 2 and hopes to be discharged next
> Wednesday. I'm going out to Fort Hayes in Columbus, Ohio
> to see that they treat him nicely etc. on Wednesday and we'll
> stay over until Thursday night. We <u>hope</u> that this two weeks
> duty will relieve him from a year's service <u>but</u> his name (last
> Thursday) was 14th from the top of the Reserve officers list
> - 400 have already been called and there are only 200 more
> to go. As of January 15 he will serve in the National Guard.
> I feel sort of weak when I think he may be called and would
> have to give up his office space (probably) and office girl, as
> well as his practice. As for me, Dohrman is leaving for
> California on Wednesday and I can't see myself running this
> big house for my three youngsters (and if you want to
> include Wanda and Violet, my help, it makes <u>five</u> children).
> I think I'll get a trailer - won't you join us? But if we do go
> it will be fun or at least something to remember for the rest
> of our lives.*
>
> *Marilyn was <u>delighted</u> with her store. We've played store
> - drug store, dress store; where to buy baby things store;
> daddy' clothes store etc. hour on end. She simply loves it and
> my only objection to it is you should have sent Bobby with
> it. (I assume he has less pressing demands on his time than
> I do).*
>
> *The day before Christmas (Howard S. being less than a
> month old) I let Wanda and Violet <u>both</u> go home. Mary had
> left a week before - and from then on did we have our hands*

full!!! I spent the day getting a man sized breakfast (sans fried eggs and sausage) for Doc and Dohrman, and Marilyn's consisted of slightly less. Katharine's pablum and bottle and Howard's formula; and from then on it was nip and tuck giving bottles, changing panties, winding up toys, listing who gave what to each, giving baths, unwrapping gifts, opening stocking, getting dinner, making formulas, dressing and undressing babies for naps, etc. and so on thru the day. It was surely a very <u>merry</u> Christmas. Wanda and "Vi" both arrived back in time to ask if they could both have the evening off!! Peace, it's wonderful!

You would be interested to know that our little Howard is no longer the baby of the family. Kathy LeVan has a new daughter, four days old, (Andrea born January 8) who will hold the honor until about next May when Frank and Dot receive their bundle from heaven. (Also Margaret Arms Mason has a new daughter born December 18).

The old home town moves along at an even pace. Catherine Miles (Katharine's cousin) and Stanley bought a new home on Belleview Boulevard where they used to live. Virginia Biddle Rogers (later Meyers) was in Florida for Christmas and Florence Henderson hopes to go down to be with her sister-in-law for a couple of months. Wilma and Garry are leaving next week with Garrett and Kay's two youngsters (Garrett and Katharine) to spend a peaceful winter. Wilma has resigned as president of the bank (Behind the curtain - the bank has steadily increased each year and last year more than doubled the income that the average bank of its size made, and the government has ordered her dismissal because she is "not of their choosing" and they need the job for a democrat). That man Roosevelt and his cohorts are traitorous and worse! Mr. Sharp replaced Wilma. There is a lot to it so don't repeat it unless you know all the details. Must to bottle and to bed. Again my many thanks and the very best of everything to you all for 1941.

Importance of Prepositions

Doc Minor seldom repeated personal information, but one morning he called his wife from the office to say that Mrs. Sarratt, Betty's (Irvine) mother had died. The elevator girl had told everyone as they went to their offices in the Sinclair Building. Katharine relates, "I quickly put on my coat and walked to the Sarratt's home located at 612 N. Third Street. Betty met me at the front door in her bathrobe. She apologized for her appearance and said they had had quite a bit of excitement that morning!! As we talked I realized that something was not right and finally told her the story being broadcast about her mother dying. She assured me her mother had not died but fainted." The truth emerged when it was learned that the elevator girl had said, "passed on" instead of "passed out." All was well.

At Home

Katharine had her hands full with the three children. One day Howie had climbed up on the trellis of the laundry building next to the garage in the back yard of the N. Fourth Street house and had almost reached the second floor. His mother heard his cries coming from outside. She came running and climbed up the trellis to get him. Katharine reached him and began carrying him down holding him in one arm and trying to hold the trellis at intervals with her other hand. She was very close to the bottom as the trellis pulled away from the laundry building. Escaping injury, she jumped in time with the baby in her arms.

Another day, young Howie was found standing on top of the grand-father's clock. He had discovered that by holding onto the outside of the staircase railing, he could walk up the edge of the steps and get to the top of the clock. His mother considered standing at the bottom of the clock and catching him as he jumped, but in the end, she lifted him off the top of the clock by standing on the stairs. Night time took on a new challenge, for young Katharine (called Keekee by her brother) would get up at night and wander around the house. Finally a solution was found by putting the mattress on the floor and putting the crib over it with a net to enclose it.

Start of War

On Keekee's birthday, December 7, 1941, the Japanese bombed Pearl Harbor and suddenly the United States found itself at war. It meant the lives of many would be changed forever. In 1940 the United States army was 18th in the world and had 5% (504,000) of the American population on active duty or in the trained reserve. This had been improved over the last year but the United States was still not prepared for war.

In December, 1941 Katharine wrote to her friend to thank her for a gift and continued,

> *Do come soon and help us use it in our new house - yes, we bought a house and a car a couple of weeks ago!! (The Depression has started for us - the house is 730 Lawson*

Avenue, across the street from where we lived before and we don't know when we're moving - maybe in a month, maybe in 6 months - the car is another Chevy two door green etc.)

Marilyn, Patty Miles and Richard Miles played with the bean bags most of Christmas night. They had a grand time. That blue duck is one of the cleverest things I've ever seen. From the amount of attention it attracted we're not sure whether it was a gift to the youngsters or adults.

There are eleven in our household now, and yesterday three more came for the day. There were 5 children of which Marilyn and Katharine were the two oldest.

We have had the very nicest Christmas. Surely a house full but each and everyone having themselves a grand time.

War Response

Katharine and Doc had a nice visit with the Pattersons in Chautauqua in July of 1942. Katharine was familiar with the area from a story about her mother and sister visiting the area. Early in the century Marie was on a boat on Chautauqua Lake. Near Bemus Point her trunk fell off the boat into the lake. When it was rescued everything was soaking wet. It was quite the display of pantaloons, long white cotton petticoats, and other clothes drying on the line. "Today's washers, dryers and nylon materials are a vast improvement," said Katharine. After their visit to Chautauqua, she wrote to thank Gertrude.

It was a double oasis for us. We didn't mention it, and tried not to think of it, while we were there, but Doc is going to Columbus next weekend to volunteer for the army! It's a long story, and I feel like your mother's friend, Scarlet O'Hara. 'I'll think about that tomorrow.'

We collected Marilyn the day after we got back and brought her 16 year old cousin, Lynn Drake back too. She's here and her 13 year old sister, Diane Drake, is coming today so they can go home together in a few days. Dohrman is coming tomorrow for a few days, before he goes into the army August 8th as a lieutenant.

Dohrman was in California most of the time during the war and did government service work after the war.

Mary Carolyn was keyed up for school in the fall of 1942. An article in the October 9 *Herald Star* newspaper reported that Mary Carolyn Minor, a first grader at Garfield, had personally accumulated 223 keys in the drive to collect metal for the war effort. These were extra keys she found around her home on N. Fourth Street.

The United States army took the Minor volunteer and asked him to report to San Antonio, Texas on October 8, 1942 as a captain. Kay drove down with Doc when he reported for duty. They were on the base and Doc had gone into the PX while Kay waited in the car. There was a car parked behind her with children playing loudly. Suddenly there was a loud bang and everything went quiet. A woman rushed out of the PX and took a limp child into the PX. Doc took a look and knew there was nothing to be done. Apparently there had been a loaded gun in the glove compartment which one of the children had accidently discharged.

Katharine had planned to stay a week but the army had different plans. Dr. Minor was on call after the first day and could not get off the base, so she went home the next day by train. Her sister-in-law, Evelyn, had volunteered to watch both the Drake and Minor children.

Letters from her husband were to follow her north.

> *My Dearest, I love you so much and sitting here this p.m. looking at the pictures I have makes me feel kinda homesick.*
>
> *The weather is lovely, warm and bright but was rather cool yesterday. Your letters have been awfully welcome and let me know that you still love me.*
>
> *I got away from here yesterday afternoon and evening and it helped break the tension. I believe I had been sticking too close. (There are about 6 sleeping around me now though). I took two other fellows, one named Slripps (Jewish, 2 children from Philadelphia) and one named Weeks (1 child & from New Jersey) to Brackenridge Park and to the sunken gardens. I figured it would be worth while as it is on about all postcard displays you see. They really were lovely. We then spent quite a long time in the zoo. It is a good one but I had to laugh when I thought how many times I had passed the Philadelphia zoo and had never been in it. We then went to the Gunter and had smorgasbord. All you could eat for 90 cents. I talked to the assistant manager in charge of the food while there and he said it is one of the ways they can practically solve the help problem. It was quite good and at the next table was Eyrman (the fellow who has the bunk under mine and comes from St. Louis) and his wife and about 4 or 5 others from our barracks. The Eyrmans invited us all to come out to their place afterwards*

which we did. They were in an old high ceiling house which I think from the conversation, their relatives own. It is the oldest brick house in San Antonia I understood them to say. The widow who lives there apparently goes with the doctor's cousin as they came in (to her own house) after the 10? of us had been there for a long time. We had a couple of high-balls and everyone seemed to enjoy it immensely as it is about the first social contact we've had. Henry was there and provided considerable amusement. I think I'll go into church with him this evening.

Sorry to take up so much of my letter writing silly details but unless you want to know about a gas mask, military law, how we drill or pages on how much I love you there is little else to write. They have been working us hard, that was the first time off the post for a week. My ankle is better. There is no use sending that card to the board of elections (I got it to-day) as there wouldn't be time for me to get a ballot and return it. No money as yet.

Take good care of our children and happier times will be coming, my own. When I think of you I go sort of soft inside.
Love, H.

Katharine wrote to her friend in the fall of 1942.

We've been having more or less of a siege here. Over five weeks ago (the week after I came back from seeing Doc 'off to the wars' at San Antonio) Marilyn took sick and briefly she's had mumps and scarlet fever and has been in bed ever since. They have cleared up but her scarlet fever has left 'signs' on her kidneys and the doctor says to keep her in bed ten days more and he'll check her again. Howard has had mumps during our siege but Katharine still leads a charmed life and has gotten neither (I've never had either to further complicate possibilities).

We are living out of suitcases all prepared to move to the hill but this (another 10 days bedfast) will throw any move too near Christmas. Doc called last night from Texas to say he hopes to be in Sherman, Texas permanently for a couple of months!! How soon do I think I can move!! I told him - for the first time what a busy time we've been having here. He's so built up on our coming I hated to disappoint him but when you can't you just have to grin and bear it!

> *Having a joint birthday party for my two and three year olds tomorrow for 14 small fries. I discovered before it was too late that K & H had blown out the gas fire - we're all fine!! Really will write soon.*

Soon afterwards, Kay wrote,

> *Don't mean to be A Calamity Jane but I'm just citing a few reasons why I don't think Marilyn (Mary Carolyn) and her mama will be able to remember in any concrete way Bobby and his mama at Christmas time this year. I've had to scratch my Christmas list to practically nothing. Personally I don't see where I'll find time to go shopping even for the children and Doc. To be apart at Christmas seemed terrible at first but now it fades and if only we're all well we can ask no more. No cards so a very especially merry Christmas to you and a happy new year.*

Christmas Apart

As much as the Minors wanted to be together for Christmas, the Christmas of 1942 they spent apart. More letters arrived from Captain Minor at Perrin Field. The military could send letters with no stamp by writing *free* in the upper right hand corner.

December 15 Doc wrote,

> *I hope you are well settled and happy. I was worried when I saw by the paper that there was a flu epidemic among babies at the hospital. I pray you are all well and stay that way. It sounds like Mary Carolyn is coming along all right which is the important thing. If you think it better for her to stay out the first semester and start back the second it is just as well as she will have a long while to go to school. Did she at any time show any evidence of heart trouble or swelling from kidneys? She is such a lamb but I have a hunch will be all right.*
>
> *I have a feeling my letters are a little dull but there is a good deal of routine and repetition. I find your letters so full of the kind of news I hunger for.*
>
> *Did I tell you I spent an hour in a link trainer one evening, very interesting. Hoffner, who is a flyer but had never had instrument training for blind flying was as excited*

as a kid at the circus. As far as I was concerned it was like riding a novel gadget at a carnival.

The new Commanding Officer just arrived and we chatted with him - his name is Ryan - he's a major and a rather young guy but most of these fellows from the school of aviation medicine have to be and they are the ones that usually draw the top administrative jobs. As for me, I'm not looking for any more paper work.

Love, H.

Another letter from Doc related,

*One draws some strange jobs. (*He enclosed the *Perrin Field Daily Bulletin* which listed him as the lecturer for the sex morale lecture*). I might as well be discussing the strange customs of the inhabitants of New Guinea - I have heard of such strange things as sex but thought it had been outlawed. These assignments turn up like a lottery. The first Wednesday I was here I was O.D. and that day whoever was officer of the day was scheduled to give a lecture on first aid at the post theater. They'll make a public speaker out of me yet. A movie helped on the other one but I'll have to get something to lecture about tomorrow. There is a movie and the chaplain will also probably take a few minutes.*

It's fun right now. The fracture services (part of orthopedics) is the busiest one and I drew it here as chief which I think is OK and have done a little of the general surgery which is slow. Not too bad when I have so little formal training and it looks well on paper. The hospital here is roughly (we don't mention too accurately size as it's restricted information) the size of the Ohio Valley Hospital.

Since you and I are going through all our separation etc. so that they'll (the children) have what we think is the right kind of world we mustn't subject them to anything harmful. I worry quite a bit about you all when you are so far away. Are you warm enough this winter? Can you get coal? When I think of those dear cherubs my tummy turns flip-flops and I would be extremely grateful to you for being their chief usher even if I disliked you and you know I love you and always always will. H.

Keekee, Howie, Marilyn

On Friday, December 19, 1942 he sent the following letter to Steubenville.

> *Darling, I got your air-mail letter today written I believe about Tuesday. It was a lovely letter and I feel good since reading it. It is nice to know that my family is settled and comfortable, and likes our <u>home</u>. It sounds like you have had a hectic time with the furnace. I think the trick is to fill it very full when the fire is hot but you are probably an expert by now. It also lifted a weight to know that Marilyn had no swelling, it indicates that she didn't have a great deal of kidney involvement and when she looks well I feel sure (since her fever and everything is OK) that the weekly check of her urine is the only really important check that she needs.*
>
> *You mentioned about my Christmas and when I finished the letter I found I was still grinning because the only present I want is to see you (and of course the children too would be nice). Let me know when you'll be coming if it works out, as I would want to be sure we had a room engaged.*
>
> *It would make it a real Christmas just looking forward to seeing you. You could look around, scout the town, see how the army lives etc. I got you only a tiny present. I believe you'll know I want to get you lots of things but I'll save the money for the trip. I think after we get the repair bills and money paid it should be a cheaper and easier place to live (the Lawson Ave home over the N. Fourth Street house). I'm glad Frank (Sinclair) will be in the same*

*town as there will be another who you could call on for pro-
tection if needed. Frank's advise is probably pretty good
except where there is a financial angle. I suppose his coming back means more tough luck. I'm glad there is the Fourth
Street house for them. Hope you and the bank finally wound
up your business.*

*You see I'm O.D. this weekend. There is a separate
weekend roster (Saturday and Sunday) from the week-day
one. That probably means I won't draw it again for 6 or 7
weeks.*

(The second sheet of the letter is on the back of the *Perrin Field Daily
Bulletin* listing Dr. Minor as Officer of the Day and includes such things as
the times for the movie, *Gentleman Jim* with Errol Flynn and Jack Carson,
Christmas parties coming up, and the official notice, 'Effective immediately all senders of Congratulatory and Greeting Services such as: Felicita-
tions Greetings for Christmas, New Year, Easter, Father's Day, Jewish New
Year, Mother's Day, Thanksgiving, Valentine's Day, Congratulations on the
birth of a child, Graduations, Weddings, Anniversaries and birthdays will be
accepted until further notice.')

When I think of all those babies lost (because of the flu)
*at the Ohio Valley Hospital I know how thankful we should
be for our blessings. This separations is at least of temporary nature. All my love, Doc*

Another letter from Doc said,

*My Darling, I guess the old man is still an old sissy. I
just finished hearing Eddie Rickenbacker talk on the radio
and had to give a few quick eye-wipes.*

*I sent about 10 Christmas cards to people I probably
should have written to, and composed a letter last night to
Fred (Slaughter). I suppose he is back in El Paso by now.*

*I wonder if I've ever thanked you enough for the picture
of the three children that you had finished for me. I find my
eyes stray to it and your picture many times when I'm in the
room. This is a little like being an intern except for the men-
tal attitude. If I remember correctly as an intern I spent most
of my time getting ready to go out or something and here I
just stay put. I've studied more than anytime since medical*

school. They have a rule that we must take exercise three times a week and its probably a good thing.

I am looking forward to having a report (in person) as to how our infants liked their Christmas.

There is little for me to write as, except to walk about three blocks and have dinner at the officers' club I don't think I've been out since I wrote last. Even though I was the officer on duty, I was only up once last night.

Major Henry who is commanding the hospital got his orders this a.m. and is now about to move. I'm at present the official head of orthopedic surgery and helping with the general surgery. I did a hemorrhoidectomy today and like it fine. Most of the staff are sort of lazy but good guys.

Love, H."

After Christmas Katharine was able to visit Doc and in the process had a chance to get some presents for their children. The following letter was written to her husband from Steubenville after her return from Sherman, Texas and dated January 14, 1943.

Your little lambs are all tucked in and in the land of nod. Marilyn made a bed for her doll under our dresser and we had to be very quiet so we wouldn't waken her. Howard took an old belt to bed with him and Katharine has a doll on either side of her, her toy sweeper under the covers and an assortment of crayons, blocks, a ribbon, the tin top to her coffee pot, etc., under her pillow!! They have been very good today, only broke two dishes.

Howie is so cute - he has a new trick of biting Katharine, for which he was twice spanked today and had a return bite once. I hope he's cured. They played around building tents out of chairs, their rocking horse, a stool, and a card table covered by my afghan. A rolled up large calender and two calender mailers made excellent horns for them and we had innumerable noisy parades all day.

While I was washing the dishes Marilyn made cocoa and Howie not to be out done, made his by mixing coco malt in a pan I had been soaking clothes (before washing them), and would have devoured it if I hadn't rescued it in the nick of time.

Ray McKinley fixed the toilet upstairs which they had

entirely clogged up with molding clay - cute aren't they? Howie's nicely newly painted walls have been quite generously covered with self expression murals in red crayons! The two bunnies on the dresser lamps still stand but the lamp pedestal is in the trash box.

At their breakfast this morning, they ate among them twelve pieces of toast so you don't have to worry about their appetites.

Keekee and Howie are talking much better than when you left. Howie copies and repeats everything you do and say, and is forming sentences himself now. While I was at my desk he started upstairs and said, 'I go up tairs - I be back - wait minute,' which is pretty good for a two year old.

They are all so delighted with the things I brought home. Marilyn and Howie particularly. Marilyn keeps her pin in the table beside her bed at night and wears it all day. I brought a little book about chickens etc. to Howie and Keekee and Howie gets exuberant when he sees it. With his little high voice he runs the gauntlet of gleeful sounds as he sucks air both in and out!"

A lovely letter arrived from Doc written January 25 after Kay's visit.

My Darling, I'm looking at the picture of my girl when she was about fifteen. She is a nice level eyed frank and honest looking youngster and I remember her as being rather full chested and straight-legged at that time when I began to be acutely conscious of her. I was still an adolescent and not very sure of my feelings nor their significance. Over a period of time I became more aware of my girl and can well recall when being home from school that merely riding by her house made me feel taut inside and all squirmy around my middle. And those early dates, I must have seemed a very awkward lout, sort of tongue-tied because of inner emotion and making inane conversation. And a little later becoming more possessive and so jealous to think that you might not be with me always or could be interested in anyone else. And then we were married my dear. I sometimes wonder if you really wanted to get married. Through the years you have grown to be a part of me. We have indications around of our mutual love and sometimes they are a handful. They at times can fray a mother's nerves, and there's the business of living and working and sometimes it crowds more important things aside and there is little time for demonstrable signs or the telling. There are times when illness strikes and personalities are strained and unreal, and some of the things above mentioned require faith; the little boy can't bring the teacher an apple every day but she should know his heart. And now I'm away from you and I hate that but we've got to keep things right for those three little ones and if it comes down to it I'd much rather be killed than have my children have to take orders from any Japs. Oh hell dear, I love and miss you an awful lot and I hope you've been pretty happy so far and better times are coming. I'll dab my eyes and give you the current events. I'm afraid you can't read my letters at any party, they seem to be a little on the mushy side.

McGee, I think I wrote you, got his promotion to captain a few days ago and Dailey got his yesterday. He certainly is a funny guy. We all went down to the club yesterday about four and had a few drinks to celebrate. The Elliots then had a stag party. A good ham dinner for eight of us. We played poker afterwards and I won four or five dollars. That's the first 'card' gambling I've done. The games down at the club are too steep. Most of those guys down there are about like college students and have no financial responsibilities. The 'card' insert above was to keep the record straight as I did take a couple of passes in a craps game coming out even and quitting.

It seems Shennon's brother-in-law's story was written up as the tale of a modern Robinson Crusoe in the N.Y. Times a few weeks back. He was on this South Pacific island for three days and on the fourth the natives came out etc. Finally the natives got him back to an island which had soldiers stationed on it.

Darling, I enjoy your letters and cards so much.
All my love, dear, your husband

An example of Katharine's day from one of the letters to her husband read,

Howie got me up at eight, right on the dot. I don't know how he does it but he always knows when 8 o'clock comes and Houdini fashion, gets out of bed and trots over to wish

me 'Good morning.' I get up and dress Howie and myself then Katharine and Marilyn, down stairs to get breakfast for them, took care of toilets, made the beds, straightened up the rooms, pared potatoes, cut up a chicken for stewing, prepared broccoli, made fruit Jell-O, washed the breakfast dishes, swept the porch, got dinner and had dinner, undressed the trio and put them to bed, washed the dinner dishes, scoured the stove and sink (which was badly needed) swept the kitchen, dressed the trio, made their beds again, and by that time they had 'made cocoa' and K. officiated. I threw it out, cleaned up the mess and they took over.

Marilyn made paste and made chains, K. got the paste later and I cleaned it up. H. contented himself with riding the cradle, upside down all through the house and M. played house with some of her salvaged doll house furniture. I next cleaned up the paprika and chili sauce which they'd dragged from the shelves and the potato that H. had squeezed over his little iron engine.

While I sewed a button on H.'s overalls M. & K. had an orange "fight" in the kitchen. In the meantime I had made a bolster case out of some material I got at Penny's yesterday. After I cleaned up the graham crackers they had stepped on I made paper hats for them and myself and we all had a parade. H. dropped out of the parade unnoticed and was gnawing at the remains of a T-bone steak from dinner last night when next seen. There's still enough left for stew on Tuesday. After they had smeared tooth paste on our bed room clock I got their dinners, washed the dishes and so to bed. H. has gotten out twice and K. once (for a longer period) and came down stairs with tomorrow morning's dress on and her shoes in her hand. I guess that was about all except their romping all over me every time I sat down - and sliding down my legs. Oh yes, we played several games of Farmer in the Dell etc. It's been sort of fun and I don't think I'll mind it. Marilyn was over at Ginny Hennings this morning and had lots of fun. H. & K. both have the sniffles but it doesn't seem to slow them down any.

It's a problem to mail letters. The mail man won't take them, so I've been very irregular but maybe a better way of mailing will present itself. Think I'll take this to the corner

*if all continues to be quiet upstairs. I'm hoping for a letter
or two in the morning. I love you darling. All our love. K."*

In another letter she mentioned,

> *I hung Dohrman's long French mirror which was
> between the windows in the library on N. Fourth Street, at
> the foot of the stairway last night. Its been leaning against
> the refrigerator. It looks quite well. I also put the knob on the
> drawer of my desk, washed your globe, switched the old
> fashioned pictures of the children in the dining room so the
> larger picture would be in the larger space, hung my needle
> point picture over the chest in the dining room, nailed a
> corner on the steps that the children had pulled off etc.*
>
> *I went down to the Civic Service League Monday night
> to their Valentine Party. We all had to take several sand-
> wiches dressed in Valentine array. Mine didn't win a prize
> but it won honorable mention. It was a red, white, and blue
> corsage (heart flowers etc.), much lace etc. It was a nice
> party with about 80 there. Last night I was over at Mary
> Agnes' (Gray) to Contract Literary Club. We had two tables
> of bridge - I made the eighth. I gave our Civic Music tickets
> to Betty Kelly. I offered them to Dot Smith Sinclair, June
> Loggie, Cahills, Hennings and Punkes and am glad they
> were used. I'd hate to see the Club disintegrate and there
> were only seven there the time before. I think they are keep-
> ing it going largely for me, which I appreciate. Mary Agnes
> asked me to go to the movies with them tonight but I don't
> know whether "my" Wilma Stopp can come over or not.
> She's an awfully nice, capable Senior - crazy about children
> (that's all she does - take care of them). She is coming all
> day Saturday and I'm going to take M.C. to Pittsburgh to see
> John (Hamilton) then we are going to see "Jr. Miss." Effie
> Afton Smith Hill Milford etc. has given us a couple of tickets
> for the Saturday Matinee. I hear it is very good.*

The Contract Literary Club had been organized in 1934 with the purpose of playing bridge and having books as bridge prizes. The winner
would receive a book and report on it at the next meeting of the group.
Katharine won a number of books including *Catherine the Great*. Katharine
said when she played bridge the women who came were always interested

in hearing the stories of what her children had been up to since the last meeting. Putting a little humor in a problem situation helped to deal with discouraging situations and trying times. Effie, who was referred to above, was Dot Sinclair's sister and was on the New York stage for many plays.

On February 22, 1943, Katharine wrote her friend from 730 Lawson Avenue.

> *Your letter surely did boost civilian morale around here. I'll spend the next six months trying to come close to all the nice things you said about me. M.C. is still out of school - nephritis this time with a tonsil operation coming up. The babies are grand. Doc got a wonderful break and we're very elated. He was chosen to take a course in Post Graduate surgery at Columbia Presbyterian Medical Center, New York. It lasts six weeks. He was <u>home</u> for two days, met his children again and saw his <u>home</u> for the first time furnished. I have no girl so I'm reduced to the penny post card stage.*

During the separation Kay and Doc managed to get together a few times. The trip down together, the trip she made after Christmas, his stopping on the way to New York, and her visit there where they stayed in the Hotel Lincoln. The following letter was written by Doc after that visit.

> *I hope you didn't have too tough a ride home. You must have been tired after all your activities including blood donating. You just gave and gave and gave. It is lonesome without you but I will see you again soon. (He took the train the following week to Steubenville on his way back to the base in Texas).*
>
> *One day when Dick and I were at Belleview we rode over together and he wanted to send two and a half cases of whiskey to his hospital as North Carolina is dry. New York has some rationing, Macy's has a few rules of their own etc. They would only send 15 bottles on one transition so I had to pay for one and Dick gave me his check for that transition plus his money for dinner.*
>
> *When there is only one week left to go it certainly seems like it is about over. We have had a couple of very good days this week, repairing severed nerves in dogs one day, Kings County in Brooklyn yesterday (its a regular city with 9600 beds) and the staff at Belleview this morning was good.*

Texas Living

In April, 1943, Katharine and the three children took the train and joined Dr. Minor at Perrin Field, Sherman, Texas. Shortly after that, a letter arrived at her friend's home written from 1726 N. Ricketts Street, Sherman, Texas.

> *Not a letter - just a 'quickie.' As you may have noticed I'm deep in the heart of Texas. A month ago I had no idea of coming - and since then I've packed, unpacked, re-packed, rented the house with all that implies, brought the three babes down by train (two days and nights) and been here three weeks tomorrow! Confusion is an understatement - to make a long story short we all stayed at the hotel a week, quite an experience all sleeping in one room! There was not a house or apartment or trailer to be had furnished or unfurnished. (The army canceled the transfer orders of the officer and family whose house we were to have, the reason we left in such a swirl was to get his house, then didn't). We are the essence of happiness in a new house which we have had to furnish from curtains and rods to mops and clothes pins. We rent our furniture. More about all that later but I thought a note now would save you a stop in Steubenville on your way to Cadiz. Delighted to hear of Mary Margaret Lippencott Reline's new son, Bruce. Frank and Dot have another boy too born May 5. They are calling him Frank Bruce Sinclair.*

The Minors stayed in Sherman, Texas the longest. Their stay at the Grayson Hotel when Katharine and the children first arrived entailed three moves in the first two days, and Marilyn referred to the bell boys as "those boys who move us all the time." Their house in Texas had most of Texas west of it. There were fields behind the house where the children flew kites, which their Dad helped them make. There were field mice which often came into the house uninvited and took the labels off the cans. It made for mysterious meals at times when the cans were opened, since one didn't know if the can contained soup, green beans or corn beef hash. During the war there were coupons for food and one day one of the children put parsley among the food being purchased. A valuable coupon was used to buy it.

Later from the same address in Texas Katharine sent a real letter.

> *I'm that girl you used to know a long long time ago - the mother of Bobby's first girl may place me in case you've forgotten!*

Souvenirs of World War II

Life is just a bowl of cherries! We're all together and well. Since I last dropped you a card we've gotten a house and are a real family unit again. The house is: new, two bedrooms, one floor (was) unfurnished and is Home to us. We were at the hotel for a week (about which I could write a book) when this house became available. We've rented most of our furniture from the store and have had to buy (rent or borrow) curtains, rugs, dishes, all kitchen utensils, silver, broom, mop, pail, scrub brush, cloths line, cloths pins, curtain rods, mail box, pillows etc. ad infinitum. I feel like a bride - with three children! Its been loads of fun (if a little hectic at times). I have no help but I send out the washing.

The house is one of forty odd new ones on a newly opened street only three blocks long. They are available only to army personnel, and as the street is practically dead end at both ends there is no traffic to speak of, and I dress and feed the youngsters in the morning and turn them loose. The thermometer hovers around 100 degrees every day so we've done quite a bit of swimming. The town has several parks of which it should be justly proud. There are two swimming pools and three or more wading pools for our younger fry. Marilyn is learning to swim and to hear her talk you'd think she could.

Howie fell in the eight foot end one day and a young boy got there first and pulled him out by the hair. It was quite exciting. It was the same day we stopped in the Sherwin Williams paint store to get a picture or two (to replace our pages from Esquire we had tacked up) and he got hold of a can of varnish!! While we cleaned up him and the store, Keekee took French leave and we located her a block or so down the street.

The youngsters have taken Perrin Field by storm. The first day we were at the Officers Club for dinner, Howie grabbed the ball off the pool table where Commanding Officer Bob Arnold was playing and ran like a scared rabbit. Everyone, including the C.O. thought that it was very funny. Last Sunday, however, when we were there for dinner the <u>new</u> C.O. was half dozing and Howie lifted a slightly filled discarded Coca Cola bottle to the C.O.'s mouth and started to tilt it. Only split second timing saved us from a cleaning bill and a demotion.

Yesterday morning the generous little soul brought me a big bunch of yellow flowers, from our garden, which would have been cucumbers if they had been allowed to pursue their own way of life! We've had beans and beets from our garden, which Doc watches over every evening when he comes home. I'd like to have a picture of it - it would be a wonderful study in still life!

There is quite a gay social life with dances, picnics, golf, bridge, supper dances etc. Everyone seems bent on getting as much out of life each day because no one knows how long it will last. Transfers are frequent and sudden, and the occasional crash makes us all realize how temporary we may be and somehow adds impetus to making each day as full as possible of pleasant memories.

This is where we belong and we're staying together as long as possible - I hope for the duration. Doc's going home for a couple of days to straighten up unfinished business and to see his mother.

The only way the Minors could attend church was to take their children to the services. Although the children were relatively good, there were instances such as the one during communion. People were going to the front of the church and Keekee said in a loud voice, "Why are they getting to play games and we aren't?" The base decided to open a nursery for the three Minor children and others during church.

The army base Officers' Club Saturday dances every other week and tea dances on the Sundays in between were fun and a good diversion for friends being called up to go overseas. These orders were traumatic for the families and the rest who sympathized. The Minors would also attend medical picnics where Jim Hoffner would fry about twenty chickens out in the open near the lake and the medical staff and families would eat them all. One good friend who the Minors continued contact with after the war was Dee Daily. Dee and his brother went to a restaurant one time and ordered turkey. The waitress asked if they wanted light meat or dark and their reply was, "We want turkey." She brought in a whole turkey and when they finished there was nothing left of the turkey but bones. Dee and his wife Marian were from Elcho, Wisconsin.

Army Stories

Mary remembered her father talking about the doctor in his late 30's or early 40's who was called up to serve and given his physical. The doctor told the army he was too old and the reply was, "You'll be rejected." However, later he was given his overseas physical and again repeated his plight of being too old. He might have been too old but the army sent him overseas anyway. Around the Minor house the saying "The right way, the wrong way, and the army way" was often heard.

The war was big business, and on the street where the Minor children lived it was fun for them to act out what they heard and saw. Mary loved the planes and had seen the soldiers practice parachuting. Inside the Minor garage was a loft where the youngsters would climb up and play. One day Mary found some of her Dad's handkerchiefs and tied strings to the corners. She and her sister were going to make the loft a plane and use their home-made parachutes. Mary landed fine but her three year old sister wasn't quite so lucky, breaking three bones in her foot. Doc set Keekee's broken leg and made the first walking cast using a bicycle tire embedded in the plaster to make a heel. It was a good walking cast and Keekee chose to test it well. Two days after she had the cast on, a neighbor ran in the house to tell Kay that her daughter was up on the hood of the car, cast and all!

Keekee was often on the move and often with young Howie in tow. One day their mother left them in the car saying she was going into a store and would be back in five minutes. Keekee decided that her mother was gone too long, and she went looking for her with her brother. Katharine discovered them missing when she returned to the car. They had just completely disappeared. Katharine called the Sherman police and they did not seem too concerned. She then called the Perrin Field Military Police and said she was the wife of Major Minor and could they help her locate two missing children. The Military Police found the two, who were two and three at the time. When they were found they said they had taken a walk. However, the walk crossed train tracks and took them to a lumber yard over a mile away.

Life moved rapidly during these years and the next letter was written from 1304 Oak Knoll, Ft. Worth 3, Texas where Dr. Minor had been transferred to Tarrant Field. He later was transferred to Selman Field, Monroe, Louisiana, where he remained until the end of the war. The housing shortage was extremely acute, and moves to better their housing conditions were frequent. One year they moved five times, and Marilyn started second grade on three successive Monday mornings in three different schools and two different states. Katharine still found time to write occasionally to her friend.

> *I was so glad to get your letter - I've written so very few for the past few months that my incoming mail is nil. Briefly, I've become practically <u>extinct</u> since coming to this delightful spot "where the West begins." We are all together and well. I'm writing during "the duration."*
>
> *I'll give you the high spots of the past few months. Doc got orders February 1 to report to Ft. Worth February 3. He did. He got a house the 4th. I packed the 5th and we (small fries and I) moved the 6th, completely settled and mailed the valentines the 7th! Houses are impossible to get. We're twelve miles from the field, one closet in the house (and the rain pours in that), cheese cloth covers the lathe and papers pasted on that etc. etc. but we are most lucky to get anything.*
>
> *Doc got a marvelous break. He's head of the surgical service for this big regional hospital. He's flown to make "emergency" consultations at other hospitals under this one, and operates or advises and then is flown back. It has many ramifications, but suffice it to say he's very busy, very happy and doing very well.*
>
> *I've been busy doing all the cooking, cleaning, serving, baby watching and nursing since we've been here. I've had <u>no</u> help.*
>
> *Just now Howie & Keekee are recovering from chicken pox. Incidentally Howie calls them chicken pops even as Gertrude (the Patterson's daughter). Marilyn finished with hers last week and I'm hoping she'll be over her measles before H. & K. get them! They've been pretty good. On our 'zero day' the temperatures ranged from 104 degrees to 105.4 degrees. Oh me! Spring is here, it is 92 degrees this afternoon and we had the heaters on this morning.*
>
> *Can't plan ahead to this summer. We live from day to day. Doc took his "over seas" physical two weeks ago but*

we don't think about that. We may all come home for a two weeks leave after school.

The minister of the First Presbyterian Church here (ours) just resigned. It is a marvelous church - North and South combined.

The Oak Knoll house, as with many other houses, did not have plastered walls but rather the lathes were covered with cheese cloth and wallpaper was pasted on the cheese cloth. It was thrilling when the wind blew in the right direction and the wall paper would bulge as if to knock someone down. All the clothes had to be taken out of the one closet when it rained, and buckets placed on the floor to catch the water. The Minors were about a block from a wooded area which Kay referred to as the Garden of Eden. One day Katharine took the children to Miss Regans so she could enjoy the sun in her own back yard. She put on her sun glasses and started in on her stack of *New Yorker* magazines. Ten minutes later she felt something strange on her legs. Looking down she looked into the eyes of a big long muddy colored snake crawling across her legs. The Garden of Eden had reached out to her. Superman never moved faster. Katharine rushed into the house and the snake went under the porch steps. Perhaps the snake frightened the two scorpions which later were killed in the house. Doc kidded her about the snake getting bigger every time she told the story.

In a more civilized experience with nature, one Sunday all the Minor family spent the afternoon at a privately owned buffalo farm. There they saw a herd of buffalo, hundreds of new kids, goats, caves, horses, colts, chickens, many cages of pheasants and many more of quails, pigs and a huge herd of cattle. Doc had operated on Major Robertson who was the head MP officer at Ft. Worth and roomed at the farm owner's home. The major had extended the generous invitation.

Dining with Children
One of Katharine's treats was eating at the Officers' Club on Sundays, since she didn't have to cook. As she said, "I loved being waited on and I think that is when I started to eat at a slower pace." She had techniques to keep the children entertained. She would wiggle her ears, make dolls and animals from napkins, and lift spoons by putting one finger in the bowl and her thumb on the end. The family all loved it when she intertwined her hands to do the wood cutters chopping wood and picking up logs. The circus stories kept the children captivated as she asked with a high pitched voice the little girl's question, "Mama, do we have to pay to get out of the circus?" Then Katharine would respond in a grownup voice, "Why no

child, what makes you ask that?" "Well we had to pay to get in didn't we?"
"I'm never going to bring you to a circus again, never as long as you live,"
said the frustrated mother. The high-pitched voice of the girl said, "You
can't bring me when I'm dead, can you?" "No!" "I'll be an angel then. Will
I look like a bird?" "No!" "Will I be wrestling with people?" "What makes
you ask a question like that?" "Well, Jacob wrestled with an angel."

She probably could have made up her own stories from what her
children said. The humming sound made by the telephone wires along the
streets, led young Howard to say, "The noise was God turning on the stars."
When Howie was learning to cross the street, he was told to look up and
down the street before he crossed. As his mother watched, Howie looked up
to the sky and down to the ground, then walked across the street.

Radio

At this time a form of news and entertainment in people's homes was
the radio. The president used the radio for his fireside chats. There were
such programs as *Jack Benny, Amos and Andy*, and the *George Burns and
Gracie Allen Show*. The younger set listened to *Hop Harrigan* and *Terry
and the Pirates*. Katharine referred to them as "trash." One day Keekee
rushed into the kitchen and said, "You know that trash Marilyn
listens to? Well, someone just got saved instead of killed." Mary remembered listening to *Jack Armstrong, the All-American Boy*, after school one
day in April when the announcement was made that Franklin D. Roosevelt
had died.

Katharine's friend next received a note from 3008 Goldenrod, Ft. Worth
3, Texas.

> *Not a letter - just to tell you we've moved from our four
> room house at long last, and now have four bed rooms so
> come down n' see us some time.*
>
> *What do you think of our Texas cow hands? (A picture of
> the children on a horse was enclosed). Their (mis) use of the
> King's English startles me sometimes! Mary Carolyn had
> been someplace where they had a piano and she told me she,
> 'just played myself away on the piano and just kept on a goin.'*
>
> *Howie and Keekee were a bit under the weather from
> their typhoid shots and K. said, "Marilyn not be real sick
> like we do she?" And lastly I was examining an infected
> place on Howie's foot and he blurts out, "Don't mash the
> risin." Guess I better get me a book and write things down*

to show you all - Anyway, Drop us a note from Chautauqua - we're thinking of all of you.

Louisiana

A card written on October 19, 1944 stated,

We have had three houses in three weeks. We just moved from a house in W. Monroe that was glued together. Our address now is 505 Stubbs Avenue, Monroe, Louisiana. Doc is head of surgery at Selman Field here. Mary Carolyn attended three schools so far this term. Near school, stores etc. No help still. (Laundries take from three to four weeks so I'm laundress, cook, nurse, scrub woman etc.) Think we'll like it here.

Summer Results

There was a great swimming pool on the Selman Field army base in Monroe and the Minor children enjoyed it greatly. Marilyn really learned to swim there and Doc would often dive off the diving board. He had been the diving champion at the YMCA years before the war. Doc enjoyed watching the three children and giving Katharine a chance to have a little time to herself. It was time she needed even though Doc had come home with the results of the rabbit test which showed she was not pregnant. She had asked her husband, "Well, do you believe me or the rabbit?"

Everyone wanted to believe the news flash on August 14, 1945 that the war with Japan had ended. It made for a wonderful birthday celebration for Doc who turned 40 on August 15. The war had started on one family birthday and just about ended on another. There was excitement everywhere. At last fighting had ceased and the country was directed towards peace. Soldiers would be returning to their private lives. Shortages would lessen and coupon books would not be needed anymore. Adjustments would come for all, but in peace time rather than war.

It took time, though, before the military would be sent home. When Keekee started school in Monroe, Louisiana that fall she didn't particularly like it. Her solution was to go out for recess and find the swings where she played until she saw the children going home. She would then file in with them. For a period of time she was able to maintain her own schedule and get away with part-time school.

Chautauqua House

In the fall of 1945, Katharine wrote,

> *We have a chance to buy a house at Chautauqua and I wondered if there was the remotest chance that you might be going up again and if so, could you give it a quick once over and see what it is like?*
>
> *It's at 33 Foster, corner Wythe with a living room, fire place, piano, dining room, kitchen with an electric ice box and gas stove etc. and a lavatory and toilet on the first floor, three bedrooms and sleeping porch and bath on the second floor, and two bedrooms and bath on the 3rd floor. It sounds like our size! They want to sell it furnished for $6,000. It is an awful lot of money and we'd like to get some other opinion - other than the real estate man! Mr. A.S. Gifford, 38 Scott Avenue is the agent (phone 3-075). If you are there we'd surely appreciate any light you could shed on the subject!*
>
> *We're going down the home stretch neck 'n' neck and expecting a three way tie! Our house is sold and December 1 is the deadline to get out; the field is due to close December 5 and little 'Conestoga Pete' is due December 3! Boy, oh boy what a race!*
>
> *Our delightful (?) summer fortunately is over and now I'm in the throes of unpacking blankets, winter clothes etc. which I'd carefully packed to send on somewhere, either home or another station, and letting down sleeves and hems of coats etc. Don't know whether to buy northern clothes or southern for our three young ones, and our coming bambino. To date 'its' layette consists of one dozen diapers!!!*
>
> *No help so gotta go to bed early.*

New Family Members

The war made it difficult to take part in normal family milestones. During 1945 two of Katharine's siblings were wed. Katharine was not able to make Wilma's wedding when she married Walter Baker May 26, 1945, in New York. Later that year her brother, Dohrman, married Victoria Crowell on December 12. She failed to make that wedding also for there were much more pressing things in her life at the time.

Margaret Sinclair Minor was born December 6 in Monroe, Oaichita Parish, Louisiana. Katharine went to the hospital and delivered at 6:58 a.m.

The anaesthetist came on at 7 a.m. and gave her two Demerol (a new experimental drug and she was used as a guinea pig). She stayed three days and went home to pack and leave for Ohio in about a week. Mary remembered her mother being in bed and giving orders for things which needed to be done.

As 1945 drew to a close Major Howard H. Minor, M.D. appeared with his wife and three children on a Christmas card which had added a small stork announcing Margaret's birth. The card was signed "The Major Minors and the Minor Minors."

When Margaret was fourteen days old, her father drove the family car home to Steubenville, and her mother brought her and her sisters and brother home on the train. Trains usually had *Parlor Cars* with individual over stuffed seats that had swivel bases so *well to do people* could watch the scenery from their comfortable seats. However, most people sat in regular seats facing forward, two people to a seat. At night the seats and backs were adjusted into a double bed. Above was a *drop down* bed creating the effect of two bunk beds. People were *strapped* into both beds and would call the porter to bring a ladder to descend from the top bunk. Drawing rooms were located at one end of each sleeping car. The five Minors headed for home in one of these rooms which boasted not only

Merry Christmas *from* THE MAJOR MINORS

THE MINOR MINORS *and*

Margaret Sinclair Minor
DECEMBER 6, 1945

bunk beds and a side sofa but a small private lavatory.

For the trip to Ohio Katharine and her four children left Monroe, Louisiana Tuesday afternoon, December 20, and arrived in Steubenville at 1:30 a.m., Friday, with a change but no waiting in St. Louis. The St. Louis station was jammed with thousands of people trying to get home for the first Christmas after the war. It was bitterly cold and every train was overcrowded. The aisles were choked with passengers perched on upturned suitcases and soldiers sleeping in the luggage racks over the seats.

Katharine and the children worked their way through the crowd at the station headed by a redcap carrying Margaret in her bassinet, followed by Howie clutching a box of disposable diapers. Next came Keekee and Marilyn with their assigned packages and then their mother and another redcap bringing up the rear. The trip had many interesting sidelights including one soldier looking at this parade and asking, "Madam, is this trip necessary?" Afterwards, Katharine wrote a letter to the Railroad company thanking them for all their help. Later she learned that the letter was published in the company's annual meeting newsletter.

Sound the Alarm

The house at 730 Lawson Avenue in Steubenville again became home for the family. Katharine took her three older children to McKinley School to enroll Marilyn. Somehow, while Katharine and Marilyn were discussing matters with the principal, Keekee and Howard left the room and the next thing everyone heard was the fire alarm sounding its urgent message. Keekee had found one more way to escape school.

Chautauqua

On April 2, 1946 a letter of thanks went to Gertrude Patterson.

> *It was wonderful to see you!! When I close my eyes and think of our dinner in New Castle; the group listening to Bere Rabbit; our midnight supper and the delightful scent of squabs etc. etc. We're all fine. Doc's on the surgical staff at the Veterans Hospital in Aspinwall, Pennsylvania. He goes to Philly next fall for an additional year of surgery. We are arriving in Chautauqua the middle of June and Doc will be there on weekends.*

The house in Chautauqua was to play a great part in the lives of all the

Minors. As Katharine related to a Chautauqua *Daily* newspaper reporter years later,

> *My husband, Dr. Howard Minor and I came to Chautauqua in the early 40's. We just stayed for two days with some friends, Dr. & Mrs. Meade Patterson. He was a Presbyterian minister. We thought this was just our cup of tea. We made arrangements to come back for some time the following summer with our three children, Marilyn, Keekee, and Howard (Margaret arrived later). As for so many others, even carefully crafted plans fell through with the advent of World War II. Family lifestyle changed and, temporarily, we had to leave our hometown of Steubenville, Ohio. My husband enlisted in the service. He didn't have to, but he felt he should. Luckily, we didn't have to go overseas. But we still moved all over the country and lived in both Louisiana and Texas. The brief initial visit to Chautauqua remained central to my post-war aspirations of returning. Near the war's end, I again thought about returning to the Chautauqua Institution.*
>
> *I wrote the Institution and asked if there were any rooms for rent. I never heard back from them the entire summer. Then I got a letter in the fall from a real estate person up at Chautauqua. After the season was over, there was a house for sale. Were we interested? Anyone who has ever rented or owned a house knows the possible problems that can incur. An old house remains filled with secrets that may range from hidden attic treasures to leaky pipes and bad flooring. We had our doubts. But a sense of fortune reigned.*
>
> *I had just gotten cash from a bad debt that I had inherited. It was for almost the same amount as the house itself. We pondered, for sure. We were still in Louisiana. And we thought, 'Let's buy the house and see what happens. Maybe we'll sell it when Mary is ready for college.' And we went ahead and bought it, sight unseen.*
>
> *Doc's sister, Evelyn and husband Earle Drake did take a look at the house. Earle's comment after looking at the house was, "The kitchen floor was put down by a person who had an eye for beauty."*
>
> *After the war was over, my husband and I came to see what on earth we had bought. It was January. Have you ever*

been in Chautauqua in January? Oh my, it's cold and bleak. In January, the only light we could find was in the hardware store. Dr. Minor and I went in, asking about where we could find the real estate man.

"He usually comes in around now," the hardware man said. It came out that we had bought a house for sale on Foster. Suddenly his eyes bulged "You bought the Hazlett's

The Minor Family in 1946 at Chautauqua.
Top row: Doc holding Margaret, Kay; Middle row: Marilyn; Bottom row: Keekee and Howie.

The Minor Cottage at Lake Chautauqua

house?" The hardware man had this look on his face. We thought something must be very wrong with the house. We didn't know, we had never seen the place.

"I think I've got a key to that house," the hardware man said. We certainly wondered about that. Then we learned that he kept keys for working on the plumbing and things like that. He asked again, "You bought the Hazlett house?

We didn't know that Mr. Hazlett was the president of the Institution. As far as the house, we expected the worst, and I think we got the best. Everything was there in place, as if it had been waiting just for us. Everything in the house except food and clothes.

The first Chautauqua summer was a treat for everyone. Dorothy Twaddle came up with the family to watch the children and fix meals. It did not take long before Marilyn, Keekee and Howie found friends and spent great times at Girls' and Boys' Club which was the oldest continuous day camp in the United States. Campers attended from 9 a.m. to noon and 2 until 4. The two hours in the middle of the day were for lunch, resting or playing. As the years passed, all the children completed their beginners, intermediate, swimmers, and advanced swimmers tests and received their badges and their cards. They learned to play capture the flag in the woods; play kick ball, dodge ball, baseball, and run races on the fields; play tennis on the courts; craft belts and bracelets and make ashtrays in art; bowl; canoe, row, and sail on the lake; and in general have a very complete day camp life. The age groups were divided into red and blue teams which competed in the groups and Club totals were kept during the summer. Each summer all the children would receive their Chautauqua Girls' Club or Chautauqua Boys' Club badge. The groups also presented an honor award yearly and often a few merit badges. Marilyn set the record for the family by getting three merit badges and two honor badges. Margaret attended nursery school when she was old enough and went through Club like her siblings. All the Minor children became counselors when they became eligible.

Clyde and Mary Chalfant were very good friends of Kay and Doc. The Chalfants rented the house next to their's in Chautauqua for a few summers. It was nice for Margaret who had Carolyn Chalfant to play with and go with to Nursery School. Her brother, Pete, was a good friend of young Howard.

After the War

The end of the second world war brought unemployment, strikes, deflation, and economic Depression. Dr. Minor decided to take post graduate work in surgery after the war and spent a year in Philadelphia getting his masters at the University of Pennsylvania medical school. On his occasional trips back to Steubenville he would take the train. Katharine had a wonderful sixth sense and would often be at the train station to meet him even when he was going to surprise her. The Steubenville station had an underground tunnel to get from the east bound to the west bound trains. Although Doc didn't make the trip to Steubenville often that year, he was home for Christmas to see his wife and children. Katharine made trips over to see him as well.

Gertrude gave Katharine a lovely nightgown for Christmas, and in January, 1947, Katharine wrote,

> *You should see me in my glamourous gown - I'm keeping it to wear on our next honeymoon - the Ohio State Medical Convention in Cincinnati the last of March. Mr. Doeright died. Mrs. D. is President of the Chautauqua Bird & Tree Club. They live next to the Vances who live across from us on Wythe Avenue in Chautauqua.*

Howard, Marilyn holding Margaret, Keekee

Season's Greetings

FROM OUR HOUSE
TO YOUR HOUSE

The Minors

Margaret was awake when I started writing this and I should have known better than to start. Took all four youngsters into Kaufmann's to the miniature circus on Saturday and lost all but Margaret on the escalator between the first and eleventh floors. Keekee's tears created terrible turmoil on the fourth floor of the lingerie department.

Doc Graduates

In a letter written June 1947 to her brother, Dohrman, Kath wrote,

I suppose when I'm a grandmother, or great aunt, I'll have loads of time to get all caught up on my letter writing, but until then anyone who rates more than a penny post card really rates. I'm again 'helpless' but it was nice while it lasted. I'm getting to be the best 'short order cook', wash woman, cleaner, baby watcher, governess, plumber, carpenter, sewer, etc., that you ever saw. It's really not bad unless it drags out too long.

Doc finished May 23, 1947 and I went over to Philly. I'm so proud of him - he made 98!! He says not to tell it, but I saw it posted with all the others outside the dean's office, and I'm awfully proud of our years' work. We had quite a trip - down to Atlantic City for one day and into New York another, and came home via Chautauqua, New York. It was loads of fun. We went down to Frank's for over the 30th and all the little Minors and Sinclairs had a very gay time.

We may go to Chautauqua this Saturday for a couple of weeks and come home for the Sesquicentennial week. By the way, think you might like to read the papers about it, so I'll order it for you tomorrow. I'll also enclose a souvenir wooden nickel and a snap of Frank's side yard. I hear that Father is to be mentioned as one of the ten outstanding men and women including Steuben, the General for whom it was named, and old Bazaleel Wells, the founder, etc. It really should be something. I hear I'm on the Reception Committee to meet the Governor, etc. - probably will greet him at the station with a babe in my arms and three others pulling at my skirt! Much love to you all. Kath

Sesquicentennial

Mrs. Howard H. Minor was one of the members on the Steubenville Sesquicentennial Old Timers Committee. Others on the committee were Mrs. Carl Goehring, Chairman, Mrs. Charles Bunch, Mrs. H.C. Cook, Mr. John Criss, Mr. Everett Ferguson, Sr., Mrs. John Irvine, Mr. E.E. McCauslen, Sr., Mrs. H. Earl McFadden, Mr. J. Easton McGowan, Mr. Robert R. McGowan, Mr. George Robinson, Mr. Alexander Sharpe, Mrs. George Sharpe, Mrs. Fred Slaughter, Mr. Charles Specht, Jr., Mr. John Sherrard, Mrs. J. C. Williams, Mr. George Wisener, Mrs. Harold Zeis, and Mrs. Will Zink. Fifty years later in 1997 she was one of the Old Timers herself as she road in the Bicentennial Parade as an honored citizen. As Katharine said, "All these people were substantial, worthwhile people who really helped when needed."

The Minor family returned to Steubenville for the Sesquicentennial week in July, 1947. They experienced the exciting program at Harding School stadium and were able to see the parade go by their old homestead on N. Fourth Street. The Minors then returned to Chautauqua for the remainder of the summer. On the way they stopped for a Sinclair family gathering.

The Sinclair Family Group in 1947 at the LeVan home in Titusville, Pennsylvania
(From left to right) Back row: Dohrman J. Sinclair, II, Garrett B. LeVan, Jr.; Third row: Dohrman S. Grant, Jr., Marian (Phinny) Grant, Katharine (Sinclair) Minor, Katharine (Armstrong) LeVan, Wilma (Sinclair) LeVan Baker, Dorothy (Smith) Sinclair holding Margaret S. Minor, Frank D. Sinclair; Second row: James D. Grant, Dohrman J. Sinclair, III, Howard S. Minor, Andrea W. LeVan, Katharine W. LeVan, Mary C. Minor; Front row: Frank B. Sinclair, Katharine E. Minor, Peter H. LeVan.

Frank Dohrman Sinclair

As the summer in Chautauqua drew to a close Katharine's brother, Frank, stopped on his way to Buffalo, New York. He was going to a business meeting and was not feeling well. He stayed about a week and then the Minors left for Steubenville after he was feeling better. His wife, Dot, was there with him and they expected to leave within a few days. Instead, Frank Sinclair died shortly after the Minors left on August 31. Frank's obituary appeared in the Steubenville *Herald-Star* and follows in part:

> *Frank Dohrman Sinclair, 58, industrialist, whose activities covered many fields of business and industry, will be buried with military rites at noon, Wednesday, in Union Cemetery. The interment will be preceded by services at 11 a.m. at the family home, 523 N. Fourth Street.*
>
> *Mr. Sinclair died suddenly of a heart attack, while visiting at the summer home of his sister, Katharine, wife of Dr. Howard H. Minor, at Chautauqua, New York. When death overtook him, Mr. Sinclair was on his way to Buffalo, New York, for a conference with executives of the American Industrial Company, of which he was a Director. He was preparing to continue the trip to Buffalo Sunday afternoon when he was suddenly stricken, and died within 15 minutes. Mrs. Sinclair was at his side.*
>
> *Like his father who was responsible for the building of the Market Street bridge, Mr. Sinclair was one of the original promoters of the Fort Steuben bridge. It was through his efforts that the mill of the Liberty Paper Board Company was not removed from Steubenville after it had been acquired from the Hartje interests. Mr. Sinclair was also one of the original group of business men from which grew the Steubenville Chamber of Commerce. While an officer of the Union Bank, his keen foresight led him to propose and promote the opening of the Toronto branch, now a thriving division of the banking concern here.*
>
> *In later years one of his chief fields of endeavor was the coal business. He had various and extensive coal interests in West Virginia and Ohio, directing their operations from Clarksburg, West Virginia, and Steubenville. Besides the directorates in the American Industrial Company, he was vice-president and director of Hammond Bag and Paper Company, a director of Steubenville Pottery Company and a*

director of the Columbia Firebrick Company of Canton.

A 32nd Degree Mason, Mr. Sinclair was a member of the American Legion, and one of the original members of the American Legion Band. He belonged to the Elks Club, and was a member of the Sons of the American Revolution. His religious affiliation was the Westminster Presbyterian Church.

Another Move

During the school year of 1947-1948 the family lived in Aspinwall, Pennsylvania where Dr. Minor was Assistant to the Chief of the Surgical Service, and head of the Orthopedic Department. The older children started school. Because the family lived on the grounds of the Veteran's Hospital, it cost $12 a child to attend school in Aspinwall. One day everyone was going to an Aspinwall ball game but Keekee didn't want to go. She said anyone could tell you tomorrow who had won!

Shortly after school started for the children, Doc came down with hepatitis and became a patient in the hospital. He made a good recovery. This was a busy year for him, for he was studying to take his Boards in surgery. He carried on his work at the hospital and studied at home.

Seasons Greetings from our house to your house

Margaret, Keekee, Howard, Mary   The Minor Family

Adjusted in her new home on the grounds of the hospital Katharine wrote,

> *We've had all the paper taken off seven rooms and all walls and woodwork painted in our house on the Veteran Hospital's grounds. We look very scrumptious but it was almost a month of 'ordeal.'*
>
> *Doc and I hope to go to Cincinnati to the Ohio State Medical Convention March 28-April 1. He passed his American Boards in Surgery!!! There were eleven who were eligible and took them here in Pittsburgh (came from a radius of about 400 miles) and as near as we can figure Doc was the <u>only one</u> to pass!!! We are sure of six who failed and think we surely would have heard if any of the other four had passed. Isn't he wonderful?*

HOWARD H. MINOR, M.D.

ANNOUNCES THE REOPENING OF HIS OFFICE

IN THE SINCLAIR BUILDING

STEUBENVILLE.

OHIO

> *Doc has office space about May 1-15 at home but we expect to stay here till school is out then on to Chautauqua.*

American Board of Surgery

A word of explanation should be added here relative to the American Board of Surgery which means little to the average layman, but it is quite a distinction to be recognized as a member of this organization. It was founded in 1937 and there were only 2000 members in the entire United States when Doc became a member. To become a member, one must have a minimum of 5 years post graduate training in surgery in approved hospitals and medical centers, after which a very rigid written exam must be taken, a technical exam during an operation in the presence of a picked group of surgeons, and, a year later, a rigid oral exam by a picked group of surgeons. About 60 per cent of all eligibles fail the exam but may apply a year later. Howard passed it the first time and was the only representative of The American Board of Surgery in Steubenville for a number of years.

Back to Steubenville

In the fall of 1948 the Minors returned to live at 730 Lawson Avenue. Katharine relates, "I came home one day to find the living room a disaster area. There were toys, dolls, *dress up clothes* etc. all over the place. I couldn't believe it, but when I got my speech back I told the children (mine and the neighbors) that it looked awful and they would have to clean it up. Little Peggy Smith quietly replied, 'But Mrs. Minor, it has such a lived in look.' She was right."

The house on Lawson Avenue had a clothes chute which became a seat when closed. One day it became the scene of a good story. Keekee either persuaded Margaret to get into the chute or helped her. Katharine heard cries coming from the room and rushed in to find Margaret hanging by her finger tips inside the clothes chute. There never was a dull moment!

The Minors frequently played a game during dinner around the dining room table called, "What have you done to help someone today?" The children gave many repeats like "took the garbage out" or "hung up my clothes without being told" etc. to their father's "saved a life today." One night when the game started one youngster dashed to the kitchen and back. He was glowing with satisfaction when his turn came. He proudly announced, "I put water in Skippy's dish." Skippy was the Minor's beloved dog.

Kay and Doc always seemed to get along just fine. However, they both agreed that their worst argument was over how to teach their children to tie shoes. According to Doc, making loops and tying them together was the way, while Kay thought you made one loop and brought the other lace around it and through to make the bow. Whatever the best way, all the children learned to tie their shoes.

Community Involvement

In the late 40's Katharine was back in Steubenville and taking part in the fabric of the town. She was one of the Jefferson County Medical Association Auxiliary committee members who helped organize an essay contest for junior and senior high students. She also served as an officer of the local American Medical Auxiliary. Dr. Minor was likewise involved in medical organizations. In 1949 Kay and Doc went to Los Angeles where Howard attended a medical convention. They visited Katharine's brother, Dohrman, and wife Vicky with their young daughter, Wilma, in La Jolla, California.

In 1949 Katharine noticed that the name *Sinclair* had been removed from *The Sinclair Building* on the northeast corner of Fourth and Market Streets where the Union Savings Bank & Trust Company was located. The name had been replaced by the Union Bank Building. Not to let such a slight to her father, who had built the building, pass without protest, Katharine immediately complained to the bank and marshaled her strengths. She let her sister, Wilma, know about the change. Wilma Sinclair LeVan was Steubenville's first and perhaps the United States' first woman bank president when she served for eight years as president of the Union Savings Bank and Trust Company in the early 1930's. Wilma sent a letter to the Directors of the bank.

A report has reached me that the name of The Sinclair Building has been changed to that of The Union Bank Building, and the name Sinclair removed from the entrance.

My Father, Dohrman J. Sinclair built the corner half of the present ten story structure, largely at his own expense, and the records will show that it was turned over to The Union Savings Bank and Trust Company, at a fraction of its actual cost.

The many large industries which are now located in the Steubenville district, Wheeling Steel, Weirton Steel, Follansbee Brothers, and countless others, are there solely because of my Father's untiring efforts, and bear mute evidence of his foresight and unselfish interest in the city he loved.

The Sinclair Building was, and is, his monument - the one tangible land mark to bear his honorable name.

It is inconceivable to me, that live men could condone or permit the obliteration of the name of a dead man who certainly did them no harm, but who, on the other hand, is largely responsible for the thriving community from which they are deriving their livelihood today. Surely the Union Savings Bank and Trust Company is in dire need of advertising, if it must stoop to the robbing of a dead man's memory.

I spent almost ten years of my life in the rehabilitation of The Union Savings Bank and Trust Company, and many of you who worked with me through those agonizing depression years know that were it not for my persistent refusal to admit defeat, the institution would not be operating today. Knowing most of you as I do, I cannot believe that you gave your sanction to removing my Father's name from The Sinclair Building, but I am writing you as a director of The Union Savings Bank and Trust Company, and The Sinclair Building Corporation to ascertain whether you approved this shameful act, and if so, why?

> *I shall await hearing from you before taking any further action.*

The name Sinclair promptly reappeared over the entrance to the Sinclair Building. Katharine had known how to alert expert help, in this case her sister.

❧

Christmas Pictures Through The Years

The 1950-1959 Era

South Korea was invaded by North Korea and the United States aided South Korea using jets and helicopters for the first time in combat. The United Nations moved to its permanent home in New York. Stalin died in 1953 and Khrushchev became leader of the U.S.S.R. Nasser took over leadership of Egypt when Britain left Egypt after 72 years, then took over the Suez Canal. Sputnik was launched by the Soviet Union. De Gaulle came to power in France, Fidel Castro took control in Cuba and Indira Gandhi became the leader of India in 1959.

Eisenhower was named NATO commander. The United States presidency was limited to two terms and Truman fired General MacArthur. Eisenhower was elected president in 1952 and 1956 with Nixon, and the McCarthy era ended when the Senate condemned him in 1954 for his Communism witch hunts. The Supreme Court ordered school integration. Alaska became the 49th state and Hawaii the 50th. The St. Lawrence Seaway was opened for boats.

Sixty-three cities had TV stations in the early 50's and parents were worried that their children were watching more hours of television than being in school. Alienation from social and literary conventions was the way of the beatniks. 3D movies such as *House of Wax* were new. Sir Winston Churchill received the Nobel Prize for literature. Seuss' *Cat in the Hat* was a success. Sinatra won an Oscar for *From Here to Eternity,* the first Newport jazz festival was held, *and Rock Around the Clock* was a hit for Bill Haley. Disneyland opened in California, and the Mouseketeers were popular on television. Television programs such as *Gunsmoke* and *Father Knows Best* were popular, and quiz shows were found to be rigged. Joanne Woodward stared in *The Three Faces of Eve*, *Bridge on the River Kwai* was popular at movie theaters, and songs from *West Side Story* and *Music Man* were hits. Rock and roll was played on the jukeboxes.

Hillary became the first to scale Mt. Everest, Bannister broke the 4-minute mile record, and Rocky Marciano retired undefeated. The New York to London flying record was seven hours, 48 minutes. Suburban housing tracts changed the way Americans lived as consumer goods and motor vehicles greatly increased. Frozen food sales passed the billion dollar mark. G.M. produced its 50 millionth car and Boeing's 707 made its debut. The AFL and the CIO merged. The United States showed an increase of 19 million people in the decade. Atomic tests were being done in Nevada in 1951 and the Atomic Energy Commission released a 438-page guide of how to defend against an atomic attack. The Salk polio vaccine was used successfully. Smoking was shown to promote cancer and Thalidomide was shown to cause birth defects.

VI.

Children Off To School In The Fifties

Parties

Katharine liked to give parties and for Howie's 10th and Keekee's 11th birthdays she planned a skating party in Follansbee, West Virginia. Little did she know that the weather wanted to be a part of the activity. It began snowing the day of the party and parents who were going to drive to the roller skating rink began calling to say they did not think they would be able to drive. Undaunted, Katharine called and hired a bus to take everyone. The ten and eleven year old party goers gathered at the house and the bus started out in the snow with them. Everyone had a great time skating for a couple of hours. Then there was ice cream and cake. The bus was waiting for the return trip and was nice and warm as the snow continued to fall. No one else seemed to be on the road when they arrived in Steubenville. Roads were blocked off and the bus was only able to get within nine blocks of Johnnie Griesinger's home. He was asked to walk those last blocks. The roads continued to worsen. When the bus tried to get up Adams Street the police stopped the celebrating group. The bus driver explained it was a private party and the bus was allowed to proceed.

Halfway up the hill it became apparent that the bus would not make it. Howard certainly remembered the party and how much fun everyone had getting to the back of the bus to help weigh it down for better traction. Not making it up Adams Street only added to the excitement for the party goers. Trying another route, the bus was finally successful and all the children made it home, much to the parents' relief.

The snow fall measured 30 inches at noon Sunday. At 6 p.m. Sunday it measured 31.1 inches and during the night there were 2.1 inches more. The storm, which paralyzed all forms of transportation, business and industry, started at 4:45 a.m. Friday. It snowed continuously until 2:10 p.m. Saturday. It resumed snowing Saturday night. The snowfall was the heaviest recorded at the city filtration plant since records started, January 1, 1919. Heavier snowfalls were reported only in March 1913 and March 1907. The blizzard's snowfall was estimated at 33.2 inches by J. Shelton Scott, city chemist and Steubenville's *weatherman*.

The newspaper account of the storm included headlines such as *City Battles To Clear Record Snow* and *Buses Start Moving as 3-Day Blizzard Brings 33.2 Inches*. Articles appeared which related facts about the late November storm of 1950 and how Steubenville was smothered by the heaviest snowfall in 37 years. The city struggled to clear snowbound streets and roads in its efforts to restore the crippled transportation system. As partial transportation slowly emerged, the city's industrial, business and professional life strived for ordinary movement but it took days before normalcy was restored.

Doc Minor Grows Professionally

Dr. Minor was busy practicing medicine. He was able to walk the few blocks from home to the Ohio Valley Hospital during the storm. Weirton Hospital and St. John's Hospital, where he was on the staff, had to wait until the roads were clear for his services. In 1951 he became the vice president of the Ohio Valley Hospital Medical Staff. This was the year when, in April, a bus went out of control on a Weirton hill crashing and killing over 50 people. One day Doc came home to say that he had lost his brakes going from the Ohio Valley Hospital to the mill but luckily, by honking the horn and driving very carefully, he was able to avert an accident.

Dr. Minor was active in the Ft. Steuben Academy of Medicine and was program co-chairman and chairman between 1949 and 1951. In 1952 he was elected president. He served as a Trustee of the Ohio Valley Hospital during 1952-53. In 1959 he was again vice president of the Ohio Valley Medical Staff. The following year he became president. Dr. Minor was on the Board of Trustees and also the 1961 Building Committee when the north and west wings were completed at the Ohio Valley Hospital.

Dr. Minor had limited his practice to surgery after he passed his Boards in Surgery and he said that being ambidextrous was a great help in some situations. In his early days of general practice he had delivered twins and the parents named them Howard and Katharine after the mother asked what Doc's wife's name was. Doc had a very caring method of medicine and knew when to operate and when not to operate. A nurse told the story of seeing him fight back tears at the nurses' station when he could do nothing for a young girl he was treating. His children would often find him arriving when they were getting ready to go to school. He had been called out at night and was just returning home for some breakfast before a busy day. Mary remembered seeing her father studying his hand during church. She was later to hear a story of an operation he performed on a young girl who had great damage done to her hand and wrist, but today has full use of them both because of his skill and his insistence that she be able to use her hand before he dismissed her from the hospital. The family thought it was great to have a father who knew medicine for their medicine cabinet held only aspirin, Mercurochrome and band aids.

Katharine's Father's Portrait Hangs at Hospital

In 1951 a portrait of D.J. Sinclair was presented to the Ohio Valley Hospital. Katharine Sinclair Minor took part in the presentation. Years before when Katharine's father had headed the committee to raise the money to build the Ohio Valley Hospital, the nurses of the first graduating class of the temporary hospital at the Lacy Hotel decided to give the new hospital a portrait of D.J. Sinclair. Father Hartley, who was a young priest at Holy Name Church in the old Sixth Ward in Steubenville at the time and whose parishioners had been helped quite often by D.J. Sinclair, agreed to help the nurses. He took a photograph of Sinclair to Europe and had a famous Italian artist paint the portrait. Alas, World War I broke out while he was there and it became practically impossible to get reservations back to the United States. When Hartley finally landed safely in the States he had lost his baggage. In his hand, however, he carried the large rolled canvas portrait of his friend.

Doc's Mother Dies

The last surviving parent of the Minor couple, Carrie Evelyn Holland Minor, died March 26, 1951. Howard's mother was born August 17, 1871 in New Cumberland, West Virginia to Samuel and Jane Erskine Holland. Carrie and her husband, Howard, had moved to Steubenville from Toronto, Ohio in 1918 living first in the 300 block of N. Fourth Street, then 504 N. Fourth Street. Later they moved to Pleasant Heights. During World War II she sold her home at 805 Lawson Avenue and moved to 303 N. Third Street. She was able to visit her granddaughter, Mary Carolyn, when she was so sick, and help her daughter-in-law, Katharine, while her son and Katharine's husband was in the army. Just before her death she went to live with her daughter Evelyn Drake, in State College, Pennsylvania.

Early Television

In the 1950's the Minors bought their first TV. The test pattern was on the screen much of the time. Getting a good picture was always a challenge in those early days, so everyone had an antenna on their roof for better reception. One day young Howard came in the house a little bruised. He had gone up on the roof to fix the antenna and had slipped. As he said, "I thought I could grab the gutter, but it went past too fast." Television in those days had such people as Lucille Ball and Desi Arnez in the *I Love Lucy Show*, the *Jackie Gleason Show*, and the *Ed Sullivan Show*. Every once in a while the family would go out for dinner at a place which had a TV and at dinner time the channel would be tuned to *Kukla, Fran and Ollie* or *Howdy Doody*. In the 1970's *M*A*S*H* became one of Katharine's favorites and later she loved the reruns.

School Activity

Katharine became active in McKinley School serving as President of the McKinley Parent Teacher's Association (PTA), head of the McKinley Child Study Group, and committee member on the PTA By-Laws for Jefferson County Council. A few years later she was on the local committee for the National Library Week.

Keekee took school with a bit of humor. One April she instigated an April fool's joke which involved most of her classmates in Miss. Quinn's class. As many as could were asked to bring alarm clocks and they were hidden around the room, set to go off at different times during the class. Virginia Quinn thought it was funny, thirty years later!

During the 50's and 60's the Minor children spread out for schools elsewhere. All the children spent the first two years of high school at Steubenville High School known as *Big Red*. At noon the school buses would take students home for lunch. For those going to Pleasant Heights, it was possible to get off before the Ohio Valley Hospital loop and catch the bus as it headed back, as Mary would occasionally do. However, most lunches were a bit more leisurely and often included the *Bob and Ray Show* which Katharine would have on the radio.

In the fall of 1953 Mary started school in Pittsburgh, Pennsylvania at Winchester Thurston School. It was an all girls school, a change from all her twelve previous schools. During the week she would stay at *The House* with the other boarders. She studied hard and returned home usually by bus on Friday afternoon. Sunday afternoon her father often drove her back to Pittsburgh. The two years were busy with many things happening on the weekends in Steubenville. Weekends also included staying at friends' homes in Pittsburgh. By attending so many schools she had the ability to

Margaret, Mary, Howard, Keekee

make friends and enjoy new situations. At the end of her junior year she found herself with invitations to five proms.

Mary entered the College of Wooster after graduating from high school. It was here where she started writing what would become a lifetime of weekly letters written home. They would arrive on Thursdays. Those letters set up a routine where Doc would come home for lunch on Thursdays and together her parents would catch up on the news of Mary and her family over the years. Mary graduated from The College of Wooster in Ohio. Keekee went to Laurel School in Cleveland to finish her high school. She graduated from Colorado College in Colorado Springs. Between her junior and senior year at college Keekee spent the summer in Switzerland in the Experiment in International Living program.

Howard went to Shadyside Academy in Pittsburgh for a year and then graduated from Linsly Military Institute in Wheeling, West Virginia. Howard went on to Yale for three years and then transferred to Ohio State where he completed his college education. Margaret followed her oldest sister first attending Winchester Thurston in Pittsburgh and then the College of Wooster where she graduated with a history major.

As Kay and Doc's children and their friends' children began to go off to college, a group of parents got together to plan parties for both the adults and those coming home from school. They were held at the Steubenville Country Club and were wonderful dances. Mary always looked forward to the parties and the chance to waltz with her Dad. It was the one dance Doc did, and he did it well.

Katharine not only became involved in her youngest daughter's PTA but she also became active in her oldest daughter's college. In 1956 she started her eleven years on the Women's Advisory Board as the Presbyterian Representative for the College of Wooster. It provided a good excuse to travel to Wooster, Ohio to see her daughters. Of course, there were the many times she made the trip and returned home with a daughter for a semester break or a vacation.

As the mother of children away at school, Katharine found an ingenious way to keep in touch. She discovered carbonless carbon paper and all her children would receive the same letter with one getting the original and the rest receiving copies. It was a wonderful way for all the children to keep up not only on their parents' activities but their siblings' activities as well.

Chautauqua and Church

When school was out the family would drive to New York. Summers in Chautauqua provided wonderful evening programs in the amphitheater and days of summer camp for the children. To this day, this summer colony limits cars and the post office and book store are still the meeting places for many. Everyone walks to lectures, the lake, and the variety of activities. Porches are where friends sit and chat.

With her strong tendency towards duty, Katharine became active in the Chautauqua Women's Club becoming vice president in 1952 of the 1,000 member organization. She also continued her church activities by becoming a board member of the Woman's Auxiliary of the United Presbyterian Association of Chautauqua, New York and a board member of the Chautauqua Presbyterian Women. In 1958 Katharine became part of the Woman's Association of Westminster Presbyterian Church in Steubenville and the following two years served as president. She also served on the Sunday School Council of this church where she had taught Sunday school years earlier.

Special Easters

Wonderful memories are held by the Minor children of the trips the family took on Easter vacations. One year they went to New York and watched the Easter parade. They also went to the circus at Madison Square Gardens, enjoyed Times Square and went out to the Statue of Liberty before breakfast. All the Minors had intended to go to a restaurant for a nice breakfast one morning but they did not find a restaurant that was open. They could see the Statue of Liberty so decided to go there first. Mary chose to walk to the top and because it was so early in the morning she was the first to reach the top that day by way of the stairs.

In Philadelphia another year, they absorbed the early history of the country, saw the cracked Liberty Bell and learned about the early drafters of the government. When the family went to Gettysburg they drove around the monuments and relived the battle. During WWII the family had gone to

The Minor Family
Rear: Katharine Sinclair Minor, Dr. Howard H. Minor, Mary Carolyn Minor.
Front: Katharine E. Minor, Margaret S. Minor, Howard S. Minor.

Vicksburg and learned about the battle which took place there. Doc had a great interest in the Civil War and Mary remembered him telling his children about the Civil War veteran he had known as a kid and whose stories he had heard. Mary had done a scrapbook on the Civil War, so Gettysburg was particularly interesting to her. She knew all about the bloodiest Civil War battle with 51,000 casualties which took place on July 1, 2 and 3, 1863.

The trip to Washington D. C. was taken when Truman was president. As good Republicans, the children were on the look out for trouble. When they heard a bang and the tire went flat, it was easy to suppose that one of Truman's friends had shot at the car and caused the flat, although all knew it was not true. The family drove around and around the streets of the capitol. At times they saw the spot they wanted to reach but were prevented from getting there by one-way streets going the wrong way. The Washington Monument, the Thomas Jefferson Memorial, the Smithsonian Institute, the Lincoln Memorial, the Capitol and the White House were all spots the whole family enjoyed.

Williamsburg provided a wonderful spring vacation one year when the Minors toured the historical 18th century Williamsburg with its Colonial homes, Governor's Palace, and the Busch Gardens. The family saw the Jamestown settlement and Yorktown. Charlottesville provided everyone with the chance to see the University of Virginia and nearby Monticello, Jefferson's home.

Although most of the summers were spent in Chautauqua, a few times in June the family took trips before the summer activities began there in July. In 1952 all six drove west in the Minor car. They set out one morning from Steubenville to drive to Chicago and were on the road for fourteen hours with stops for gas and food. It was a challenging start to the trip. They arrived at the Dohrman Grant's home to spend the first night. On their way west they stopped to see the Corn Palace in Mitchell, South Dakota. The four president faces at Mount Rushmore shown down on them as did the early carving of Crazy Horse. All spent a lovely time hiking around Yellowstone National Park seeing Old Faithful Geyser and the Paint Pots, and fishing in the river. The family ate in the lodge with all the college students as their waiters and waitresses. Then it was on to a dude ranch at Jackson Hole where everyone rode horses and enjoyed the West with its rodeo and great scenery. Mosquitoes were certainly a problem in some of the western towns the family visited. A postcard with a huge mosquito on it told the story well. Katharine was driving when the family drove to the top of Pike's Peak. It was only afterwards that the children learned she could not see where the side fender of the car was on the narrow winding road. She could not see it but she knew where it was.

Margaret, Keekee, Mary and Howard   *Mary, Howard, Margaret and Keekee*

Travel days were usually long. One morning the family planned to leave by 6 a.m. Everyone was busy getting ready and the car was packed. Then someone accidently shut the car door with the locks on. The keys hung from the ignition. It was Sunday and after a futile attempt to find someone to get the car unlocked, Doc broke the window. It was almost more than he could take since his nature was to fix things, not destroy them. As the family started out on the day's journey, Doc said that no one was to say a word and all knew it was better that way. Floating in Salt Lake later that day relieved a lot of pressure and things were fine for the rest of the trip. On the way back to Ohio there was a stop in Kansas for a famous steak dinner.

The trip in June to Florida was one with lots of sunny hot weather. The family drove the miles down through West Palm Beach, Miami Beach and on to Key West staying on different islands at motels. Motels were fairly new at the time and made traveling easier when a whole family had to find rooms at night. Pools were popular and everyone did a great deal of swimming. The children learned about tourist traps, alligators stops, shells of all kinds, and stores with plenty of summer wear. There were spans of bridges and picturesque sunsets to add to the palms, pines, and pools. It was a good introduction to a southern state.

In 1959 Katharine and Doc rented their Chautauqua cottage for July and the two of them flew to Europe for a month of travel and vacation.

633 Belleview Boulevard

In 1954 the Minors made another move to their newly purchased home at 633 Belleview Boulevard in Steubenville. The Minors had put a $500 deposit down on the Spies home in October 1953. It was a lovely home located on the corner of Belleview Boulevard and Oregon Avenue. The long brick covered porch entrance with the open area to the right in front of the living room led into the spacious hall. To the left on the south side of the house was a large dining room complete with fireplace and mantel, small windows above the enclosed built in shelves, a marble window seat and a beautiful crystal chandelier. A lovely sunroom looked out on the city and the Ohio River. At the back of the house there was an eating area and the kitchen. From the spacious kitchen with attached pantry, doors led outside, to the second floor, the basement and the front hall where a den and small lavatory were located. The living room faced the city and had a molded dying lioness above the fireplace. It was a detail from the Ashurbanipal's lion-hunt series of stone bas-reliefs. A replica of Assyrian art, the original from Nineveh dated 645 B.C. can be found in London's British Museum. In the two floors above there were four very large bedrooms, a sitting room,

The Minor residence in Steubenville

*Keekee, Mary, Howard
and Margaret*

Mary, Margaret, Keekee and Howard

*Keekee, Mary, Howard
and Margaret*

*Margaret,
Mary, Keekee and Howard*

two small bedrooms, an enclosed porch, a screened in porch, and an open balcony. Both floors have large halls.

The home has seen many parties, the first of which was a pre-moving party for Mary's friends when a game called sardines was played. This large house without furniture provided a perfect setting for the hide and seek game in which a person would hide and when others found the person they would join the group until all were together.

At the beginning of Mary's senior year nineteen members of the Winchester Thurston senior class came for a weekend house party. Everyone was presented with a key to the room where she would be sleeping. Katharine had set up the party by naming the bedrooms with such names as Buckingham Palace, the White House, and the Taj Mahal. Of course, there was not much sleeping with a house full of teenage girls. Dinners, a picnic, games and outings made for a great weekend. Katharine and Doc's room had a sign on the door *Doctor in the House*. Katharine's love of entertaining shown through by how well she had organized this fantastic weekend. She learned from her house parties of many years before and gave a new generation a bit of what the past had held for her.

Civic Activities

With all Katharine's children in school she became more involved in civic activities. In 1953 when W.C. Sterling was mayor, she worked on the Mayor's Committee for the Preservation of the Stanton-Pierce Home. Edwin M. Stanton was born in a home across the street from First Westminster Presbyterian Church in an area that is now part of a drive-up bank. Later he moved to a home at 612 N. Third Street. Stanton was Lincoln's Secretary of War and today his statue stands in front of the Jefferson County courthouse. Getting involved in historical matters led Katharine to become part of the Ohio Historical Society in 1959. She also taught two hour weekly sessions which contained information on how to be good citizens, to the Girl Reserves, a group at the Y.W.C.A.

All these activities were administered from her desk in the living room. Here a phone and an old fashioned desk provided what she needed to take charge of the things that were of interest to her. Many were the times when her children would hear the skillful way she managed to get things done over the phone by presenting a good case and listening to the person she was speaking with for their concerns. Her letters were always beautifully written both in content and penmanship, so were her lists. She used legal sized pads and would list things she needed to pay, people to call with the phone number, letters and notes to write, items to get fixed or new items to purchase and reports etc. for her many organizations which needed to be

done. Then along the margin she would put the date when it was completed.

For many years Katharine was a member of the local Junior Woman's Club which she had started. In 1958 she transferred to the Woman's Club of Steubenville where she joined the Garden Department, the American Home Department, and the Civic Department. In 1959 she became First Vice President of The Woman's Club of Steubenville and was on the Membership, Memorial, and Year Book Committees in addition to being the Chairman for the January meeting. That year she was also the registrar for the Daughters of the American Revolution chapter in Steubenville.

Family Milestones

On April 27, 1955 Kay and Doc celebrated their 20th anniversary by giving a lovely party at their home. Nearly 150 were there and people came from the surrounding area and even as far away as Detroit, Michigan. Dorothy Rietz called to regretfully decline but asked that their visitors be invited since she knew how much fun they would have. The home was decorated with lovely flowers and the dining room table held delicious food and a wedding cake. The Minor children gave their parents an engraved Bible.

The mother of the bride was a new role for Katharine and she excelled. Her oldest daughter married Robert Howard Evans in the fall of 1957. The couple had wanted a small home wedding, so Katharine had the home beautifully decorated with white chrysanthemums. She found the dress her mother had worn in 1884, 73 years earlier, for her daughter Mary to wear.

Katharine and Howard Minor
20th Wedding Anniversary

Mary Carolyn Minor in her grandmother's
wedding dress.

For the reception she prepared a marvelous dinner to serve the guests in the dining room and the sun room after the late afternoon wedding. Music played in the background and Keekee served as Mary's maid of honor. Doc met Mary at the foot of the stairs and walked his daughter to the fireplace for the ceremony. It was a grand occasion.

Less than a week before Katharine turned fifty she was presented with her first grandson. She and Doc were able to visit John Howard Evans at Magee Hospital in Pittsburgh and be the proud grandparents. On her actual 50th birthday Doc gave his wife a pipe capped at each end which contained fifty silver dollars.

❦

The 1960-1969 Era

The U-2 spy plane broke up the Big Four summit and Gary Powers, the pilot, was indicted as a spy in Russia. The Berlin wall was erected in 1961. The Vietnam War raged and the United States sent 16,000 advisers. The Soviet Union put the first man in space, and the United States followed with Alan Shepard. Israel beat the Arabs in the Six Day War, and the British left South Yemen after holding it as a colony for 128 years.

Nixon and Kennedy met in the first TV debate. The Cuban missile crisis brought the U.S. and the U.S.S.R. near war. The Peace Corps was formed to help developing nations. John Glenn was the first American to orbit the earth. President Kennedy was assassinated November 22, 1963. The average income was $6,249, a new Ford cost $2,500, gas was 30 cents a gallon and bread was 22 cents a loaf. Weight Watchers was founded. In 1964 the Civil Rights Act was passed and King was assassinated in 1968. President Johnson pushed his *Great Society* programs with the Water Quality Act, Medicare, and the Higher Education Act. Feminism became a cultural and political movement. Opposition to the Vietnam war sprung up especially on college and university campuses but more troops were sent to Vietnam.

Ty Cobb, who was the first baseball player elected to Baseball's Hall of Fame, died. Wilt Chamberlain and Bill Russell were stars in basketball. The Houston Astrodome opened. Jack Nicklaus won his second Masters. Jean-Claude Killy won three Olympic skiing metals at Grenoble, France. Rod Laver achieved the Grand Slam in tennis, Billie Jean King won her 3rd Wimbledon title and Arthur Ashe won the United States Open.

Psycho played in the movie theaters, Liz Taylor and Richard Burton starred in *Cleopatra, and* Sidney Poitier won an Oscar for *Lilies of the Field.* Clark Gable died and Hemingway committed suicide. Chubby Checker introduced *The Twist.* The Beatles recorded *I Want to Hold Your Hand* and the Supremes and the Beach Boys were singing. Andy Warhol blurred lines between pop and fine art. *Sesame Street* first appeared on PBS television.

The limbo was the new dance, the mini skirt and Twiggy were popular and skateboards became prominent. A *counterculture* developed where marijuana and hallucinogens were used. Hippies attended outdoor concerts such as Woodstock and sported daisies, buttons and guitars.

The GNP figure doubled in the United States in this decade. The birth control pill became available to American women. Scientists explained continental drift. Metal tennis racquets were patented. Polaroid introduced color film and Kodak marketed Instamatic cameras. The first heart transplant took place in 1967. Lasers and integrated circuits were developed. The first weather lab was launched into space. The Concorde made its first flight, and Neil Armstrong became the first man on the moon in 1969.

VII.

Travel and Community Involvement In The Sixties

Woman's Club

*I*n 1960 Katharine became president of The Woman's Club of Steubenville, Ohio. Her grandmother, Mrs. W. B. Donaldson had been the first president of the Club from 1899 to 1900 and Mrs. H.H. Minor became its 35th president. The object of the organization is the mutual improvement of its members in Literature, Art, Science and the vital Issues of the Day. Katharine was very active over the years and attended the annual meeting with her daughter Mary in 1997 where she sat at the past presidents table.

Another Grandson

The Evans family of three were at the Minor's home before Bob started graduate school at Indiana University in Bloomington, Indiana that fall. Mary was trying a Hula Hoop, which was popular in the early 1960's, just before her second son and Katharine's second grandson was born in Steubenville, Ohio. James Robert Evans was born on September 6, 1960 in the Ohio Valley Hospital where his father had worked construction on an addition the previous summer. This was one hundred years after the birth of Dohrman James Sinclair who had made the hospital a reality. Dr. Minor would visit his daughter there when he was on hospital rounds.

Shortly after Jimmy's birth, Bob Evans packed up a trailer and headed for Indiana. His mother, Eugenia, arrived to drive young John to Bloomington. Doc drove his son Howard back to Yale. On the way he checked with a doctor friend in New York and called to have Kay fly over and have a lump checked, which she did. Doc and Katharine returned with good results. Kay had a party at her home for all the new teachers that fall in Steubenville, something she did for many years. Mrs. Howard Minor was given an honorary membership in the Alpha Mu Chapter of Delta Kappa Gamma Society, for being active and making worthy contributions in many educational fields according to a *Herald-Star* May 28, 1975 article.

Mary and Jimmy left Pittsburgh for Indiana on a plane when Jimmy was two weeks old. The Minors were slated to fly to Hawaii which they did when everyone had left. In Hawaii Katharine learned that the name used for grandmother was Tutu. She has been called *Tutu* by her grandchildren and great grandchildren ever since.

Flowers on Route 7

Beauty and flowers were favorites of Katharine. She found the routes leading into Washington D.C. lined intermittently with rows of huge bright yellow forsythia bushes lifting the spirits of all who drove to the capital. They welcomed spring as well as the people who arrived. Almost every private home, park and landscaped building had these bright bushes with each stem supporting swaying yellow flowers. Katharine was inspired by this. She thought that the care Steubenville citizens took in their town had diminished. She decided she wanted to improve the appearance of her town and the home town of all the others from Steubenville.

On February 14, 1962 twenty-five interested citizens gathered and the idea of Project 7 was born. Under the leadership of Mrs. Howard H. Minor a campaign was launched. Many people of all ages, political parties, colors, races, nationalities and social groups donated money from their pockets to make their city an even better place to live. This project was not done through government grants nor taxes. The money raised went for over 1,000 forsythia plants which were planted on 2.6 miles of Route 7 through Steubenville. A ground covering of crown vetch completed the project. The bushes never needed to be pruned and the ground cover never needed to be mowed. Simultaneously at the south end of the town on the west embankment opposite the Wheeling Steel plant thousands of yellow crocuses were planted in block letters five feet high spelling SPRING IS HERE. This did not happen without a hitch. While the city maintenance people were planting, one evening Katharine received a call from Charles Wilson, the city maintenance manager, saying they had run out of crocuses. Katharine asked how much was finished and he said, "SPRING IS H". More money was raised for the remaining three letters and the sign blazed for many springs. "Fifteen years later the City Fathers paid with tax dollars to have those beautiful healthy plants dug up and thrown away. Why? No one will say. Will people have the heart to build again, will the *City Fathers* destroy

Sinclair Family Reunion – June 17, 1962
(From left to right) Back row: Judith K. LeVan, Peter H. LeVan, Wilma I. Sinclair, Margaret S. Minor, Dohrman J. Sinclair, II, Garrett B. LeVan, Jr., Dr. Howard H. Minor, Howard S. Minor (holding John H. Evans). Middle row: Garrett J. LeVan, Katharine A. LeVan, Wilma S. LeVan Baker, Katharine S. Minor, Mary M. Evans, Robert H. Evans (holding James R. Evans). Front row: Frank B. Sinclair, Dorothy S. Sinclair, Andrea W. LeVan, Dohrman J. Sinclair, III, Katharine E. Minor. (Family members not present for photo: Katharine W. LeVan, the Garrett J. LeVan children, and Grant family.)

again?" asks Katharine.

A Sinclair Reunion

Family was always important to the Sinclairs and on the weekend of June 17, 1962 the family gathered. Saturday night there was a lovely formal dinner at the Minor's home. Wilma Sinclair LeVan Baker, her son Gary and wife Kathy Le Van, their children Garrett (Cricket) Le Van Jr. and wife Judy, Andrea Le Van, and Peter Le Van, Dorothy Sinclair and her sons Dohrman III and Frank (Buzzy) Sinclair, Dohrman J. Sinclair Jr. and his daughter Wilma (Corky) Sinclair, and Katharine Sinclair Minor, her husband Howard, and children Mary with her husband Robert (Bob) Evans and their children John and Jim, Katharine (Keekee) Minor, Howard Minor, and Margaret Minor were all present. On Sunday a relaxed outing at Dot Sinclair's home included swimming at their pool in Steubenville.

Wilma Sinclair Le Van Baker

The following May, Katharine's sister Wilma Sinclair LeVan Baker died in Pittsburgh, Pennsylvania. Wilma was twenty-one years older and had been like a mother to Katharine when she lived next door on N. Fourth Street. There was a service in Pittsburgh which family including Margaret who was there at school attended. Katharine made arrangements for the funeral in Steubenville. Mary and Bob, who was working on his Ph.D. in philosophy, came from Pittsburgh for the Steubenville funeral.

From the May 6, 1963 Steubenville *Herald-Star* page one and four the following appeared.

Mrs. Wilma LeVan Baker, Woman Leader, Dies at 76

Funeral services for Mrs. Wilma Sinclair LeVan Baker, 76, a member of one of Steubenville's most distinguished families, will be at 11 a.m. Tuesday at the McClave Funeral Home chapel. The Rev. Dr. Charles W. Fulton, pastor of Westminster Presbyterian Church, will officiate. Burial will be in Union Cemetery.

Mrs. Baker, whose talents and accomplishments were many and varied, died about 11 p.m. Friday at her residence, Kenmarr Apartments, Shady Avenue, Pittsburgh. Death was attributed to an apparent heart seizure.

Wrote Book About Her Father

In later life after an eminent career in the financial, political and civic life of the community, Mrs. Baker turned author. She published in 1961 "Father And His Town," the story of her father, Dohrman J. Sinclair, and his community, Steubenville.

In a series of narrative sketches and personal memories, Mrs. Baker showed in her book how her father's resourcefulness, courage, imagination and respect for Steubenville promoted the economic and cultural welfare of its citizens.

Her reason for writing the book, Mrs. Baker said was "to tell something of my father's humanity, his vision, and his driving energy, which overcame seemingly insurmountable obstacles and translated vision into reality."

In 1957, Mrs. Baker published "The Silk Pictures of Thomas Stevens," which grew out of an interest prompting her to gather one of the most complete collections of Stevens' third dimensional woven picturers, many of them preserving scenes and objects of historical significance.

Mrs. Baker, born April 7, 1887, in Steubenville, was educated in Steubenville public and private schools, and at Ogonlz School in Elkins Park, Pennsylvania.

Went On African Safaris

As a girl she starred at tennis and later continued her interest in the out-of-doors by going on several African safaris. She lectured on her travels, using stereo-realist pictures which she took herself.

At home she filled many positions of responsibility as an officer or trustee of business and professional organizations, of the Daughters of the American Revolution, and of philanthropic and church organizations.

Like her father, Mrs. Baker was a staunch Republican. She founded the Ohio Council of Republican Women, served as Republican National committeewoman for Ohio and was active as a delegate to various Republican national conventions, where she advocated important legislation.

Reopened Closed Bank

Most notable of her achievements were her bank activities. When the Union Savings Bank & Trust Co., which her fore-bearers had founded, closed during the depression in the early 30's she was chosen chairman of the committee to reopen the bank. For eight of 10 years which she devoted to its welfare she was president - at a time when a few women held top level posts in the business world.

Mrs. Baker was married on June 30, 1909 to Garrett B. LeVan, vice president and general manager of the LaBelle Iron Works, now Wheeling Steel Corp. Mr. LeVan died in 1943.

Later she married Walter H. Baker, founder and president of Universal Cyclops Steel Company. Since his death in 1951, Mrs. Baker devoted herself to travel and writing.

She leaves a son, Garrett B. (Gary) LeVan of Warren, Ohio, who was an All-American halfback on the 1936 Princeton football team. Mr. LeVan also starred for Steubenville's Big Red football teams during his high school days. Other survivors are a sister, Mrs. Howard H. Minor of Steubenville; a brother, Dohrman J. Sinclair of Steubenville, four grandchildren and four great grandchildren. Her parents were Dohrman J. and Mary Donaldson Sinclair. Mrs. Baker was a member of the Shadyside Presbyterian Church in Pittsburgh.

In 1909 Wilma was head of the first Red Cross Tuberculosis Seal Campaign held in Jefferson County. She was one of the organizers of the Junior King's Daughters of Steubenville, and has held office or membership in the following organizations: Daughters of The American Revolution, National Association of King's Daughters, Jefferson County Children's Home, Phyllis Wheatley Association, Daughters of America, Women's Benefit Association, Ohio Valley Hospital Board, Red Cross, Query Club, New York World's Fair Committee, Business and Professional Women's Club, Circle No. 1 of Westminster Church, American Legion Auxiliary, Ohio Banker's Association, Ohio Chamber of Commerce, United States Chamber of Commerce, American Institute of Banking, American Bank Women's Association, American Club, Pike Run Country Club (Westmoreland County, Pa.), Steubenville Tennis Club, Legislative Committee A.B.A., Republican Progress Committee, Women's National Republican Club of New York and the Twentieth Century Club of Pittsburgh. Two years before her death she qualified for membership and was accepted as a member of the National Society of the Colonial Dames using Francis Stanfield, a Member of the Provincial Assembly, 1685 as the relevant ancestor.

In Wilma and Katharine's mother's will, a ring had been given to Wilma with the understanding it would be left to Katharine. However, this did not happen upon Wilma's death for it was given to another through Wilma's estate in 1963. It was a lovely ring and her husband and brother knew it should have gone to Katharine. So together Doc Minor and Dohrman Sinclair had another ring made to match the original ring with the two diamonds and this copy was given to Katharine with great love.

Graduation and Grandson

The beginning of June had great activity. Margaret, Katharine's youngest daughter who had attended Winchester Thurston for two years graduated and was making plans to go to the College of Wooster in the fall. Katharine also had the opportunity to watch her two grandsons, John and Jim Evans, while her third grandson, Alan was born June 5 in Pittsburgh. The weather was warm and she and the boys had a picnic outside one day. John and Jimmy enjoyed playing in new surroundings. It had been a few years since Katharine's children were young and two year old Jimmy was adventurous. He checked out the neighborhood on his own one day but had an escort coming back to 633 Belleview Boulevard as he stood between two policemen in the front seat of the squad car. The police received much thanks. A short time later Jim and John came down with chicken pox and the dilemma of alerting the police presented itself.

Travel

Travel was a love for this adventurous couple. Perhaps it dates back to Katharine's early travels and Howard's first attempt to leave home. When Doc was about five he and his friend, Whitney Irons, decided to run away from their homes in Toronto, Ohio. They got as far as the street and knew they were not allowed to cross it. This ended their trip.

In 1962 Kay and Doc took a trip on the Delta Queen down the Mississippi and had a wonderful time. Kay's ancestor had Dohrman's Line, a boat and coach company, which traveled between Wheeling and Pittsburgh. The distance by the Dohrman Telegraph Line was sixty-three miles. Twenty-three miles of this distance was on an elegant light-draught steam boat to Steubenville from Wheeling. The Telegraph Line then took the passengers to Pittsburgh on splendid post coaches. This was also the route for the daily mail in June of 1831. Doc's grandfather, Samuel Minor, had been a pilot on the Ohio River until 1861 when he was 33. With this family background, the love of the water came naturally for Kay and Doc. In fact, they took more than one trip on the Delta Queen. One year they went to the Mardi Gras on the Delta Queen and used it as their hotel. They were glad to escape the noise and return to the boat after some time in New Orleans.

Other trips the Minors took were with their friends the Kirks. Young Howard was at Yale and Zane Kirk was at Princeton so when the football teams played each other it became a wonderful opportunity to visit their sons together.

In 1963 the Minors took a Mediterranean cruise which included north Africa and the Holy Land. They had written their daughter, Keekee, who was in Jordan that they were coming on a certain date and had given her the name of the boat. Keekee made arrangements to cross the border from Jordan to Israel since three days notice was required. She took the bus to Haifa, Israel instead of hitch hiking and arrived at what she thought was the boat, only to be told that Dr. and Mrs. Minor were definitely not on board. Keekee admits that she did look like a hippie who just wanted to get aboard. As she was leaving her parents came walking down the gangplank. There was a great reunion which might not have taken place except for good timing on everyone's part. Keekee stayed for dinner, overnight, and then left the next day to sign up to work on a kibbutz.

Another day Doc went to a Rotary meeting while Kay stayed on board the ship. She later went with a group from the ship to a little cafe on shore. As she was eating, much to her surprise she heard, "Hello, Katharine Minor." She looked but didn't recognize the man. He said, "Why don't you know me, I just live down the block from you." Of course she did not know him and he knew it. He had asked one of the group what her name was.

It was on this trip that they met Irene DeMartin's family in Greece. Irene was then living in Steubenville and a good friend. On the day through the Corinth canal they had a chance to look up and see the bridge where the day before they had been. The Englishman next to Katharine on the ship said, "It looks the same as the last time we saw it."

Alaska

Howard was anxious to drive to Alaska but Katharine wasn't too sure. After all, the state could be reached by plane. The day Doc arrived home with a sleeping bag and said, "I'm going to Alaska and you are welcome to come" she knew the die was cast. Doc set the date. Kay said he would not leave on the stated date but she purchased a sleeping bag. The appointed day arrived for leaving and lo and behold they did delay their departure. The car had to be modified because the station wagon was too low for some of the bumps on the Alaskan roads and plastic covers had to be placed on the lights and gas tank to protect them from the stones and dust on the twenty year old dirt road. It took them days to drive to the beginning of the Alaskan highway. On the highway when they infrequently passed a car, they let the dust settle before proceeding. The mile posts showed them how far it was to Alaska and there were signs such as *62 miles to sleeping accommodations*. Sometimes there were no sleeping spots so they slept in the car using their sleeping bags. This happened at least five times. Meals were often eaten along the Alcan highway and these meals consisted mainly of Metracal. At one stop they found a house with a room at the back where they slept. At breakfast the next morning Katharine asked why they had chosen the spot. "It is so near the school," the woman answered. The school was just 26 miles down the road! On one of their travel days they drove all day and only passed one car. When they said this to the filling station fellow his reply was, "Oh, a traffic jam."

One little restaurant had a sign in the window which said, *If you lost everything you now have and got it all back, how happy you would be.* At one point they discovered they had left their Visa card at a gas station about 250 miles back. When they asked at another filling station if they could use the phone the reply was, "Well it worked last Tuesday." It only took four long distant operators to reach the filling station where they had left their credit card and it was charged as a local call! Along the way to Alaska they saw elk, moose, deer, and lots of interesting scenery. The day they arrived at Fairbanks certainly was a Red Letter Day. There the workers were putting bricks down over the dirt road. They had a chance to stop at the home of Robert William Service, the author of *The Cremation of Sam McGee*. They came back via the inland passage to Prince Rupert, Canada and drove home from there.

Dr. Minor said that he was the only man he knew who had been in all 50 states - with the same wife! Katharine maintained that Doc had a keen sense of humor. He would say to his friends, "My first wife said I was a good kid."

Pollution Problems

Intermixed with travel was community work. A 1964 article in the newspaper stated that the Steubenville Woman's Club under the chairmanship of Mrs. Howard H. Minor of the Community Improvement Committee did a visibility and odor survey. Steubenville did have a pollution problem as did Pittsburgh and other steel cities at the time. Steel mills bellowed smoke into the sky and soot descended on the area. At one period Steubenville had the distinction of being the dirtiest city. Laws were passed, attitudes changed and efforts to clean up mills brought pollution down considerably. Effort on many levels made this happen.

Katharine was appointed to Steubenville's Shade Tree Committee about this time and became a board member of the Civic Music Board. She was very active in the National Association of Parliamentarians too and provided expert help to her many organizations.

Income for the Next Generation

In the spring of 1964 Bob Evans started his teaching career as an instructor at the University of Minnesota in Duluth. That fall the Evans bought their first house at 1832 E. Fifth Street and moved in over Labor Day weekend celebrating Jim's fourth birthday. Katharine and Doc soon made a trip to see their daughter, Mary, and her family in their new setting. Their house warming gift was a guest book. It proved to be a great gift which has multiplied into more than eight filled guests books at the Evans' home in Duluth.

Christmas

In the early years Christmas cards contained pictures of the children. As the children grew and left home letters replaced the picture cards. The following is taken from the Minor's 1964 Christmas letter.

Dear Friends, We hope you and yours have had a good year. Since our last Christmas letter, in '62 Mary and Bob and their three sons have moved to Duluth where Bob is on the faculty of the University of Minnesota, Duluth Branch. Keekee has returned from 14 months in Europe, Africa, and

The Minor Family
(1964)
Back row, left to right: Margaret Sinclair Minor, Howard Sinclair Minor, Katharine Evelyn (Keekee) Minor, Robert Howard Evans. Adults seated: Dr. Howard Holland Minor, Katharine (Sinclair) Minor, Mary (Minor) Evans. Children: John Howard Evans, James Robert Evans, Alan Frank Evans.

Asia and is living in New York. Howard has graduated from college and Margaret is a sophomore in college.

We have been busy with church and civic affairs, the practice of medicine and homemaking. The travel bug has bitten us and in '63 we enjoyed a Mediterranean Cruise and also drove to Alaska, and back - enjoyed that too! This spring we flew to Spain and Portugal - so beware!! You may get a phone call from us, if we're in your town in '65.

Our very best wishes to you for a very Merry Christmas, and a Happy and Peaceful New Year.

Howard and Katharine Minor.

Katharine's travels were enjoyed by many. An article in the April 16, 1965 Steubenville *Herald-Star* states, "Mrs. Howard Minor will show slides of her travels to the Holy Land." On January 25, 1966 the following appeared: "Mrs. Howard H. Minor will address the Steubenville Y's Men Club members and their wives tonight at the YMCA. Mrs. Minor will speak on *The Federal Land Office and Its Pride.*"

Federal Land Office
Katharine was busy in the 1960's. Another of her projects was to save the National Federal Land Office. When Sunset Boulevard was to be widened the spot where the land office was located across from the county infirmary, now the Jefferson Community College, was slated to be used for the road. Katharine Minor decided to approach Mayor Targoss to get help. Today we would say this project was done by a public-private partnership. Many meetings with dedicated citizens were held at Katharine's home on Belleview Boulevard. Help came from the city, from citizens and from the Ohio Power Company which moved the land office to the vicinity of the railroad bridge on Route 7. Some of the bottom logs were rotten and a barn was being demolished in the country. It was worked out that logs from this barn were used to replace the rotten ones in the land office. A top section which had been added later to the land office to watch for Unidentified Flying Objects (UFO) was removed and green shutters were added for protection. Later when the Veteran's Bridge was built the land office was again moved to Third and Adams Streets where it is located today within the reconstructed Fort Steuben. Names of people who first bought land were obtained from Washington, D.C. and placed on a plaque which was hung on one of the walls of the Land Office. A tape was made by George Wilson describing the Land Office and Fort Steuben. It was dedicated and opened to the public on July 4, 1965.

The Steubenville Federal Land Office administered the Northwest Territory which had become United States territory in 1783 by the Treaty of Paris. In 1786 Congress ordered the surveying of the territory. The first U.S. Regiment, under the command of Major John Hamtramck, chose a site north of Mingo Bottom on the banks of the Ohio River to build a fort. With the river on its east and the hills to the west the spot made an ideal site for military defense against the hostile Indians in the area. Cornell Harmar wrote on December 15, 1786, "With 33 men from each company, the rest being unfit to work for the want of shoes, on the 27th of October, we commenced our fortification and promised as a reward, six gallons of liquor to the first house completed...and in eight days, the houses of my company were completed and the men moved in that evening. The forwardness of my company on this occasion can only be attributed to their great attachment to whiskey." Hamtramck named the fort after General Friedrich Wilhelm von Steuben, organizer of the army in the Revolutionary War. The pioneers who located around the fort made the first permanent settlement in Ohio.

On July 13, Congress passed the Northwest Ordinance of 1787, a legislative measure creating the territory as the first commonwealth in the world recognizing every man as free and equal, encouraging free public education, and guaranteeing religious freedom. It forever prohibited slavery in what became the states of Ohio, Indiana, Illinois, Michigan, Wisconsin and part of Minnesota. Land sold for one dollar an acre. President Adams appointed David Hoge as Land Title Registrar for the Federal Land Office which was opened July 1, 1800. The log building which Hoge built was first on the east side of Third Street then moved to Third and Washington in 1809. In 1821 it was moved to the opposite corner where about seven years later it was enclosed in a brick building. In 1941 it again surfaced when the brick building was being torn down. It was at this time the log building was moved to Route 22 along Sunset Boulevard.

In 1797, a government surveyor named Bezaleel Wells was offered his choice of cash or land for his services to the government. He chose the latter, taking 1,100 acres on the west side of the Ohio River, including the site where Fort Steuben had stood. James Ross, a Pittsburgh businessman, owned a large adjacent plot and the men laid out a town in 1797 naming it Steubenville after the fort. Lots were sold in August and later the city of Steubenville was incorporated on February 14, 1805, two years after Ohio became a state.

New Grandson

In early April Katharine made a plane trip to see her fourth grandson in Duluth, Minnesota. She had expected snow which she found but she had not expected to see the whole family, new baby and all, there to greet her at the airport.

An April 20, 1966 letter from Gertrude Patterson responding to a letter sent by Katharine mentioned,

> *I am very happy over the arrival of Matthew Minor Evans and I am sure you are too. I am glad you could go and help that dear little mother get organized. She is so precious and I know the older brothers will give Matthew good training. I figure you took the Panama trip. I read in the paper that they are going to dig a new ditch so I figured that the old one did not suit you. Where is Howard taking his basic training? I figure that they are going to drive us out of Vietnam before long. Mary tells me that Keekee finds the summer weather very hot in India. I imagine she is acquainted with Indira Ghandi by now. I imagine Margaret is working her head off at Wooster. It is one hard school.*

At Christmas letters went out to friends which said,

The Minor family brings to you their best wishes for a very Merry Christmas, and also news from various places. Howard and Katharine bring greetings from Steubenville, Ohio. We have been busy in church, civic, home and medical fields. Last February we sailed from New York to San Francisco by freighters, with a week stop-over in Panama, and home via Las Vegas. On January 26, 1967, we expect to sail from New York on the S.S. Coronia, Cunard Line, and go around the world.

The Evans family brings greetings from Duluth, Minnesota. There is never a dull moment with the Evans tribe. Bob teaches Philosophy at the University of Minnesota, Duluth. Mary referees a Cub den and teaches Sunday School. On March 22, 1966, they made it 'four of a kind' when they welcomed Matthew Minor Evans. John, age 8, and Jimmy, age 6, are both enthusiastic students. Alan is 3 and loves everyone and everything.

Keekee brings greetings from halfway around the world, Bombay, India. She could write a book about her life and experiences doing social work there as a member of the Peace Corps. She will finish her two years next October and we hope in 1967 she'll be home for Christmas (not only in our dreams).

Howard brings greetings from Pittsburgh, Pennsylvania. He too, has had a busy year. He completed his Army service and is now with the Fisher Scientific Company, of Pittsburgh, in the Sales Department. He will be located in Cleveland, Ohio, after January 1, 1967.

Margaret brings greetings from the College of Wooster, Wooster, Ohio. She worked at the Union Bank in Toronto, Ohio, this summer and commuted to our cottage in Chautauqua, New York, on weekends. She has taken to the water at college, not only as a crew in the Sailing Club but also as a member of the swimming team. P.S. She also studies and loves her history major.

We all join in hoping that 1967 will bring Happiness to you, and Peace on earth, Good will to men.

Round the World Trip

In 1967 the Minors took an around the world trip by ship in ninety three days, stopping in South America, South Africa, Kenya, Kilimanjaro, Malagasy, Seychelles Isles, India then to Ceylon, Thailand, Okinawa, Japan, Hawaii and Panama. When the Minors left New York they traveled to Florida then on to Trinidad and Rio. On board they had a "meet your neighbor" party which was done by regions. Those from Ohio met passengers from Arkansas, Illinois, Indiana, and Iowa. A Caribbean Ball where everyone wore crazy hats and a Valentine dance where the women wore red and white dinner dresses added to the boat activity along with many many cocktail parties given by the passengers. The Minors were invited to have dinner at the captain's table shortly after the trip started.

"Howard said I was the most naive person he had ever known and he was probably right," Katharine recalls. "When we left on our round the world trip on the *S.S. Caronia*, we had a lovely little Bon Voyage party in our stateroom. One of the guests said he had a friend in Johannesburg, South Africa and would I call him if I stopped there? He gave me a card with the man's name on it and I said I would call him. When we got to Johannesburg I dutifully called. A man answered the phone. I explained I was Mrs. Minor from the United States and was he Mr. So and so. He said he wasn't and to wait a moment. Another man answered and said my friend was at his summer home and he would connect me. A third man answered and I repeated that I was Mrs. Minor from the United States. He said to please wait that he would call him! Next a lady answered and I apologized for disturbing her and asked her just to relate the message that I had called and that my friend from the Bon Voyage party would be there in February. She said her husband would want to speak with me. He was most gracious but said he couldn't recall my friend from the States. Naive me! I had called and talked to the Prime Minister of South Africa."

When they were in Kenya they went to the Kenya National park and had a chance to take a picture of an elephant who had had too many fermented bites of fruit and thought he could charge towards their jeep. They weren't allowed to get out of the jeep until they reached the compound. There they were protected from the wandering animals by a high fence. They had a nice lunch before going on for other night arrangements.

At Victoria Falls Katharine was crossing the hotel when she heard a voice say, "There is Katharine Sinclair!" She turned to find Muriel Ginger from Steubenville who she had not seen in over thirty years. Muriel joined Doc and Kay when they went to look at the falls.

Katharine and Howard visited their daughter Keekee in India who was with the Peace Corp. They spent a night at the Ruparel's in Bombay where a party was given for them. Indira Ghandi's doctor had been invited to meet Dr. Minor. Probably twenty-five people were there with the men talking in groups and the women sitting quietly. During the evening Katharine lost a contact lens in her eye but being the lady she was never mentioned it until the party was over and the guests were gone. She was able to retrieve the contact lens before she went to bed. Each hour on the hour throughout the night the watchman would sound a gong to let every one know that things were all right. Howard said afterwards, "If we had stayed another night there would have been twenty-three not twenty-four servants left in the house."

The three of them traveled to Delhi and saw the red fort and other sites then went on to Agra and saw the Taj Mahal. In Udipur they stayed at the Lake Palace which had been a residence of a maharaja before it was converted into a hotel. They were the only guests except for a group of Vogue models. Taking advantage of the opportunity, Doc asked his wife to take pictures of him with some of these gorgeous women. Much to his disappointment these pictures were the only ones that did not turn out. The weather was beautiful and they traveled to Jaipur where they stayed at the Palace. There were riots erupting and this prevented them from leaving the Palace. They had drinks out on the lawn and in the Polo room. Katharine liked to refer to this as their "Palace arrest experience." Needless to say, they did not see much of Jaipur. With their daughter as guide they spent about a third of what others traveling from the Cunnard ship had spent.

In the Seychelles Isles they obtained a coco de mer which is a double cocoanut found only in these islands. It is the largest known seed weighing about forty pounds and has a diameter of twelve inches.

When they were in Bangkok, Thailand, they took a three hour trip via tender from the Gulf of Siam into the most colorful, rapidly changing fairy tale of unreality. Bangkok's sky was pierced by spires of 400 temples. The Minors learned that Buddha temples have five basic precepts: to abstain from taking life, not to take what has not been given me, to abstain from sexual misconduct, not to tell a lie, and to abstain from intoxicating beverages.

When a group from the ship went ashore in Japan a bus took them around sightseeing. Katharine noticed the name of McAdoo on the fence of one of the houses on the street where they were stopping. While others looked at the site which brought the group to the spot she went down the street to Hester McAdoo's home. Alas, her friend was not there but a young girl was. Katharine Minor introduced herself and said, "You don't know me." Much to her surprise the little girl replied, "I know who you are, you taught my mother in Sunday school." And so she had.

"On our trip around the world, each day brought tranquility or tragedy. We stopped in Hawaii where we had previously alerted a doctor who Doc had known that we would be there and hoped to see him. As we came down the gang plank, the doctor was standing at the foot of it with a gorgeous bouquet of flowers for me.

We had a delightful day seeing him and his summer home where we went fishing. By wading into the water I was able to eliminate the splashing and could see the fish swimming around through the bottomless, topless box I inserted partway into the ocean. Our host served a delicious seaweed concoction. Two days after we had set sail again word reached the passengers that one of the stewardess who took care of the rooms adjacent to ours had jumped overboard, creating a tragic drowning at sea. The ship had to be turned around and retrace its course. Four hours later they found her body floating. They brought the body aboard and after contacting her family in England, it was decided to have her buried at sea. My stewardess asked if I would like to give the bouquet of flowers that the doctor in Hawaii had presented to me, to the crew's quarters where the captain gave the eulogy. The body and my flowers slid down into the sea."

Of all the places the Minors visited on their trip around the world, Katharine liked home best. Back in the United States there were interesting places to see. A childhood friend, Virginia Pearce Glick, invited Kath and Doc to Louisville, Kentucky to the Kentucky Derby in early May. They were immersed in the weekend staying with people who owned horses and had a dog. As far as they could tell this dog would go out with the horses and herd the horses as a sheep dog might do. A lovely dinner party the night before the Derby provided a wonderful opportunity to meet some of the natives of this popular horse country. The parties, the mint juleps, the highly competitive horse race at Churchill Downs all made for an exciting weekend. The Kentucky Derby had begun over 30 years before Katharine was born. She liked to watch the horse race but the one time she went to the Indianapolis 500 she said the noise was too loud for her.

In December of 1967 Keekee returned from India after completing two years with the Peace Corp in Bombay, India. She arrived in Duluth in December to experience a very cold weather welcome but a warm one from Mary and Bob Evans and their four sons.

CLSC and *An Ohio River Anthology*

The summer of 1967 Katharine Minor became a life member of the Chautauqua Literary and Scientific Circle. Members of CLSC had required reading which stretched over four years. Those completing the assignment, would become part of a graduating class. Each summer at Chautauqua there is a Recognition Day parade with present and past graduates walking behind their year banner. The graduation takes place at the Hall of Philosophy and then the procession walks on the brick walk to the amphitheater. There the banners are displayed and an address is given. The organization dates back to 1874.

Mrs. Minor was one of fifteen persons who collaborated to write informal memories of their life and times in The Ohio River Valley, with special emphasis on a few decades prior to and following the dawn of the twentieth century. *An Ohio River Anthology* was written and published in 1968, under the direction of George Mosel, a former Steubenville citizen. Katharine's section appeared in the Steubenville *Jeffersonian* November 7, 1968. Mrs. Minor also wrote an article on the *Pains and Pleasures of Reestablishing Our First Federal Land Office in the Northwest Territory* for the magazine *Our Public Lands* which was published by the United States Bureau of Interior during the winter of 1967. The article was requested by them, and showed the excellent cooperation received from local, state, and federal agencies. She has written other items for newspapers, clubs, etc.

Brother's Brother

On April 26, 1968, the Minors became volunteers for Brother's Brother and had a rich and rewarding experience vaccinating 800,000 Costa Ricans. They inoculated those between the ages of one and twenty one and any others who desired to be inoculated. Doc and Kay Minor stayed in the capital city of San Jose and were driven to the surrounding areas. One Sunday they were outside a church with a table set up and a sign saying *get your vaccination here* (in Spanish) and as people came out of the service they used the new vaccination gun which vaccinated at 700 miles per hour leaving no scratch, causing no pain, and relieving those who did not like needles. At schools they were greeted with "Good morning, Dr. & Mrs. Minor." People would come to the schools from all over the area to be vaccinated for tuberculosis and leprosy. Some of the schools were located over stables because through the floor boards they could see straw and horses. With the ability to vaccinate 2,000 an hour they vaccinated customers, cooks, and waitresses in restaurants; men having lunch after working in the fields (they did not even stop eating); those in stores and even people walking along dusty roads. The jeep would use a megaphone with the message *Get your vaccinations.* An article appeared about the inoculations in the local paper which stated, *Dr. Minor was here with his legitimate wife.* Although most of the shots were done by Doc with Kay providing the tender loving care, she did a few at her legitimate husband's request so she could say she vaccinated too. A post card to her friend Gertrude said,

> *Think of you often. This is quite an experience! Dinner last night with missionaries here; met the Vice President of Costa Rica; had our pictures on the first page of today's paper (wish I could read what they said about us). Weather perfect.*

There was so much work Doc sent word to Dr. Jane Schaffer from Toronto, Ohio to come down and help. When they were about to leave to go home the man at the hotel desk called their room to thank them for all they had done for his countrymen.

1969 Letter

Greetings from The Minors was sent to friends the beginning of January, 1969.

> *We hope you had a good Christmas and will have a happy healthy and peaceful New Year.*
>
> *We've had an interesting year. Wedged between an active surgical practice and church, civic and club activities we have had several trips. In April we had a rich and rewarding experience as volunteers for Brother's Brother. With Dr. Hingson's Guns of Mercy we helped vaccinate 800,000 Costa Ricans against tuberculosis and leprosy.*
>
> *We took a quick trip to Europe with the Pittsburgh*

Surgical Society of which Howard is a member. The remainder of the summer we enjoyed at our cottage in Chautauqua, New York. This fall we have been in Washington, Cleveland and Florida.

Our children have been busy too. Mary and Bob's new addition this year is a Ph.D. after Bob's name. It's now Dr. Robert Evans, Assoc. Professor of Philosophy, University of Minnesota, Duluth, Minnesota. Their four sons are thriving.

Keekee arrived home after completing her two years with the Peace Corps in Bombay, India, where we saw her in 1967. She is working in Washington where the action is.

Howard is living in Cleveland and sells for Fisher Scientific during the week and skis and sails during the weekends.

Margaret's big day came in June, when she graduated from the College of Wooster complete with signed diploma and a teaching certificate. That makes a college certificate for all four children.

Thank you so much for your Christmas wishes. We hope that 1969 brings the best to you and yours. Howard and Katharine

Projects

A June 4, 1969 article in the *Herald-Star* reported "Progress reports on beautification projects and the anti-air pollution campaign highlighted a meeting of the community improvement committee of the Woman's Club of Steubenville, OFWC, held at the home of Mrs. Howard H. Minor of 633 Belleview Boulevard, chairman of the committee. Mrs. Minor reported she went to New Philadelphia for a meeting with Levi Kimble, Division 11 deputy director of the Ohio State Highway Department, regarding the scenic pull-off on Route 7, north of Toronto.

Mrs. Minor also attended the seminar held in Cleveland under the auspices of the General Federation of Women's Clubs, co-sponsored by the Division of Air Pollution Control Department of Health and Welfare, in cooperation with the National Air Pollution Control Administration. While in Cleveland, Mrs. Minor toured Jones and Laughlin Steel Corporation where air pollution control experiments are in progress."

Katharine also continued her focus on history. She became an honorary incorporator of the Meadowcroft Foundation which set out to preserve history by recreating a rural life village with many old buildings in Avella, Pennsylvania.

Doc and Kay and the doll collection.

Social Fun

Kay had a active social life and one noon she was a bit late going to a luncheon. She did not check the address but knew the street. With gloves and hat on she knocked at the door of a home and saw a number of familiar faces upon entering. Then someone asked her what she wanted to drink. At that moment she knew the Medical Association never had drinks at their luncheons and excused herself, finding her right meeting down the street.

Katharine had a wonderful doll collection of between 80 and 100 dolls dressed in native dresses from the countries where the Minors visited on their trip around the world. A favorite was a *Waltzing Matilda* doll she brought back from Australia. Katharine found them very useful at parties, for church programs, and for giving presentations. One day Katharine shared her experiences through a talk to a school. She received a note from the class which said, "Thank you for making your **trite** (*sic*) so interesting."

Her dolls often helped make her parties more interesting. She would use them as table decorations and have place cards of small cardboard suitcases for the guests. Her parties were occasions where people had fun getting together. When those coming did not know everyone she would print cards with a line description of everyone present and then people would get acquainted as they matched the person with the description. She had word games, guessing games, and find the object games. A game which everyone loved was the adjectives game where a story was completed as people called out adjectives.

During 1969 Katharine wrote her friend.

We are all fine. Margaret seems well launched in her new school and apartment. Keekee still loves her job, although it's most exacting - and of course, they may pull the rug from under that particular department (Office of Economic Opportunity) at any time - then she'll just look for another job. Dohrman got over his surgery very well and has driven east to Washington (to occupy Keekee's apartment while she's 'in the field,') then he will go over to Millville to check on Margaret, then home again. Howard is getting over a touch of the flu. Mary and her tribe are busy as busy can be! Doc and I are back in the rat race!

❦

The 1970-1979 Era

The 1970's began with the first Earth Day on April 22. Four students at Kent State University were killed during a war protest. In 1971 the voting age was lowered to 18 years. The 1972 *Roe vs. Wade* decision permitted legal abortions. *Life* magazine published its last issue. President Nixon visited Beijing and became the first United States president to visit Moscow. The United States agreed to stop fighting in Vietnam at the beginning of 1973. Watergate hearings were held in the Senate. Vice President Spiro Agnew resigned and Ford replaced him. Nixon resigned and Ford assumed the presidency choosing Rockefeller as vice president and later pardoning Nixon. Carter and Mondale defeated Ford in the next election. The New York harbor filled with tall ships to celebrate the Nation's 200th birthday. The twin towers of the World Trade Center were completed. Boston was ordered to bus 21,000 children. The Trans-Alaskan oil pipeline finally opened, and the Energy Department was created. Proposition 13 saying that excess spending and taxes should be cut won at California polls. The worst United States nuclear accident occurred at Three Mile Island and India set off a nuclear bomb.

Margaret Thatcher became Britain's first woman Prime Minister and John Paul II became the first non-Italian Pope in 455 years. In Guyana, 909 died in a mass suicide. The Suez Canal reopened after eight years. It was disclosed that the world was spending $300 billion a year on arms, and humankind had wiped out slightly over 1% of the world's species since 1900. Sixty-three Americans were taken hostages in Tehran, Iran. Egypt and Israel signed a peace treaty.

Jimmy Connors and Chris Evert were top tennis stars. A. J. Foyt won his fourth Indy 500. Mark Spitz won seven Olympic gold medals in swimming and Dorothy Hamill won the gold in freestyle skating at the Innsbruck Olympics. The Pittsburgh Steelers won the Super Bowl in 1975, 1976, and 1979. Hank Aaron hit his 715 homer, beating Ruth's record. Lou Brock stole a record 938 bases. Muhammad Ali knocked out George Foreman to regain the world heavy-weight championship. Jack Nicklaus won his fifth Masters. *Affirmed* took the Triple Crown.

All in the Family and *Happy Days* were big hits on television. *Dallas* began on CBS. *Jaws* scared many, and *Star Wars* played in the movie theaters. De Niro acted in the Vietnam movie *The Deer Hunter* and Woody Allen made *Manhattan*. *A Chorus Line* was a success.

Easier credit and more career opportunities for women led to the trend of leaving home early and marrying late. Weekend marriages with spouses living apart were becoming more common. One in three food dollars was spent in restaurants or fast food outlets.

In 1971 the Dow Jones industrial average closed above 1,000 for the first time. The first test-tube baby was born in London. A $1.5 billion loan was given to Chrysler Corporation. U.S. Steel closed fifteen plants, and 13,000 lost their jobs because American steel was uncompetitive.

VIII.

Mother of the Year
In The Seventies

Contagious Disease Aboard

*A*s the new decade began, the Minor couple decided to celebrate their 35th anniversary a little early by taking a cruise. The happy pair drove to the airport for what was to be an extremely interesting trip. "We left Pittsburgh on a non-stop plane at 8:30 a.m. on a frigid -15 degree day, January 9, 1970, and arrived in Los Angeles, California," said Katharine. The Minors had luncheon at the Biltmore, then went to San Pedro, the port of Los Angeles, where "We boarded the *Oronsay,*" continued Katharine.

> We settled into cabin B41 and sailed at 6 p.m. At the dinner table for twenty-four at 8 p.m. we received the first announcement that this would be a *unique cruise*. As we sipped our champagne, a present we shared with our table mates, Engineer Coughey and Mr. and Mrs. Darrell Neale, the loud speaker announced, 'This is the Captain.' He then told us he regretted to say that a crew member had suspected typhoid and had been taken off the ship in Los Angeles. He went on to say that all members of the crew and passengers must be inoculated! Later all were queued up waiting for our inoculations (the first of many 'queuing ups') when word came that passengers were not to be inoculated, but would be given little 'Health Alert Notice' cards which we were to carry for six weeks.
>
> We got our yellow health cards, and were free to leave the ship and see San Francisco, which we did. While in San

Francisco we attended the Old First Presbyterian Church at Van Ness and Sacramento Streets, we rode the Cable Car, spent time at Fisherman's Wharf and toured the Balclutha, a Cape Horner of the 1880's.

Our yellow *Contagious Disease Aboard* flags flew high above the ship. While we toured San Francisco many people went aboard the *Oronsay*. There were those invited to farewell parties, those curious to see the ship, and groups of school children taken aboard to see the big ship. All these people were later advised to be inoculated against typhoid, especially if they had eaten any food or had drunk any water while on board.

On Tuesday, January 13th, the day before we were due to land in Vancouver, we began to get *Health Notices* along with our *Good Morning Sheets*. These were cautions, asking that we be inoculated as a *precautionary measure*. We were advised that the Port Quarantine Doctor would interview all passengers upon arrival in Vancouver. All passengers were inoculated.

We steamed into Vancouver Harbor, with our yellow *Contagious Ship* flags unfurled. We had our Vancouver map, notes and information pamphlets ready to see as much of Vancouver as possible in the eight hours we expected to be there. We waited! The tour was canceled. Those leaving the ship queued up for their final *Oronsay* health check, then left. The rest of us awaited developments not knowing that our view of Vancouver would be from the boat from January 14 to January 28.

Headlines in *The Sun* on January 15, 1970 read,

Unless Typhoid Carrier is Found Liner Feared a 'Floating Bomb'. *Oronsay* warned against sailing. Six crew members taken off the vessel at California ports are being treated as confirmed cases and another 20 suspected cases were taken to Vancouver hospitals after the ship arrived here Wednesday. The company has agreed to hold the line in Vancouver for at least 48 hours with a possible extension.

Dr. G.A. Mott, one of the medical sleuths, said the cost of keeping the *Oronsay* in port will probably be horrendous. "We have asked people who have suffered from typhoid in the past to come forward for tests. About 30 passengers volunteered and some four or five crewmen," said Mott.

The ship took on about 40 Genoese crew members in Southampton, England before she sailed and it is likely one of them is a carrier of typhoid," said Dr. R. David Thompson. George Turner, president of P and O Lines North America Ltd., flew to Vancouver from San Francisco Wednesday night to decide the company's next move, and Dr. J.H. Newnham, is en route from London to take over medical investigation for the company. The last disease outbreak aboard a ship in British Columbia waters occurred in February, 1939, when crew members on the British freighter *Rugeley* contracted smallpox. The quarantine station was closed in 1961.

A newspaper article carried the headline, **No present vaccine gives all-out Typhoid Protection.** The use of antibiotics in the past had reduced the death rate from a one-time high of 14 percent of those who contacted the disease to no more than one or two percent. A hunt was pushed on *Oronsay* for the typhoid carrier. The garbage was being kept on board the ship. The cruise entertainment went on with contract bridge, fitness classes, table tennis, slide shows, Scottish country dancing, *progressive horsie* (a way to bet) and movies such as *Sam Whisky* and *Alaskan Eskimo*. However, notices like "scrub your hands every time you visit the toilet" and "use four layers of toilet paper together each time" accented and underlined the potential danger the passengers were in. One day a quote from Robert Louis Stevenson appeared in the ship's paper, "For my part, I travel not to go anywhere, but to go. I travel for travel's sake. The great affair is *to move*."

The Sunday Sun on January 17 ran a headline, **It's Going to Get Worse on Typhoid-Stricken Liner** and went on to say that there were twelve confirmed typhoid crewmen and passengers. In the *London Times* on January 17 a headline read **Nearly 7,000 deaths from flu in month**. On the 19th five more persons were due to be moved to the hospital, bringing the total from the stricken ship in the hospital in Vancouver to 43 (33 crew and ten passengers). The typhoid strain on the *Oronsay* was identified as a K-1 phage type. The disease had spread through the ship's water supply, where fecal organisms were found on Friday. New crew members were flown in to replace those who had become ill.

The passengers were notified that unfortunately, it was impracticable to allow the public baths to be used when the ship was stationary. The water used in the baths was salt water, gathered from the sea, into which the ship's waste was also being pumped. The showers and all baths attached to cabins had fresh water. On Wednesday, January 21, the thought for the day in the ship's paper was, "Everyone in the world at one time or another has wanted to live on a houseboat. Aren't we lucky?" Then came the not completely unexpected news: *Oronsay* **to stay another week**. The incubating period for typhoid averaged from ten to fourteen days. Fifty-five crewmen and passengers were in the hospital (thirty confirmed and twenty-five suspected) and five others were suspected carriers but were not in the hospital.

On January 25 there was a Burns' Night dance. The next day the ship's passengers received good news, although it was conditional.

> If the carrier responsible for the typhoid outbreak aboard the P & O Line ship has been located - and health authorities are *reasonably certain* he has been - the ship will continue its voyage to Hawaii and Australia on February 2. Arrangements are being made to allow passengers who wish to disembark, to leave the ship within a few days.

The number of confirmed or suspected cases of the disease stood at 71. The ship carried on its regular entertainment program just as if it were at sea, and added a few twists which included a series of movies on Vancouver. These, of course, were augmented by the ever present view of Vancouver itself, live and in color.

On January 26 the passengers received notice that a medical team from the Port Health Authorities would check out all passengers in the Tourist Ballroom on B-Deck for the Charter Flight. On Wednesday, the 28th of January, those leaving gathered and proceeded onto the Pier. The flight was scheduled to depart Vancouver at 5 p.m. on the 28th and arrive in Sydney at 6:45 p.m. on the 30th with stops in Honolulu and Auckland. Fifty-two passengers including the Minors, took the plane from Vancouver to Hawaii, then Australia. Kay and Doc saw Vancouver via post cards, from the ocean and from the air but not on their planned excursion from the boat. Their vacation in Australia and New Zealand was wonderful and full of flowers and down-to-earth activities. Their trip to celebrate their 35th anniversary ended much better than it began.

Family Changes

Back home the Minors took up their regular routine. On May 20 Howard Minor had skipped playing golf because he had not felt well. However, he had gone to the Williams Country Club and was about to have dinner with Howard Brettell, Steve Harris and John Bevan. Suddenly he collapsed. Dr. Brettell had just gone into the shower when he was called to help Doc Minor. Males gathered around the two men in the hall, one an ailing doctor and the other a naked one, as Dr. Brettell administered help while waiting for the ambulance. It was a fast ambulance ride to the hospital. Dr. Harris called Kay from the Ohio Valley Hospital saying that Doc was there. Kay's trip there was very speedy. Dr. Minor's ability to speak suffered greatly from the stroke he suffered, but he was able to regain his ability to walk. Katharine says of the time, "He was very courageous. He did as much as he could." It became clear that he would have to give up his surgical practice and limit many of his activities. Doc's first bank board meeting after his stroke was difficult for him to make, and when he entered the room all conversation ceased. Katharine related, "He did look terrible but he was determined to attend the meeting." He traveled, spent time in Chautauqua during the summer, and learned to listen to tapes instead of reading. His son-in-law, Bob Evans, tells the story of reading to him and stumbling over a medical word. Doc quickly gave it the right pronunciation.

That fall Doc and Katharine's son Howard married Pauline Paciorek. The wedding took place in Cleveland on Howard's 30th birthday. His three sisters, his parents, and other family and friends attended the lovely wedding held at St. John's Cathedral. The reception was held in an elegant room at the Lakefront Airport. Howard and Pauline left for a honeymoon in Ocho Rios, Jamaica, stopping on the way in Ft. Lauderdale, Florida.

Nomination for Ohio Mother

In 1972 Katharine Minor was nominated for *Ohio Mother of the Year*. The following is part of the nomination letter from Mrs. Stanley Slee, a past president of the Steubenville Woman's Club, which recommended Katharine for the honor.

> *Katharine has shown our members, particularly our Mothers, that 'it can be done.' She is dedicated to her husband, yet committed to all things and all people when there is need. She can serve on a church committee or a community project with equal enthusiasm and thoroughness. Any assignment is never too big or too small. She finds easy rapport with a young mother or an International Ambassador, - for she has rocked the cradle and circled the Globe.*
>
> *Today's world demands much of a woman, and even more diversity of a Mother than ever before. By family*

tradition and growth, Katharine is a woman who dares to be
<u>*a lady*</u>*, whether it is a civic meeting in a smoke-filled room*
or a tea at the club house. This is her heritage, her basic
attribute, that quality that makes her a real Mother, our
nominee for the Ohio Mother of the Year.

Letters were received from the minister of Westminster Presbyterian
Church, William M. Perry who wrote,

> *My wife and I came to Steubenville in June (1972). At the*
> *time Dr. and Mrs. Minor were away and I learned soon*
> *afterwards that Dr. Minor was still recovering from a major*
> *stroke. However, awaiting us on our arrival was one of the*
> *most gracious notes of welcome we have ever received in*
> *any city. Katharine Minor, in spite of illness in her own*
> *family and absence from the city, had taken the time to write*
> *such a note. Right then and there my wife and I would have*
> *voted for her with all our hearts for the highest award in the*
> *land. Since that time, on many other occasions, she has*
> *shown the same warmth and graciousness - not because we*
> *now happen to be the minister and minister's wife of her*
> *church, but because this is just the sort of person she is. She*
> *manages somehow to find the positive in every situation,*
> *without either dishonesty or forced superficiality. She*
> *qualifies for the award on the strength of her many services*
> *to the church and through the church to other people, but on*
> *this ground alone, I highly and gratefully recommend her.*

Other letters came from the Martha Kinney Cooper Ohioana Library
Association and from Arthur Bowers, Ohio House of Representatives, who
had the Ohio House of Representatives commend her for receiving the
nomination for Ohio Mother of the Year. Andrew W. Miller, Mayor of
Steubenville for eight years, wrote,

> *Who ever heard of a prominent club woman with hum-*
> *bleness and selflessness as outstanding personality traits?*
> *Katharine Minor fulfills all of these roles and at the same*
> *time works constantly to make Steubenville a better place*
> *for everyone - the high and the low - to live.*

John Targoss, Former Mayor of Steubenville wrote:

I only knew this person by sight before she introduced herself to me on the third day of my tenure as Mayor of the City of Steubenville, Ohio. This was a day I will always remember. She came along with a fellow member of the Project 7 Civic Program. After a brief session I consented to her wishes and became a firm believer of the things she stood for, 'Community Dedication.'

She is energetic, pleasant, persuasive, loyal and a humble person. I know of three projects that were completed during my stay in office through her efforts. This type of person makes a position, such as the Mayor, a pleasure to work with. I recommend her highly and would be pleased to accept her on my team anytime.

One of the most beautiful spots in our City of Steubenville stands as a memorial at the gateway of our city, 'The Federal Land Office,' a project that she helped move from a desolated part of town to its present spot. She served on the Citizens Advisory Board, Project 7, and the Land Office Removal Project.

I am sure Katharine Sinclair Minor is deserving of a salute for all of the wonderful things she has contributed to the City, State, and humanity.

Letters to recommend her as *Ohio Mother of the Year* also came from Judge John Griesinger, a member of her Query Club, a bank president, a chemist and bacteriologist, Chief Judge Carl Weinman of the United States District Court, and many friends.

The Daughters of the American Revolution's letter covered her interest and her family's interest in patriotic, historical and educational activities of the Steubenville Chapter, National Society Daughters of the American Revolution.

Mrs. Minor's mother, Mrs. Dohrman J. Sinclair, was the first Regent of the Steubenville Chapter, DAR. Her older sister, Mrs. G.B. (Wilma) LeVan, followed in the footsteps of their mother and her brother, Frank D. Sinclair, was a member of the Sons of the American Revolution.

Katharine Sinclair Minor became a member of the Steubenville Chapter, DAR, in 1930, before her marriage to

*Dr. H.H. Minor, and in 1935, served as a page at the
National Societies Continental Congress. She was elected to
various offices in her local chapter and served it in many
other capacities.*

*Mrs. Minor has always believed in and fostered the
objects of the National Society, DAR, which are, 'To cherish,
maintain and extend the institutions of American freedom, to
foster true patriotism and love of country and to aid in
securing for mankind all the blessings of liberty.'*

J. Sheldon Scott wrote,

*It is a pleasure to add my word to those of others in trib-
ute to Mrs. Howard H. Minor (Katharine Sinclair Minor).
This letter is concerned mainly with her leadership in the
organizing committee of the new Jefferson County Historical Association, of which she serves as unofficial chairwoman by common consent of its members.*

*Since the inception of the Association, she has shown a
rare gift of leadership coupled with inventive imagination
and a positive genius for getting things done. Her gracious,
self-effacing and always friendly personality have much to
do with her almost uncanny ability to influence others; she
is persuasive without even seeming to be coercive, so that
one WANTS to follow her direction. As a result, the Historical Association has made steady progress toward the forma-
tion of a county-wide organization. As is well known, Mrs.
Minor, an extremely busy person, has been most generous
with her time and talent in the promotion of many other civic
enterprises. She is deserving of any special honor that may
come to her.*

*I am tempted to include in this letter a circumstance at
which I am sure Mrs. Minor would smile if reminded of it.
There is a possibility that she is descended from one of the
early discovers of America. Henry Sinclair, Earl of Orkney,
sailed to this country and landed on the shores of Nova
Scotia in 1393, 99 years before Columbus made his first voyage to the West Indies. He was in search of timber for the
building of ships, as large trees do not grow in the Orkney
Islands. He built a village and remained here for a year.
While his shipwrights labored to build new ships for his*

navy, he spent much time in exploring into the interior. At his campsites he left monuments in the form of engravings on rock faces where available. These carvings bore his name and the date underneath the Sinclair family crest. Recently one of these engravings was discovered as far south as Massachusetts.

Sinclair's navigator, an Italian who had been ship-wrecked in the Orkneys and pressed into service, returned to Italy after his two voyages to 'the large island in the north Atlantic' we now know as America. He had kept detailed records of the entire venture in his log books, which he care-fully preserved. These books, still quite legible, were discov-ered some years ago by his great-great-great-grandson in the attic of his home. They are now in the archives of the Italian government in Rome.

The following letter came from Scott McMurray who was the News Director at WSTV- Radio.

To Whom It May Concern, I'm writing to recommend Mrs. Katharine Minor, wife of Dr. H.H. Minor for Ohio's Mother of the year. Mrs. Minor has had to overcome every advantage a woman could surmount in her efforts to achieve this honor. It is customary to nominate people for this honor who have served their community well after rising to wealth or prominence or both from humble station. Katharine Minor has lacked this opportunity. Born a Sinclair she was from birth a beauty born to a wealthy and powerful family whose influence on their section of the state has been great for a century and still continues to grow. She compounded her problem by the obstacle of a long and happy marriage to a dedicated and highly successful physician, world traveler and community leader.

Her selfless devotion to charity and community improve-ment was augmented by her enthusiastic fight to preserve the history of one of the state's most historical areas against staggering odds. It's tough to campaign for preservation of the late 18th and early 19th century historical items in an area where the vast portion of the population is second and third generation foreign born from Europe. Nevertheless Katharine's continuing battle to preserve our nation's heritage through preservation of the federal land office park dating from 1802 is just one of her many community interests.

F. Scott Dimit wrote:

> *It is a distinct pleasure for me to join with those people of this community nominating Katharine Sinclair Minor (Mrs. Dr. Howard Minor) for Ohio Mother of the Year.*
> *My acquaintance with Mrs. Minor dates back to her very young Sunday School days in Westminster Presbyterian Church where she taught a class of youngsters, assisted the Secretary and did any other chore where she could help. Later she did her share in singing in the Church Choir. She has a long record of active service and generous financial support of her church. Mrs. Minor follows her mother in this respect and as she was trained to accept her responsibilities to her church and community so has she reared her family.*
> *Her influence and hard work in the community is reflected by her interest in beautifying parks, even reclaiming a former city dump on Franklin Avenue. The most ambitious idea in this area was the landscaping of Route 7, known as Project 7, through Steubenville for a distance of some two miles. Then there was the matter of preserving the original Land Office of the Northwest Territory which attracted attention state-wide.*
> *Yes, it does indeed give me great pleasure to include my name with those nominating this dedicated woman, Katharine Sinclair Minor as the Ohio Mother of the Year.*

Margaret Boyd, who was an officer of the Delta Kappa Gamma Society at the state level, wrote,

> *I have worked with Mrs. Minor in many activities and have found her greatly interested in the program of the church and at all times willing to give of her time and energy to bring success in that which she undertakes.*
> *When she was President of Westminster Presbyterian Church of Steubenville's Woman's Association in 1959-61, she was faithful in all her duties, she showed initiative in planning our activities and also qualities of leadership in*

implementing her plans.

> *Mrs. Minor is a person of high intellectual attainments, strong character, broad sympathy and high ideals. She has a pleasing personality and possesses unusual skill in working with people. She has unusual executive ability, including both competence in performing work herself and in delegating work to others. She possesses unusual emotional stability, tolerance and poise. Her personal qualities are a constant source of inspiration for others.*
>
> *Mrs. Minor has a rare sensitivity and understanding of other people and other cultures. This has been shown when she extended hospitality to visitors from other lands.*

An elder in the Westminster Presbyterian Church, Mrs. Charles Ford wrote,

> *She taught a children's Sunday School class for years and later taught a Couples class of young adults. In 1955 she was a member of the steering committee to re-organize the Women's Societies to form the Women's Association of Westminster Church. She has served on the nominating committee and was Fellowship Chairman of the Association.*
>
> *In 1960 she received an Honorarium from the United Presbyterian Christian Education Department U.S.A. She has been circle leader many times and was President of the Women's Association. In 1965 she was appointed to serve on the committee of the Fifty-Million Dollar Fund Raising Program sponsored by the General Assembly of the United Presbyterian Church, U.S.A. Mrs. Minor has recently been appointed to serve on the By-law committee to revise the Women's Association By-laws.*
>
> *She has raised her children in a Christian home and they attended church regularly as a family unit. She was always an inspiration to them, seeing they were active in young peoples work of the church. She is very humble and unassuming and has never been too busy to take on any task for her church. Her life has touched many lives in our church and has left many marks for good.*

Her children were also asked to write letters to accompany the nomination. Mary Minor Evans wrote:

When I think of my mother I think of the warmth, tenderness, and affection she has given to me. A mother is an origin yet many are origins without being a total lifelong strength; my mother has given me that strength and a friendship where give and take provide both with satisfaction. She has always enjoyed both the young and old and that attitude is reflected in her relationships with me and my siblings. She was always there when you needed her. She gave us guidance for choosing and making our own decisions while giving us freedom to learn and live our own lives.

There were the intangible things about our home that made it a place you were glad to come home to. A warm atmosphere, the efficiency of a well run home giving time to enjoy living, the open door for friends whether they be the ones brought home from school or later those stopping by on trips, and the ability of my mother to add six more to the household with an ease and welcome that has made her grandsons look forward to visiting her, give some idea of my home where I grew up.

My mother has always been energetic. She gave her love and talents to us but she also shared her talents with others outside our home. Her variety of interests extend from the Woman's Club, Project 7 to beautify a highway, restoring an old log cabin, and church work to being on a library board and PTA president. She also put her energy into the many fun parties we gave for our friends providing boxes with hidden presents when we were young and hiding objects for us to find around the house when we were older. She watched grandsons while new ones were arriving, organized picnics for grandsons and all, made marshmallow men, played games both as mother and grandmother, gave many hours of time during my brother's illness to read to him, taught us girls how to cook and crochet, fixed hair, helped in easing problems, and all in all just was and is a wonderful mother. She is extremely thoughtful and considerate remembering special dates not only of family but friends also. As we grew and moved away she gave her loving care to others who needed a little attention. Many of the wonderful things she gave to her children she has been able to re-channel towards others.

As a mother also of four, perhaps the best thing I can say

about my mother is that I'm trying to follow her example, because I think enough of the way I was raised to pass it on to her grandchildren.

Mary's husband, Bob wrote,

I hope that a son-in-law will be considered eligible to make a few remarks on my 'second' mother. I have known Katharine Minor for 15 years now, and two characteristics come immediately to mind. During the high school and college years she had the marvelous ability of being able to express her disapproval of a course of action by one of her children, while at the same time, she both allowed them the freedom to guide their own lives, and made them feel that they would be loved and accepted at home despite any mistakes they might make. This delicate balance between giving moral guidance and developing autonomy has most impressed me as a parent.

Secondly, she not only opened her home to anyone (and seemly any number) that was brought home, she welcomed them and took a genuine interest in them. The first time some of my friends stopped for overnight I was amazed at the time Katharine took to talk with them and the effort to prepare festive meals as if they were her own long lost friends.

Lastly, I think it takes special qualities to put up with a son-in-law who moved in with four grandchildren for several summers while he, in a not very pleasant mood, took over a large corner of the house to write a dissertation.

Keekee Minor wrote,

I have received your letter requesting that I write something about 'what I think of my mother.' I often think if I were given the task of choosing a set of parents, I'd certainly select the ones I have.

My mother, well she is a pretty exceptional person and has received recognition throughout the years as being such. I remember once my friends and I gave her a sportsmanship award for taking us to a football game away from home, where she sat through, and enjoyed four quarters during a downpour and later joined us on the way home with our singing.

She is able to adapt to any group or situation. She sees the best in people and magnifies it. I can't imagine her ever raising her voice to anyone. As a matter of fact, when I was a child, I used to think maybe it was because she didn't have a strong voice - later I realized that in her own tactful way, she accomplished far more than most people in getting done whatever needed to be done.

Her saying of 'What's mine is yours,' has been taken quite literally by members of the family. She derives so much pleasure from giving - far be it from us to fail her in that regard. Most of her projects involve doing for others.

My friends remind my siblings and me that since our parents are so special we must share them, and we do. Even when I am away from the United States, friends of mine will visit them. I can safely state that 633 Belleview Boulevard, Steubenville, Ohio is regarded as home in every sense, by anyone who has ever met and come to love my mother. Her warmth is universal, and acts as a magnet to one and all.

My parents, therefore, are more than my parents, they are, in addition, friends of mine, and very good friends.

A combination of love and friendship provides an ideal relationship, and ideal is not an accolade easily bestowed. When referring to my Mother, however, it does not begin to express my feelings.

Katharine's son, Howard, wrote,

I welcomed this request to tell of my mother because it brings forth a kaleidoscope of images from the past. Do I enumerate the hundreds of times when I was a child that her understanding and support minimized the many small disappointments that are part of the growing of a boy into a man? Or, is it possible to capture the essence of my feelings by relating the joy added to my life by telling of the unselfish giving of herself to her family?

Perhaps the best way is to tell of one incident which casts light on the kind of mother she is. Turn back the clock with me and find yourself a small boy of ten confined to a hospital with rheumatic fever. As visiting hours approach each day, you look forward to seeing that familiar, cheerful face coming through the door. You wait in anticipation for the four leaf clover that was picked today and each day while your mother was walking to visit you in the white ether-filled rooms. A four leaf clover to bring you luck, yes, but it is more, for unlike a toy that one buys, it represents her love in the fact that her search for it each day was a giving of her own effort.

One cannot choose their parents, only God can. In my case, God chose well.

Margaret wrote,

I'm thrilled to tell you something about my mother. The Woman's Club nominating her as 'Ohio Mother of 1972' is an honor well deserved.

She is not a mother for just one year but every year, each day, hour and minute. Words are lacking for there is feeling beyond words. A warmth that cannot be described. A love that is 'more than tongue can tell.' As a child she told me that love for me was 'more than tongue can tell.' I now have some understanding as to what that means. It is through actions that her love for me has been shown.

When I was sick her loving arms held me and made the illness bearable. As I grew her understanding and guidance were always there. One of the first things I remember was having a doll that was almost as large as me and my mother carefully explaining, in response to what may have seemed a very stupid question, that no it would not ever become as tall as I. At a little older age I remember her taking me to concerts, introducing me to music which I still enjoy. She took me to see Madame Butterfly, but took me home before the last act so I would get my sleep and would not be exposed to suicide at the very young age.

In junior high and high school who remembers the foot-ball and basketball games she attended because she took my friends and me. She provided the shoulder to cry on and the consoling words when I came home heartbroken because I didn't become a cheerleader. I, as many tanagers, went through a stage of bitter, fierce antagonism toward my mother. Never though through that period did the bond between us break as she made sure we could always talk with each other.

There were 'Parents Weekends' in college that my parents came to show they cared. There were the days she would spend all day coming out and then driving us all home from college. When I left college for a semester because of poor grades her response to the news was 'come home we love you.'

I have always felt free to bring people home for she and my father have always been gracious to my friends and made them feel welcome.

She helped to shape my character in many imperceptible ways; in conversations where the words are forgotten. Her actions did this also. I never in my life have heard her say anything negative about anyone. She shows by example how to be a good person, caring for others before herself.

Words cannot describe what it is to have a mother like mine. I've only told of a few small incidents that I remember. Many are too personal to share. It is with great joy that I find others are paying tribute to a wonderful human being that I am lucky enough to call mother.

An article in the Steubenville *Herald-Star* by Barbara Parker March 29, 1972 stated:

"Today's young mothers have tremendous courage and will be responsible for many changes for the good in the

world," according to Mrs. Katharine Sinclair Minor, the new Ohio Mother of 1972.

Mrs. Minor, wife of Steubenville surgeon Dr. Howard Minor and the mother of four children and the grandmother of four, made the statement in an interview in her home on Belleview Boulevard following announcement of her selection as "Ohio Mother of the Year."

"I think today's young mothers are wonderful - and I think they've got courage," said Mrs. Minor. "I think they'll make many changes that perhaps my generation didn't have the courage to make." "The role of mother, although

Mother of the Year Award
with four children.

fundamentally the same, changes, with the times," the Ohio Mother continued. "After all, I'm different from my mother."

Mrs. Minor noted, for example, that her grandmother, Mrs. W.B. Donaldson, was the first president of the newly formed Steubenville Woman's Club way back in 1899, a time when women did not go out of the home to meet for "club." The current club yearbook is dedicated to the courageous Mrs. Donaldson who helped to prove women could be a vital force in the community and still be good wives and mothers.

The new Ohio Mother of the Year, following the tradition of her mother and grandmother, also is active in social and civic affairs and is an avid collector and world traveler. She was elected as the first president of the Steubenville Junior Woman's Club when it was formed in 1933.

"I would say my greatest interest, however, is my husband and children," she said. With her husband, she has traveled extensively throughout the United States and around the world including South Africa, Europe, India, the Mid East and Alaska.

In 1968, she and Dr. Minor volunteered their services to the Brother's Brothers Foundation injecting program and for three weeks traveled in rural areas of Costa Rica giving tuberculosis and leprosy vaccinations. The following year they rendered similar services in Guatemala. As a result of their associations abroad, Dr. and Mrs. Minor have entertained many international guests in their Steubenville home and their summer home in Chautauqua, New York.

A member of one of the city's pioneer families, Mrs. Minor has long been interested in area history and preserving records and landmarks. She spearheaded the saving and restoration of the First Federal Land Office in the Northwest Territory which is now a public museum in Steubenville, and worked on the committee for the restoration of Meadowcroft, a restored village in Washington County, Pennsylvania.

Descended from the Donaldsons and Sinclairs, Mrs. Minor is the great great granddaughter of John Donaldson, the first man to be buried in Union Cemetery. Some of her most treasured possessions include old land grants, records, diaries and antiques handed down through the family for generations.

Although deeply involved in community life and human-

itarian work, Mrs. Minor believes her first duty is to make a good and happy home for her family. She is an accomplished needlewoman and admits to be "probably one of the valley's best short order cooks." Mrs. Minor explains a doctor husband and four children in and out constantly calls for extreme versatility in cooking.

One of her favorite civic projects was "Project 7", a Route 7 beautification project undertaken by the Steubenville Woman's Club. She also is a life member of the Westminster Presbyterian Church and an active volunteer with the P.T.A., Y.W.C.A., Daughters of the American Revolution, Ohioana Library Association, Mayor's Citizens Committee, hospital auxiliaries and the Ohio Historical Society.

The Minors are the parents of four children, Mary Carolyn, the eldest daughter, is the wife of Dr. Robert Evans of Duluth, Minnesota. Their second daughter, Katharine (Keekee), is field representative for Family Planning under OEO in Washington, D.C. Prior to assuming her present position, Ms. Minor spent two years in Bombay, India as a Peace Corps volunteer.

Margaret, the youngest daughter, is a teller with the Central Bank of Cleveland. The Minor's only son, Howard, is affiliated with the Fisher Scientific Co., of Cleveland as sales representative with the Investors Diversified Services.

"We've got the finest people in the world in Steubenville and a wonderful town with marvelous potential," concluded the new Ohio Mother of the Year.

Mrs. Minor, who was sponsored by the Steubenville Woman's Club, will go to New York May 8-12 to attend the annual conference of the American Mothers Inc., the official sponsor of Mother's Day at which time the American Mother of 1972 will be selected.

At a reception held to honor the 1972 Ohio Mother of the Year, Mrs. Katharine Minor, Congressman Wayne L. Hays, one of several officials present to honor Mrs. Minor said, "To me the word mother is probably the greatest word in the English language - women's lib not withstanding. Mothers have made America what it is. It is a great privilege to be here today to do honor to an *Ohio Mother* from my district," Hays concluded. From Ohio Governor John J. Gilligan a letter came stating, "As a businesswoman, humanitarian, environmentalist, civic volunteer, hostess and, above all, wife

Den wall with the picture of luncheon for Mother of the Year and certificates Katharine received.

and mother, you have been a true inspiration to the millions of Ohio women who have found their most important role in life as being a mother." Mrs. Minor also was presented with citations from Senator Douglas Applegate from the Ohio Senate; Rep. Arthur Bowers, House of Representatives; Steubenville Mayor William Crabbe; Peter J. McCafferty, president of the Steubenville City Council which passed a resolution honoring Mrs. Minor; Nathan Stern, president of the Steubenville Area Chamber of Commerce; Miss Margaret Boyd, president of the Woman's Association of Westminster Presbyterian Church; and Mrs. James Bruzzese, president of the Junior Woman's Club of Steubenville.

There was a luncheon at the Waldorf - Grand Ballroom in New York City on Friday May 12 at noon for all the state mothers. The Ohio hostess later took Katharine and Howard Minor out to dinner at the Butler Hall where years before Katharine had lived while attending Columbia University.

Needlework

After Doc's stroke, when he was courageously fighting to regain his speech, Katharine took up hobbies which gave her a chance to stay at home with her husband. She found that needlework was a perfect match for staying close to her husband and keeping herself occupied with productive projects. She did petit point, gross point and needle point, and finally latch hooking rugs as her eyes became worse. A lovely hooked rug with flowers

Example of needlepoint designed and done by Katharine S. Minor in 1973.

in the center and around the edge; a self-designed banner with her Mother of Year award on one side, her husband's caduceus on the other side, and their marriage dates in the middle; and a needle point of the home at 633

Belleview Boulevard are some of many hand-made items she has created and which have helped to produce the warm atmosphere to be found in the Minor home. Other items include a panel hanging in the Evans' home which says, *Have A Good Day for Evans' Sake*, a sign saying *Think Ahead*, cute clown pillows, a large cross banner for the church, a rug with sheep jumping, numerous pillows with flowers, country scenes, a clock, door pulls, and a whole variety of hooked rugs. By the 1990's she pretty much gave up needle work because of macular degeneration and the inability to see.

Jefferson County Historical Association

Katharine was always interested in the history of the Steubenville area. Around the dining room table at 633 Belleview Boulevard, work really began on creating the Jefferson County Historical Association. In 1972, Mrs. Howard H. Minor, William Brandt, J. Sheldon Scott, Mrs. Earl G. Snyder and George Barthold met to establish a historical society whose purpose was to establish a museum and to hold meetings to promote, preserve, perpetuate and disseminate knowledge of the history of Jefferson County and the City of Steubenville. After many meetings, the Jefferson County Historical Association was formed and held the first general membership meeting in January of 1974. The Association was incorporated on February 19, 1974. John O. England was the first President of the Association. Often one hundred or more attendees would be at the meetings, where both business and a program would be presented.

Much work was done to obtain a place to house the museum. Finally the home of the late Emma Carter Sharpe Zeis was purchased by the Jefferson County Historical Association in 1976. The three-story English Tudor house had cost approximately $35,000.00 to build in 1919. Colonel John Joyce Carter of Titusville, Pennsylvania purchased the land to build a house for his daughter Emma and her husband Mr. Alexander B. Sharpe. Following Mr. Sharpe's death, his widow married Reverend Harold Zeis. Mrs. Zeis lived in this house from the time it was built until her death in 1962. The house stands, as originally erected at the corner of Fifth Street and Franklin Avenue at 426 Franklin Avenue.

Beyond the living room through French doors, in a glass enclosed room which was formerly a sun porch, is a Genealogical Library which contains more than 2000 volumes of records and history of Jefferson County, other Ohio Counties, and areas of West Virginia, Pennsylvania and other states. The Library, considered to be one of the best in Ohio, has received publications from many people. It also features books by local authors including Wilma Sinclair Baker, Malcolm Brady, Oral Pflug, Dorothy Rietz, Mary

Donaldson Sinclair, Dohrman J. Sinclair II, Richard Weisberger, George A. Mosel, Walter Kestner, Robert Richardson, Dr. Robert W. Shillings, and Rabbi Harry Stern.

Many from the town and area made donations. On one of the Minors' trips Kay happened to notice in the window of an antique store in Mobil, Alabama, the ledger for the Steubenville Spencer store. She mentioned this to her brother Dohrman Sinclair, and when he was next in Alabama he purchased it for $500 and brought it back for the museum. Gracia Spencer had been Katharine's second grade teacher and taught her to write. Katharine remembered how she was having trouble with spelling *are* until Miss Spencer covered up the a and e of the word. It was Gracia's father who had the store in Steubenville.

Katharine served as a Director on the Jefferson County Historical Association until her death. She along with many from the area have put in hours of work and contributed articles of the past to make the museum what it is today. Membership rose to over 300, and meetings were first held in Judge Ralph Levinson court room Monday nights, then moved to the YWCA. In 1987 work began on the installation of a new heating system, plastering, painting, new carpet and drapes, cleaning, and relocating the genealogical library to the sunroom. Expenses exceeded $30,000. Many groups have toured the facility over the years and learned of the rich heritage of the Jefferson County area. The Chamber's Business After Hours has found the museum ideal for special gatherings. Bus trips bring people to Steubenville to see the murals, old Ft. Steuben and the Jefferson County Historical Association Museum.

Trips

During the 1970's the Minors were at home at first while Howard was recovering from his stroke. He soon tired of the four walls and wanted to travel. Katharine hesitated but finally decided to try it. They purchased bus passes which allowed them to get on and off the bus as they wanted. During the early 1970's there was a gas shortage, so the bus worked well for their travel. On the Minor's Greyhound bus trips they would ride from town to town. When it was nearing dinner time they would get off the bus and find a hotel, then have dinner. If the town was interesting they might stay an extra day. When there were not two seats together they would sit apart. Katharine met many interesting people this way. Once she met a young Eskimo girl named Anna Levi who had worked at the post office in Resolute Bay. The girl continued to write Katharine even after she was married and had a child. Another time a young boy from Scotland visiting the United States was her seat mate. He talked a lot and told her his past life and goals. He mentioned that it was like talking with his grandmother, she was so friendly. He had never talked to anyone so frankly. When they reached Salt Lake City he helped them off the bus. Kay and Doc went to the hotel after checking their large suitcase at the station. Finding they were missing something when they reached the hotel, Katharine retraced her steps and found her bus friend still there with his friends. When he saw her he came over and embraced her and asked her if he could do anything for her.

The Minors traveled on to the west coast seeing the country. Howard enjoyed the trip so much that the following year they again purchased bus passes for $50 each and went west by way of southern Canada to Vancouver and then back.

Katharine also made reservations on the Delta Queen where they could travel on the Mississippi River and explore areas if they wanted when the boat stopped. It definitely was a change from the four walls of the house and proved to be a very effective way to travel. One year they cruised up to St. Paul on the river then on to Duluth, Minnesota by bus to see their daughter Mary, her husband Bob, and grandsons, John, Jim, Alan, and Matt. The Minors went through southern Canada to Winnipeg, Jasper, and Vancouver, then down through Washington, Oregon, and the northern part of California. They enjoyed Yosemite Park and the Grand Canyon, and when the snow came they headed home.

The Minors spent time during the winters in Florida at friends or motels and in Arizona, where they rented a trailer a few winters. One year they

Kay and Doc Minor in the 1970's

arrived in Arizona expecting to have the trailer on the date they said they would arrive. The owner said he did not think that they were going to arrive on their stated date, so he had not fixed the plumbing. The Minors lived with a mess for a week. On one bus trip to Jacksonville, Florida they stayed at the Hilton. During the night the alarm went off and people vacated the hotel in various forms of dress and undress. The fire was soon taken care of and all returned to their rooms to get what sleep they could. While in Florida they took a boat across the Everglades. On the swamp tour they sat two feet in front of the old, very loud airplane motor. After that trip Katharine could not hear anything, not even the start of an engine, for quite some time. She credits that experience with causing her hearing loss.

In the mid 1970's, while Margaret was living in Cleveland, she traveled with her parents to Puerto Rico in February while she was recovering from mono. Kay and Doc had the trip scheduled, and when Margaret called to say she needed help, the Minors weighed the options and decided to continue with their planned trip but take Margaret along. Katharine drove up and picked up her daughter in Cleveland. When Margaret arrived in Steubenville her father asked, "Did you bring your bathing suit?" The Minors proceeded on their trip. Coming back from Puerto Rico there was a stowaway on the plane. After they landed there was a five-minute delay, then more delays until after five such delays they were able to get off the plane in Miami and the authorities were able to capture the stowaway in the back of the plane. By this time the connecting flight was boarding. Katharine had called for a wheel chair for Doc, which did not arrive. Margaret called to ask the plane to wait until they arrived at the gate. The exhausted three people did make the plane to Pittsburgh. Katharine called the valet parking for their car the first thing upon arrival in Pittsburgh and then went to make a claim on the broken bottle of liquor that had arrived with their bags. As they were all ready to leave, Margaret came to her mother and said there was a woman crying and she really needed help, could her mother please do something? The poor woman had never been on a plane before, and had lost not only her ticket but her luggage as well. Kay sorted things out for her and by the time they got to the car, the valet man was long gone. They arrived in Steubenville where Katharine was scheduled to give the memorial service for the Woman's Club. She had ordered roses before she left for the families who had lost members during the year. With no time to change she went to the Woman's Club in the middle of winter in her summer vacationing clothes and was told that there had been another death and there would not be enough flowers. Luckily she had ordered an extra rose so all worked out well.

1975
Floor and couch: Matt Evans, Pauline holding Howie Minor, Katharine Minor, Howard Minor, Mary M. Evans, Alan Evans. Rear: Jim Evans, Howard Minor, Margaret Minor, Keekee Minor, Bob Evans, and John Evans.

In 1975 the Minors made another trip to see their fifth grandson, Howard Sinclair Minor, Jr., in Cleveland, Ohio. Howard and Pauline's son had arrived on May 6 to keep the run of boys intact.

Doc Dies

All the family gathered in Steubenville for the Christmas holidays in 1977. Doc enjoyed a special treat when his wife and three daughters sang Christmas songs for him. When winter engulfed Ohio, Doc and Kay headed south to Florida as they had done in previous winters. There were friends to visit and warm weather awaited them. Doc enjoyed attending Rotary meetings. One day they went to Disney World and afterwards Howard did not feel well. The next day they stayed in the motel, but Doc did not seem to recover. On March 20, Doc was taken to the hospital and died that day in Winter Haven. The Minors returned to Steubenville by plane, and Irene and Bob Coblentz drove their car back to Ohio. Young Howard called Mary who was in Colorado with Bob at a philosophy conference. They drove non-stop to Steubenville. Keekee had arrived in Manila a day or two before she got the news. It had spooked her staff when the call about her father came because Keekee had felt funny about taking the trip to Manila in the first place. The husband of the Deputy in the Regional office in Manila happened to be a vice president for American Express, and he arranged for the flight back for Keekee. When she arrived at the airport the flight had been canceled and he came out to the airport and made other arrangements. She transferred in Hawaii and California, arriving in Pittsburgh where Washington friends picked her up and took her to Steubenville and the packed funeral home in time for the visitation. Margaret was called by Howard and made her way to Steubenville from Chagrin Falls, Ohio. Howard came down from Erie, so all the far flung children were able to make the funeral.

The obituary appeared on page one of the *Herald-Star* on March 21, 1978:

Physician, Bank Director Dr. H.H. Minor Claimed

Dr. Howard Holland Minor, long-time area physician and director emeritus of the Union Bank, died Monday in Winter Haven, Florida, while vacationing. He was 72. Minor, a resident of 633 Belleview Boulevard, retired from his many years of practice in 1970. He had served the Union Bank for 40 years from 1936 to 1976 as a director until reaching mandatory retirement.

Dr. Howard H. Minor
Long-Time Civic Leader

He also was head of the medical department of the Steubenville, Mingo and Follansbee Coke plants of Wheeling-Pittsburgh Steel Corporation for 20 years. Born August 15, 1905 in Toronto, Ohio, he entered private practice in 1933. He interned at Allegheny General Hospital in Pittsburgh, Pennsylvania and was Resident Physician in the Ohio Valley Hospital in Steubenville in 1932. He spent ten years in private practice before going into the Army.

During World War II, he served 3 1/2 years in the Army Air Force, attached to hospitals at Perrin Field, Sherman, Texas; Tarrant Field, Ft. Worth, Texas; and Selman Field, Monroe, Louisiana. When he was released from the Army at the close of World War II, he was Major Minor, Chief of the Surgical Services at Selman Field, Monroe Louisiana. Before resuming private practice in Steubenville, he served on the surgical staff of the Aspinwall, Pennsylvania Veterans' Hospital for two years.

He was a member of The Academy International of Medicine, the American and Ohio State Medical Associations and had served on the latter's speaker's bureau; he belonged to and was four times president of the Jefferson County Medical Society; was a member and had been chief of surgical service of the Ohio Valley Hospital in Steubenville and the Weirton General Hospital in West Virginia, and held membership in the surgical staff of the Gill Hospital of Steubenville, Allegheny General Hospital in Pittsburgh, Pennsylvania, the North Wheeling Hospital of Wheeling, West Virginia, and St. John Medical Center in Steubenville, Ohio. He was a member and past president of the Fort Steuben Academy of Medicine. He served three times as President of the Ohio Valley Hospital Medical Staff and was Head of the Doctor's Staff. Minor was a diplomat of the American Board of Surgery; a Fellow of the American College of Surgeons; member of the Pittsburgh Surgical Society and the Hawthorne Medical Society, Philadelphia, Pennsylvania.

He also was a member of Westminster Presbyterian Church, where he had served as an elder, a trustee and Moderator of Deacons. He was a member of Phi Gamma Delta social fraternity, Alpha Mu Phi Omega medical fraternity, Steubenville Rotary Club, Elks Lodge 231 and also Masonic Temple Lodge 45, where he was a 32nd degree Mason. He was a Director of the YMCA and on the board of the Boy Scouts. He belonged to the Williams Country Club of Weirton and the University Club of Pittsburgh.

His education include graduation from Wells High School in 1923, from Washington and Jefferson College with a bachelor of science degree in 1927 and from the University of Pennsylvania Medical School in Philadelphia in 1931. He returned to the University of Pennsylvania postgraduate school of medicine for a year's additional training in surgery, graduating with a master's degree in surgery.

He leaves his wife, Mrs. Katharine Sinclair Minor; three daughters, Mrs. Robert (Mary) Evans of Duluth, Minnesota, Miss Katharine (Keekee) Minor of New York City and Miss Margaret Minor of Chagrin Falls, Ohio; a son Howard

Sinclair Minor of Erie, Pennsylvania; a sister, Mrs. W.E. (Evelyn) Drake of State College, Pennsylvania, and five grandsons. He was preceded in death by his parents, Howard and Carrie Holland Minor.

On Thursday, March 23, 1978 the editorial contained the following:

Dr. Howard H. Minor

The Tri-State Area is the poorer in the passing of Dr. Howard H. Minor, who died Monday at age 72 while vacationing in Florida. A life resident of the area, except for when he was away at medical school, interning or serving his country while in the armed forces during World War II, he was an immensely dedicated and popular resident of this vicinity who gave unselfishly of his time and talents so the area might benefit.

There was hardly a facet of life in the Upper Ohio River Valley which he did not touch. In addition to being a physician and surgeon, he was involved with banking, with steelmaking, and with health and with his community in many untold ways.

He was an active member in fraternal and social organizations, holding many offices in those organizations. And he was active and involved with his church, Westminster Presbyterian, where he served as an elder and trustee.

It takes an uncommon man for the involvement which he was into, but anyone who knew him well could tell another of the uncommon qualities he possessed.

Anyone who is involved - and active - in the things which interest Minor has to be of the disposition that they care about what is happening in their community and to those who reside in it. That the Toronto native chose to live and work in his home area is testimony to the esteem which he held for the Tri-State Area.

Few people have touched the history and future of this area to the extent he did and it is doubtful one will come again this way for some time to come - if ever.

Many residents of the area, regardless of whether they had contact with him in his role as banker with the Union Bank, where he was director emeritus when he died, in his role as physician and surgeon; in his role as the head of the

medical department for the Steubenville, Mingo and Fol-
lansbee Coke plants of Wheeling-Pittsburgh Steel Corpora-
tion or in a variety of other ways will soon forget him.

He was a gentle, humble and gracious person, loved by people from all walks of life. His brilliant career was cut short by a stroke. Under the watchful eye of his loving wife and family, he led a limited active life until his death. Many wrote to remember him. His sister said,

> *My thoughts are with you, Kay, and I know you will have*
> *a great adjustment after almost eight years of concern for*
> *Howard. I'm sure he would not have lived the last years had*
> *you not often adjusted your own wishes to do what he*
> *wanted so that an upset and possible attack was avoided. No*
> *man ever had a more loving and caring wife and I too am*
> *happy to have you as my sister (in law but I really feel as a*
> *sister).*

Albert Miller who was the Executive Vice President of Meadowcroft Village accepted an invitation to speak at the Jefferson County Historical Association meeting and wrote,

> *As I read your husband's obituary the one thing that*
> *entered my mind was that as I read in magazines and news-*
> *papers about the beautiful people (and I'm not sure just who*
> *these people are - the 'jet crowd' or the 'cocktail crowd'*
> *many of whom have been married two, three and even four*
> *times), I wonder why they are being called the beautiful peo-*
> *ple. My thoughts were that certainly the Minors, community-*
> *minded, devoted family-type people, are the <u>real</u> beautiful*
> *people. I know that people do not become Mother of the Year*
> *without fine husbands and devoted family relationships.*

Family Milestones
That Christmas Katharine wrote,

> *As many of you know, 1978 was a traumatic year for us.*
> *Howard and I were in Winter Haven, Florida in March,*
> *when he was called home. During the eight years since his*
> *stroke he showed tremendous courage, against great odds,*
> *and was an inspiration to many. He did a great deal of good*

in this old world and it's a better place because he was here. I'm grateful for our many good years together and thankful to each of you who knew and have expressed your sympathy.

Mary and Bob Evans still live in Duluth. They traveled to England and Wales this summer for three weeks - just for fun. Bob continues to teach Philosophy at U.M.D., is head of the Department and is Assistant Dean of Student Affairs for the College of Letters and Science. Mary is again President of the Duluth League of Women Voters, continues on the Board of Spirit Mountain Authority (the City owned ski, restaurant, camping and summer recreational area), and also received the Jr. League Volunteer of the Year Award. Their two oldest sons are attending the University of Minnesota in Duluth. John traveled east this summer to New York where he saw The Acts and Chorus Line. His grandmother enjoyed his stopovers with friends in Steubenville and Chautauqua. Jim traveled west to a camp in Colorado for a week then on to California. Alan is now in High School where he ran cross country and is the first chair French Horn player for the Trojan Band. Matt had a good Little League summer and is now attending Jr. High. He plays the Trumpet and is first chair for the 7th grade band.

Keekee is a bit difficult to keep up with. If you ask me her whereabouts, I might have to answer, "I don't know where in the world she is today!" Her home base is One Lincoln Plaza, N.Y.C. During the past year as Deputy Director of Family Planning International Assistance (Planned Parenthood Federation of America) she has been in twenty-four countries. She works hard but enjoyed a fantastic trek through Nepal and a memorable visit to Manchu Picchu in Peru. Last year she had a fascinating three weeks in China. As some of you know, Keekee doesn't believe in working straight through life, so on March 1, 1979, after three years with F.P.I.A., she plans to give herself a sabbatical from work!

Howard and his very capable wife, Pauline, and my favorite four-year-old grandson, Howard, Jr. live in Fairview, Pennsylvania (near Erie). Howard is in the Sales Department of Mogul Corporation which deals with Water Treatment. Fortunately, for me, they were in Chautauqua with me much of the summer. Howard Jr. loved his Nursery

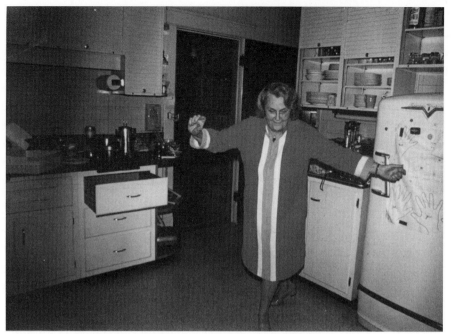

Katharine showing how she could Charleston.

School. Their big news is: they are infanticipating a play-mate for little Howard in February - and I get to babysit at the time!

Margaret is involved in Chagrin Valley Little Theater near Cleveland, where she is serving her third year on the Board. Her biggest role now is as a student at Kent University. This summer, research for her Master's thesis took her to Philadelphia, Virginia and Oxford, Ohio. This fall she moved to Kent, Ohio where she has begun work for a Ph.D. in history.

We will all twelve be home for Christmas and join in sending you our best wishes for health and happiness at this very special Christmas season and throughout the New Year.

Katharine S. Minor

The family gathered for Christmas and a chance to all be together. Much of one day was spent rearranging furniture to make room for Keekee's furniture, which she was storing at the house and also filling a U Haul for Margaret to take back to Kent. There was much excitement about the newest grandchild. Michael Dohrman Minor arrived February 5, 1979 and Katharine went to visit and help in Erie.

In May Katharine traveled to England for a wonderful trip. She stayed with her cousin, Claire Martin. They traveled to Edinburgh and Glasgow and north to Inverness and Portree. She spent several days in London with Keekee before returning to the States. Kay spent the summer at Chautauqua.

That December Katharine flew to Duluth to attend the wedding of her first grandson, John Evans, who married Sarah Oreck December 21. It was a mild winter with no snow. She was able to stay at one of the Evans' friend's home and helped with the groom's dinner held at the Evans' home. Keekee also came with her mother and as usual, the airline lost her luggage. There was a lovely church wedding and a lively reception.

❦

The 1980-1989 Era

The Brooklyn Bridge and the Statue of Liberty celebrated 100 years. The family farm depression was as bad in 1987 as it had been in 1937. A devastating fire in Yellowstone National Park burned more than 88,000 acres. Army General Colin Powell became the first black man to head the Joint Chiefs of Staff. Sandra Day O'Connor became the first woman on the Supreme Court. Reagan fired air traffic controllers. United States troops invaded the tiny Grenada island. Mount St. Helens erupted and 710 families left Love Canal in New York.

Kohl became Chancellor in West Germany and Premier Trudeau resigned after 15 years as leader in Canada. Indira Gandhi was murdered in India. Over two thousand died in a toxic gas leak in Bhopal, India and the Chernobyl accident released deadly atomic radiation. The Tiananmen massacre took place in Beijing. The Berlin wall came down.

The Americans won the Olympic hockey gold medal, and Heiden won his fifth gold medal in speed-skating, but the United States boycotted the summer Moscow Olympics in 1980 to protest the Soviet invasion of Afghanistan. Mary Lou Retton won the gymnastics gold and Carl Lewis won three gold medals in track at the Los Angels Olympics. San Francisco was struck by an earthquake as the World Series game began and 62 died in the quake.

Yuppies displaced hippies in San Francisco. Hemlines began to climb again above the knee. Skateboarding became popular. John Lennon of The Beatles was shot. Movies had new under-13 ratings. *The Last Emperor* won nine Academy Awards.

Sally Ride became the first American woman to go into space. In 1986 Challenger exploded as a horrified nation watched on television. Halley's comet returned after a seventy-six-year absence. Smoking was banned on all U.S. flights of less than two hours. Washington split up AT&T. In 1989 the Exxon *Valdez* created one of the worst oil spills in U.S. history. Computers became popular in offices.

Aids was first identified in 1981. The second heart implant was done in America and lived 620 days. A federal panel called obesity as dangerous as high blood pressure.

In the 1980 census Steubenville had a population of 26,400 but by 1990, it had dropped to 22,125. The average home price was over $100,000, and asbestos became a problem in buildings. The Japanese invested heavily in United States real estate. On August 25 the market stood at 2,722 but fell 508 points on October 20, 1989.

IX.

Enjoying The Generations
In The Eighties

Steubenville Activity

*A*lways active in the community, Katharine became the first Treasurer of the Steubenville Clean Community Board. There was a drive on to clean up Steubenville and she actively took part and did her share.

Katharine loved history and knew a great deal of the early years of the area. In 1982 she gave a talk to the Jefferson County Historical Association on early Steubenville, the oldest community in Ohio. Their newsletter listed the highlights of her talk. She gave information about the early events in the history of the town, including in some depth, contributions her father, Dohrman J. Sinclair, made toward the growth and betterment of Steubenville. She gave the background of early medical facilities, culminating in the building of the Ohio Valley Hospital. "My father always said, 'the impossible just takes a little longer.' The Ohio Valley Hospital Board wanted the hospital to be built on Fourth and South Street across from the Carnegie Library. My father wanted it at its present site, with lots of fresh air and sunshine. The Board said people would die going all the way to the hilltop location. Accident patients from La Belle Iron Works, now Wheeling Pittsburgh Steel, had to be taken to Pittsburgh or Wheeling for treatment so the argument was somewhat melodramatic. My father had his friend, Ben Sharp, who owned a livery stable, hitch up a horse and buggy and timed his run from the La Belle Iron Works Gate of the mill to the present location of the Ohio Valley Hospital. The Board was convinced and the tedious work of acquiring the land for the new hospital began. Father even went as far as to redraw the first plans larger using store wrapping paper on top of a barrel keg in a grocery on S. Third Street," said Katharine.

Dohrman Sinclair not only headed up the campaign to raise money for the hospital, but also gave five acres of land and a generous amount of money. In addition to his own contribution, he gave $500 in Katharine's name to the Ohio Valley Hospital.

Continuing with her talk, Katharine conveyed the history of Steubenville's Water Works at Alikanna and the Filtration Plant on Stony Hollow Boulevard and how they were erected against almost impossible odds. The clear need for a better water works became evident when a fire destroyed most of S. Fourth Street because there was not sufficient water to fight the fire. When the new system was finished, a twenty-inch main went from the pumping station to the Franklin Avenue reservoir, and the downtown business section had a separate system of pipes to carry water at high pressure. A picture taken in 1895 demonstrated the water power in Steubenville. It showed six high pressure streams of water soaring above the court house.

At the Historical Association meeting Mrs. J. Sheldon Scott read an account from her husband who was Steubenville's Chemist for forty years. He had written it after talking with Mr. Dillon, who was a participant in the story. Mr. Sinclair, unable to convince the City Council that they should build a filtration plant to protect the citizens against typhoid, arranged a special train to take the members of the Council and City Officials to Cincinnati to see their new plant in 1912. On the way home the Council was not ready to vote. After all possibilities were discussed and exhausted, Dohrman Sinclair insisted that the matter had to be settled before morning. A vote was finally taken and Steubenville was on its way to getting a new filtration plant, even though some of the councilors had had a bit too much to drink to remember clearly the vote the next day.

Katharine concluded by telling how her dynamic father engineered the building of the Market Street Bridge so the Follansbee Brothers could be persuaded to locate a plant and found the city of Follansbee. He brought the brothers to the area on a special train and showed them, from the hills on the Ohio side of the river, the beautiful site of wheat being tossed in the breeze. Little did they know that the proposed area for the factory in West Virginia was covered by a few inches of river water due to rain the previous day. Sinclair knew that dams would soon control the river.

In another building block for the area, Sinclair persuaded the officials of the Philip Sheet and Tin Plate (now Weirton Steel Co.) to locate in Holiday's Cove and found the City of Weirton. He had promised a streetcar line to transport workers to and from the plant which seemed a simple task since two different trolley companies had consented to put in a line for Sinclair. However, they both backed out, leaving Sinclair with a promise to construct a streetcar line between Steubenville and Holiday's Cove. He decided to organize a construction company after he collected enough capital in the surrounding cities. The company spent month after month hacking away at the rock hillside to clear a wide enough path for rail tracks and also a boulevard. It was finally completed. Sinclair then hounded Brooke County officials to pave the boulevard.

In 1982, sixty seven years after his death, a plaque honoring D.J. Sinclair was presented to the Minor and Sinclair families at the Franciscan University of Steubenville Founders Day event. Katharine accepted the plaque which read, "Once he had the vision he had the iron will and the resourcefulness to translate the vision into reality." Only one vision should not have become reality. Two weeks before Dohrman's death he called a friend to witness a *beautiful sight* in the heavens - a cloud portrait of a locomotive and cars with an engineer looking at something below the cab. Little did he know at the time it depicted his death scene exactly.

England Visiting Daughters

In November of 1981 Katharine traveled to England to visit her daughters, Mary and Margaret. Margaret was doing research in London, and Mary was with her husband, the director of a study abroad program through the University of Minnesota, Duluth. That program was stationed in Birmingham, England. Katharine arrived and spent Thanksgiving with Margaret in her *bedsit* in the Bayswater area of London. Katharine brought food to feed Margaret's friends at Thanksgiving, and they all enjoyed the American food. Katharine caught the train to Bath where she met Mary and Bob. After enjoying the area they drove to Birmingham where her grandson Matt was going to the King Edward VI school for the year in the fourth form. Margaret later came to Birmingham to deliver an academic paper. The family traveled around the Cotswolds and to Coventry, where Katharine remarked, "The cathedral has much more of *an air conditioned look* than the last time I saw it in 1924." (That was before the WWII bombing.)

For Katharine's return flight to the United States, Margaret took her to the Heathrow airport in London. That evening, after Margaret returned to her flat, she heard a knock at the door. She was surprised when it turned out to be her mother. The plane had been canceled because of the weather. The next morning Katharine again set out, only this time in the airport limousine. She chatted with the other passengers, some of whom had experienced the same delay. That evening Katharine again appeared at her daughter's flat. No planes had been able to fly that day either. The evening she did not return, Margaret knew the plane had left.

Dohrman and Katharine

Siblings

Katharine's brother, Dohrman, was a great help to her after Doc's stroke. An artist, he had his own apartment which he used for painting and writing. At night he usually joined Kay and Doc for dinner when they were in Steubenville and stayed over night at the house in case he was needed. During the day he often ran errands for Kath. He also stayed at the house when the couple was gone. After Doc's death he moved into the house and continued to help. They attended church together and often went out for dinner afterwards with friends or visiting family. As the two youngest members of the Sinclair family, they had many Steubenville interests and knew many of the same people. They both kept up their many friendships in town. Dohrman continued his travels and so did Katharine.

When Howard Minor's sister, Evelyn, was in her eighties, she mentioned to Katharine that she had always wanted to see the Grand Canyon and had never been able to go. Her husband, Earle Drake, had died October 1, 1977, and she was now living with her daughter Lynn in Cleveland, Ohio. Katharine said she would treat her to the trip and made arrangements. There were no rooms at the Grand Canyon lodge, but finally a suite became available. Katharine went to Cleveland to meet Evelyn and they flew to Reno. They were surprised to find their room with only one large bed. Evelyn wanted to go out on the town that night, wheelchair and all. The next day they took a small plane to the Grand Canyon where they could learn in English, Spanish, German, or French what they were seeing in the canyon. The plane flew between the walls of the canyon and it was spectacular. Their suite was quite an upgrade from the room in Reno. It had a

large sitting room as well as a spacious bedroom with two beds. They enjoyed walks and had their meals in the lodge. The trip delighted both. Evelyn died a few years later, on September 24, 1984.

AWOL

Finding herself with more freedom as a widow, Katharine turned to her women friends. A group called AWOL for All Women On the Loose found a good recruit in Katharine. In the winter she would join other women who had lost their spouses and head to Florida. They enjoyed bridge, companionship, good meals, and warm weather. Katharine also opened her home in Chautauqua to the group for a visit one summer so they could also appreciate this unusual setting together.

Chautauqua

In her late 70's and 80's Mrs. Minor was often found on the porch of the Chautauqua cottage waving to friends who passed and the bus driver who picked up children. It was a friendly porch and often full of neighbors, relatives, and friends of everyone in the house. The friends changed over the summer as different children, grandchildren, and great-grandchildren spent time in Chautauqua. Thinking back to the first visit at Chautauqua, Mrs. Minor exuded pride in the family tradition that she and her husband created. Her children have moved to distant hometowns but out on the front porch there are five state flags to represent the states of family residences. All still find time to return to the summer cottage. For Katharine and many others, Chautauqua's dearness stems from its comfortable atmosphere and its remembrance of history. Katharine said, "Chautauqua is the people, and

Seated: Katharine S. Minor; Standing, Mary, Howard, Margaret, Keekee

**PEACE
ON
EARTH**

Katharine Minor

Mary (Evans) Howard

Margaret and Keekee

the whole atmosphere radiates happiness. Since the 1940's it's the same and that's the way I like it."

During her years at Chautauqua Katharine became a life member of the Chautauqua Women's Club and served on the Board of Directors. She was a member of the First Family Life Institute of Chautauqua, under the auspices of New York University, and has spoken from the platform of the Hall of Philosophy.

The following is taken from the Chautauqua *Daily* for Friday, July 22, 1983:

> *Among Chautauqua houses to attain 100-year status in 1983 is the Minor family home at 33 Foster Avenue. A copy of the first 99-year lease of the land from the Chautauqua Lake Sunday School Assembly has been preserved and hangs in the cottage. Dated August 19, 1882, it substantiates the fact that Mrs. Ada T. McCollin had paid $150 for the lease which was signed by Lewis Miller and A.K. Warren.*
>
> *In 1883 Mrs. McCollin built a two-story, presumably four-room house on this lot on the corner of Foster and Wythe Avenues, facing Foster Avenue. The house had a steep peaked roof and a porch across the front. The front and back doors had glass panels in the upper two-thirds of the doors, as well as brown porcelain knobs on the outside and white porcelain knobs on the inside. The doors remain the same and even the oft-painted screen door hooks and eyes and hinges are visible and intact. The stairway originally divided a few steps away from the first floor and entered both the living area and the kitchen-dining area. The original clapboard wall is still in the old front porch which has since been made into a glassed-in-sunroom, and on the second floor which is now a sleeping porch. A porch on the Wythe Avenue side of the house was added later and became the main entrance. Sometime before the Minors bought the house, dormers were added to the third floor so that two sleeping rooms and a bath could be accommodated there, while an addition on the south side of the house provided an extra room for both first and second floors.*
>
> *Ada T. McCollin was born in 1847 and died in 1907. Her home was in Sugar Grove, Pennsylvania, now less than an hour's drive from Chautauqua. But in 1883 over dusty or muddy roads, it must have been a day's journey by horse and buggy. She and her husband are buried in the Cherry*

Hill Cemetery in Sugar Grove in a family burial ground which is surrounded by an ancient, ornate wrought iron fence with a gate at one end. Mrs. Minor visited the cemetery some time ago out of interest in the first owner of her house. She said that the excellence of the location in the center of the cemetery and the faded pretentiousness of the stones leads her to believe the family had been people of position and means.

The next owner of the house whose lease was recorded June 2, 1910, was Mrs. Alice F. McCollin, thought to be the wife of the son of the original owner, Paul McCollin. The lease also is framed as a keepsake at 33 Foster Avenue. Successive owners include Louis J. Harter (1914), Frederick F. Ingram (1919) and Mrs. Mary R. Stokoe (1920). In 1930 the property passed into the hands of Mr. and Mrs. Samuel M. Hazlett. Mr. Hazlett was to become the chairman of the Chautauqua Reorganization Corporation and in 1947, the President of the Institution. So 33 Foster Avenue figured prominently in those crucial years of saving Chautauqua in the '30's and early '40's, as the home of the man who spearheaded that effort. The Minors purchased the home from Mr. Hazlett (and have now owned it for 53 years as of 1998).

Mrs. Minor has comparative tax figures that she finds interesting. The school tax in 1884 was all of two cents while the property tax was $4.15. By 1910 the school tax was within two dollars of the property tax. In 1975, the school tax was 100 times greater than it was in 1910.

Thirty-three Foster has been much-beloved by the Howard Minor family. Mrs. Minor and the couple's four children would come for the season and Dr. Minor would spend vacations here. After he retired he could enjoy Chautauqua all summer long. He died in 1978. The children come and go as their busy lives allow them and now eight grandchildren also call the house "home." Howard, Jr. resides in Erie, Pennsylvania within easy access to Chautauqua. During this summer of 1983 Margaret Minor is working on her doctoral dissertation at Chautauqua; daughter Mary Minor Evans of Duluth, Minnesota, is in Europe; and Keekee who has been head of Services with the International Branch of Planned Parenthood of America, is doing consulting work and can be in Chautauqua only for brief periods.

Mrs. Minor continues her activity at Chautauqua, where she is a life member of the Chautauqua Woman's Club, the Chautauqua Literary and Scientific Circle and a trustee of the Chautauqua Presbyterian Association. A resident of Steubenville, she was honored in 1972 as Ohio's Mother of the Year.

Family Changes and Gatherings

Katharine's seventh grandson, Paul Donaldson Minor, was born November 11, 1980, in Erie, Pennsylvania. He joined his brothers Howard and Mike. As with the other grandsons, Katharine went to visit the family and enjoy the new addition.

On April 20, 1982, Katharine's first great granddaughter was born in Minneapolis to her grandson John Evans. They named their daughter Katherine Jane Evans after her great grandmother. Young Katherine's great grandmother

1983

Back row: Sarah Evans, John Evans holding Katie Evans, Matt Evans, Alan Evans, Jim Evans, Dohrman Sinclair.
Seated: Bob Evans, Mary M. Evans, Margaret Minor, Katharine Minor, Keekee Minor, Howard Minor, Pauline Minor holding Evan Minor. Floor: Howard Minor, Mike Minor, Paul Minor.

was delighted. Katharine's eighth and last grandson, Evan Thomas Minor, was born in Erie on October 1 of that year. All of Katharine's other grandsons were baptized at Westminister Presbyterian Church in Steubenville using the baptismal font given to the church by her grandparents, William and Emelda Donaldson in 1914. As an elder in the Presbyterian Church, Katharine was able to take part in Evan's baptism in Erie.

In the fall of 1983 the Minor/Evans/Sinclair clan gathered in Steubenville. People were assigned to rooms with names such as *The Greenbrier, The White House, Windsor, The Hermitage, The Waldorf,* and *The Athenaeum Hotel.* Activities included bridge, family movies, ping pong, darts, picture albums, a family flea market, the modeling of clothes in the big clothes exchange, visits to the Land Office and Historical Museum, and watching the football games on TV. The weather was mild for the outside activities. Everyone helped with the meals. To celebrate Howard's birthday, Mary and Bob's anniversary, and Howard and Pauline's anniversary the whole group went out to Haverland's Farm for some good country cooking. There were twenty-five there including Katharine Minor and her children Mary (Bob, John, Jim, Alan, and Matt) plus their additions (Sarah, Katie, and Maria, future bride of Jim); Keekee; Howard (Pauline, Howard Jr., Mike, Paul, and Evan); Margaret, Katharine's brother Dohrman Sinclair; and nephew Frank Sinclair and family (Peg, Gary, Bruce, Mary and David).

The following spring Katharine wrote to her friend.

> *I've had several visitors lately. Mary had a two day conference in Pittsburgh on Monday and Tuesday of this week, so she flew down on Saturday and we had a good visit together. She continues to enjoy her job as Director of the Voluntary Action Center in Duluth, Minnesota. Keekee was also here and she left for Washington this morning. Howard and Pauline and their two oldest boys, Howie and Mike, will be here over night on Friday. They then drive on to Washington for Saturday, and on Sunday they go to Williamsburg where Howard has a two day business meeting.*

On September 30, 1984 another great granddaughter arrived for Katharine. Barbara Anne Evans was born in Minneapolis and joined her sister Katie. Both girls with their parents, John and Sarah, went to Jim and Maria's wedding in July of 1986. Katharine's daughter, Margaret, drove her in her new Cadillac to Milwaukee, Wisconsin for the July 5 wedding, which was in the garden of Maria Lazowski's parents. The day before, Jim and

Maria had run a 4th of July race. Jim had proposed to Maria after finishing Duluth's Grandma's marathon by holding a sign saying *MARRY ME MARIA* which she saw when she finished the marathon.

Katharine had a great love of flowers and always enjoyed receiving them. Beautiful flowers arrived for Katharine on Secretary Day one year. The card read *Love from Avis and the Doctor*. Katharine was greatly puzzled and tried to think of an Avis she might know. She called the florist and said she did not know any doctor married to an Avis or even a doctor going with an Avis. They must have made a mistake. The puzzle was finally solved when her daughters, Keekee and Margaret, confessed. Keekee as the second child called herself Avis, the second in car rentals, and Margaret had shortly before received her Ph.D. They just wanted to thank their mother for all the mail she had forwarded to them.

Union Cemetery

On Sunday, April 26, 1987 the *Herald-Star* carried an article with the title,

Union Cemetery Among Few In Nation On Historic List.

It was approved by the U.S. Department of the Interior on March 18 and Scott Dimit and Katharine Minor of Steubenville were credited for their work. Katharine Minor, a member of the Jefferson County Historical Association and chairwoman of the Union Cemetery Association, said the idea for listing the cemetery on the National Register literally began afer church on Sunday in the parking lot. She said she and Scott Dimit, who was superintendent of the cemetery in the 1930's, discussed the idea. She said Dimit said the cemetery trustees had given up hope for the listing after hearing the National Register's criteria. She suggested trying again saying the impossible takes a little longer.

Mrs. Minor said others who helped with the nomination for listing were William 'Slim' Brandt and William Becker of the Jefferson County Historic Association; Malcolm Irwin, who was superintendent of the cemetery at the time; the late Milton McConnel, who was a local historian; Robert Greene of Weirton, who took photographs documenting the various styles of markers and building architecture in the cemetery; and John Maltese, who is a local historian.

'It really shows the progress of cemetery tombstones for a number of years. There are many different kinds there,' she said. She noted that there were a number of the old church

*burial plots in the city in the mid 1800's. 'To get all the churches to agree to a cemetery, a **union cemetery** of all those denominations was in itself an accomplishment,' she said. The process of getting the cemetery on the National Register took nearly seven years.*

At a meeting in November, 1853 representatives from the First Presbyterian Church, the First M.E. Church, St. Paul's Church, the U.P. Church, the M.P. Church, and the Hamline M.E. Church were selected for a committee to select ground for the cemetery. A Cemetery Association was formed in February, 1854, and after the dedication a Board of Trustees was elected. Katharine's father served as a Union Cemetery Trustee from 1896 to 1915.

Letting her friends know of her year she wrote,

> *In the spring of 1987 I visited my daughter, Margaret (Ph.D.!) in Rhode Island where she was teaching Tudor Stuart History at the University. This fall she is living in London, England, doing research and thoroughly enjoying it.*
>
> *For four months during the summer I was at my cottage in Chautauqua, New York enjoying family, friends and excellent programs. One week two hundred and forty Soviets were invited to live with us, mostly in our cottages, to promote fellowship and mutual understanding.*
>
> *My daughters, Keekee and Margaret, and son, Howard, his wife Pauline and their four darling well-mannered little boys were with me in Chautauqua. My daughter, Mary and her husband Bob (Ph.D.!) were in England and only one of their four boys came to the cottage. Two of Mary's sons, John and Jim, are married and she has reason to brag about her two granddaughters, Katie and Barbie. My brother, Dohrman, visited me in Chautauqua and his daughter, Wilma, flew in from California. Also from California were my grandnephew, Jim Grant, and his wife and their two daughters. We thoroughly enjoyed friends from other states and from other countries too: Alex and Margery Sharpe from Toronto, Canada; Edda Walchhofer and her family from Salzburg, Austria and David Starkey from London, England.*
>
> *This fall Keekee and I had a most interesting and inspir-*

ing trip to the Bahamas with the Norman Vincent Peale Group.

At home I stay busy with church, club and civic work. Among recent projects was helping to make Steubenville a Mural City with outdoor paintings of yesteryears of our steamboats on the river, our old railroad station, our bank, main streets and so forth. Come and see them! Also our beautiful cemetery is now registered as a historical site.

First Great Grandson and a Marathon

1988 brought Katharine her first great grandson, Joseph Robert Evans, who was born in Minneapolis on April 20. She made the trip to Duluth in June for the baptism. She had a special treat while there because Grandma's marathon was being run on June 11 and her grandsons Jim, Alan and Matt were all running. Her son-in-law also tried it for the first time. Bob, who was 50, came in 2071 with a time of 4 hours 14 minutes and 12 seconds. His sons' times were better. Jim, who was 27, placed 611 with a time of 3:21:02; Matt, who was 22, placed 612 with a time of 3:21:02; and Alan, who was 25, placed 90 with a time of 2:49:03. With over 7,000 runners these times were not bad and all have finished under three hours in other years, except Bob who only ran the marathon once. Jim had come up from Minneapolis, where he was teaching, and Alan came from Rochester, New York, where he was attending graduate school. The runners did well but so did the watchers. Katharine went with her daughter, Mary, driving to different parts of the course to watch the runners. At one spot they hiked over hilly land for about 15 minutes and then had to return again that way. They were at the finish to cheer the runners. Back at the house the runners collapsed. It was a hot day but Katharine was back downstairs with a new outfit ready to go to the marathon parties about half an hour after everyone returned to the house.

Shingles

Katharine had always experienced good health, but that summer in Chautauqua was not quite what she expected. She experienced great pain and was finally diagnosed with shingles. Alas, her shingles recurred often over the subsequent years causing her problems. Her eye sight was also a problem. "In my 80's my eyesight deteriorated to the point where I could not read," she said. Katharine dealt with her shingles, her bad back and her failing eyes by continuing to do all she could.

Seated: Katharine S. Minor. Standing: Mary, Margaret, Keekee.
July 23, 1988 on Katharine's 80th Birthday.

Organizations

The Steubenville *Herald-Star* carried an article on Thursday, October 13, 1988

> *RECIPIENTS Several members of the Laura E. McGowan Circle of the International Order of King's Daughters and Sons, were recipients of awards at the celebration Tuesday of the 95th birthday of the circle at the Williams Country Club. Receiving awards were Mrs. Malcolm McGowan, 50 and 60 year charms; Mrs. Stanley Slee, a 25-year member, and Mrs. Howard Minor, 50-year award.*

In 1989 Katharine attended the 98th Continental Congress of the National Society of D. A. R. in Washington, D.C. as a delegate of her chapter. She was able to renew old friendships.

Katharine was the chairwoman of the Miriam Circle for Westminster Presbyterian Church. During 1989 when Westminster Presbyterian Church merged with the First Presbyterian Church and became First Westminster Presbyterian Church in meant that she also became the first chairwoman of the Miriam Circle for the new church. Still active in the Woman's Club, she served as the Special Gifts Chairman for 1989. In her early eighties she also served as the president of the Query Club.

Connecting to the Younger Generation

Visits to her children were a constant joy to Katharine. She made many friends among the younger crowd, not only among her children's friends but also her grandsons' friends who got to know her in Chautauqua. Whether attending a book group, playing bridge, going to luncheons, parties and dinners, or just visiting, she brought happiness to her children when she stayed with her offspring.

Once when she and Keekee were in New York, they went to visit Mrs. Dow's School in Briarcliff, New York. Today it is the Hasting Institute. Katharine gave the secretaries and others interested a tour of where her room had been, how the walls had been moved, and where she had once dined as a student. "The tea tables were gone, the grand piano was gone, and the lace curtains and oriental rug were gone. A student wearing no shoes or shirt, and carrying a boom box walked past. Times have changed," Katharine commented.

As a permanent fixture of Steubenville and a friend of children of her good friends, Katharine often found herself making arrangements for funerals of her dear friends by working with their children. The next generation, who are her children's ages, knew her well and visited when they came to town. For many, she became their adopted mother. Pictures of numerous children accompanied cards at Christmas. She always had time to write.

❦

Katharine Sinclair Minor
November, 1983

The 1990-1998 Era

The nineties saw a decade getting ready for the next century. One of the big problems was how computers would deal with the date since most were programed only for the final two digits of the year. A peace agreement was signed in Northern Ireland. Tony Blair and the Labor party won in Britain. China regained control of Hong Kong. Kuwait was invaded by Iraq, the Persian Gulf War broke out and lasted 100 hours, and the Asian economy collapsed.

At the beginning of the decade the government was trying to reduce budget deficits with spending curbs and tax hikes and at the end was dealing with a surplus. A budget impasse brought a partial shut down of the government. House members lost their bank. Democrats Bill Clinton and Al Gore won in 1992 and in 1994 the Republicans won control of Congress. The *Brady Bill* was signed into law as a major gun-control measure. The Citadel, a military academy in Charleston, South Carolina, admitted women. Kenneth Starr began investigating the Whitewater affair and the Monica Lewinsky's affair with the president. Paula Jones accused Clinton of sexual harassment. The House of Representatives impeached President Clinton. O.J. Simpson's televised trial was watched by many.

In 1993 a powerful bomb exploded in the basement of the World Trade Building. Janet Reno became the first woman United States Attorney General. The Oklahoma City bombing killed 168 people and Timothy McVeigh was convicted. The Great Flood of 1993 covered eight million acres in nine Midwestern states. A heat wave had temperatures in Chicago reaching 106 degrees and 800 died. In 1997 fifty thousand residents of Grand Forks, North Dakota were forced to leave their homes when the Red River flooded and then the town burned. Thirty-four Florida counties were claimed disaster areas because of fires. El Nino was the cause of some strange weather patterns. TWA Flight 800 bound for Paris from New York exploded killing 230. The space shuttle *Atlantis* safely made its first series of dockings with the Russian space station *Mir* and John Glenn returned to space.

Septets were born and survived. By the last decade two hundred million cars were on U.S. roads. The Dow Jones climbed from 3,004.46 in 1991 and reached a high of 9,354.71 on July 17, 1998. The tobacco industry lost lawsuits and company documents were made public.

The baseball strike lasted 234 days. Atlanta hosted the 1996 Olympics. The Chicago Bulls won their sixth National Basketball Association title with Michael Jordan. The *Titanic* won best picture in 1997.

X.

Dealing With Aging
In The Nineties

Golden Years

*T*he golden years are not necessarily pure gold!" Katharine said. "Old age is not for sissies." By the last decade of the twentieth century there had been many changes during Katharine's lifetime. She stated, "We've seen communications go (or come) from telephones when a soft live voice answers saying, 'Number please' (which worked) to phones with 38 buttons where one presses 9 for a local call, etc. The two and three digits phone numbers expanded to eleven digits when calling outside the district. A person dialed or pushed one, then the area code and local number. The area code has just been changed to 740 for Steubenville because there were not enough numbers left for the old area code. Years ago the exchange went from Atlantic to 282. Such places as Washington, DC have run out of numbers for local calls so the area codes have to be used even when calling locally. Calling overseas is now possible by adding country numbers, so the simple two digits that the operator once heard now can add up to many many more being pushed on the phone." Now one of Katharine's phones has 34 buttons which may be pressed and Katharine has talked about *carry around* phones requiring a day's instruction to know how to make or answer a call. "It is not just calling from home or office, calls can be made from one's car, at the beach or even 30,000 feet up in the air. When reaching a business there is often an assortment of options i.e., press one for billing office, press two for advertising department, press three for....if you need help press six and stay on the line!" stated Katharine.

"Overseas transportation used to take fourteen days on a ship without stabilizers and now it is done in a few hours by plane. At the end of the 20th century planes have pilots, copilots, stewardesses and serve meals. There are movies, phones, a variety of music accessed by earphones and first class seats with lots of room. Passengers leave from well lighted airport buildings filled with restaurants, shops, bars, and even hotels. Returning from trips, their baggage awaits them at baggage carousels near acres of parking. It is still said that it is not practical to fly to London for lunch," said Katharine.

Katharine continued to compare the early and late years of her life. "In the first part of the century divorces and people suing were rare because they were frowned upon by society. Today both are prevalent because people do not assume responsibility for their actions, and commitments are not considered a priority. The Commandment, *Thou shalt not commit adultery* now has become, *Thou shalt not admit adultery*. Life was calm, happy and peaceful in the early decades compared to the last decade of this century when life is lived at a frenzy pace, with no time to think or stop to enjoy the surroundings. Words and interpretations have changed greatly over the years. When someone said, *Thank you* we used to say, *You're welcome*, and now they say, *No trouble*. It used to be that one said, *could have or would have*, now its *could of and would of.*"

With respect to health, she recalls, "In the early part of the century there was little reference to health, and daily pills were never left on the eating table as they often are today. Also, in each era there is a health cure-all that will take care of all your health problems. After the war Katharine remembers seeing a huge advertising banner that stretched almost the entire length of the end of the Grand Central Station in New York City. On it was *Haddocal*. She always wondered if its name came from "Had to call" it something. Then there was *Metracal* which would help people diet as well as getting then into good shape. Now the cure-all is *Ensure*.

"Today," Katharine said, "we have come a long way since we had to scrape ice and snow from the cars left out over night. In this last decade, when we get up in the morning we can go to a window and with a remote control we can press a button and have the engine heater go on in the car. When we get dressed and breakfasted we go to a nice warm car. As a precautionary measure, if anyone moves the car, before we get there, the brakes come on and the engine turns off."

Updates also occurred in Katharine's life. The *Emma Willard Bulletin* for Fall/Winter 1990 under 1927 contained the following:

> Katharine Sinclair Minor tells us she is still going (fairly) strong. Her four children are spread throughout the Northeast United States and England, and she has eight grandsons, and three great grandchildren. She summers in

Chautauqua, New York, and travels, as well as staying active with her church as circle leader, elder and past president of Department Three, the Jefferson County Historical Association Museum, the Steubenville and the Chautauqua Women's Clubs, Kings Daughters and Sons, and past president of the Query Club etc.

The rewards of living in the same town for decades are illustrated in the following story. Katharine recalled, "I was in the funeral home and saw a friend I had not seen for decades who embraced me warmly and told me of the flowers I had given a mutual friend years ago. I could not remember my friend's name nor the flowers. This reminded me that I usually forget kindnesses done for others and I usually remember kindnesses that others have graciously done to and for me."

Gertrude Patterson and Katharine Minor on the porch
of the Athenaeum in Chautauqua, New York.

Chautauqua continued to be her summer home where she would see her friend Gertrude. In October, 1990, Katharine wrote,

> *Hope you're getting settled and liking the St. Elmo.*
> *We've had beautiful fall days and I can just see you racing*
> *around Chautauqua taking your 'constitutionals' each day.*
> *I had hoped that I could come up this fall and see you but*
> *I'm still housebound - receiving no phone calls nor visitors*
> *- but I am getting better. Haven't been dressed, except to go*
> *to or from the hospital (two weeks in the hospital here, after*
> *I came home)."*

Barbie Evans and Katharine   *Barbie Evans and Katharine*

By spring Katharine wrote,

> *We're all fine - Margaret is packing up to move her "stuff" to Thibodaux, Louisiana now so she can stay longer in Chautauqua. She will be teaching at Nicholls State University and is all excited about it. Howard is recovering nicely from having both hips replaced - first time he has been pain free for 30 years! He and the boys will be at the cottage all summer. He'll work out of there and Pauline will be there most weekends. Keekee and friends will be there the first 2 weeks of July and Mary most of August. Dohrman is in a beautiful, caring retirement home in Sebring, Ohio but is in the medical (hospital) section and hates it. I drive the 130 miles once a week to see him. Hope all is well with you."*

Before the Christmas of 1992 Katharine sent out a letter to friends.

> *It was a fun summer for us at the cottage in Chautauqua. Nineteen of the family were there, some for a few days and some for the season.*
> *Mary and Bob have been very busy, as usual, as have*

their four sons: one added a Master's degree (Matt), one a Doctorate (Alan) and one a darling baby daughter (Jim). Keekee is adding another chapter to her unique life as the director of the Peace Corps in the Marshall Islands. Howard and his boys stayed in Chautauqua for the season while Howard worked and the boys enjoyed Boys Club. Pauline came as often as she could. Margaret teaches history at Nicholls University in Thibodaux, La. and I had a wonderful visit while enjoying the warm and gracious hospitality of her friends, during Mardi Gras."

Katharine discovered that no matter which child she visited, she found herself at home with their friends. She went to athletic events, attended parties, visited their friends' homes, and even went swamp exploring with Liz King in Louisiana. She and Liz, who was the first female off-shore oil rig operator in the world, became fast friends and exchanged many calls when they were not both in Louisiana having their Friday adventures.

Chautauqua Gathering 1989
Top row: Howard Minor, Jr., Howard Minor, Bob Evans. 3rd row: Margaret Minor, Mary M. Evans, Keekee Minor. 2nd row: Paul Minor, Katharine Minor, Mike Minor. 1st row: Evan Minor, Katie Evans, Barbie Evans.

Woman's Club

On October 7, 1993, the Woman's Club of Steubenville presented to Katharine a Certificate of Life Membership in recognition and appreciation of fifty-five years of loyal and continued service to the Woman's Club of Steubenville. In a *Herald-Star* article on December 8, 1994, the following appeared.

The Woman's Club honors Katharine Minor, Katharine Minor recognized for many years of service. Katharine Sinclair Minor was honored as a life member of the Woman's Club of Steubenville, OFWC, GFWC, at the December 5 Monday afternoon meeting at the club home. Minor is the granddaughter of Mrs. W.B. Donaldson, who founded the club in 1899.

Minor has fulfilled the legacy created by her grandmother, who envisioned the civic impact of the club in the community, and of a family tradition of community service. The honored club woman has taken a lead role in many community endeavors and especially has been interested in cultural and beautification projects. Minor has been a member of the Woman's Club of Steubenville since 1948, served as its president from 1960 to 1962 and has been active in the American Home and Garden departments of the club. Another of her accomplishments includes co-founding and serving as the first president of the Junior Woman's Club.

She is the widow of Dr. Howard Minor, a Steubenville physician for many years, and is the mother of four children.

Murals

In the 1990's Steubenville began to be adorned with murals of the past on many of its buildings. Katharine was on the committee when it was organized to raise money and find the artists to paint the historical depictions. She contributed financially to the committee's success. Today many tourist come to see old steam boats, banks, grocery stores, educational and medical facilities, Dean Martin singing, and many scenes from the early days of this Ohio River town.

Family and Christmas

1994 seemed a good time for a Sinclair family reunion with the Minor and Evans families also attending. Much organizing was done for the gathering at Oglebay Park in Wheeling, West Virginia. There were cocktails

The Sinclair Reunion in August 1994
(From left to right) Front row: Oliver and mother Dawn Sinclair with dog, Katherine Evans, Katharine (Sinclair) Minor, Barbara Evans, Joseph Evans. Back row: Frank B. Sinclair, John H. Evans, Betsy Beecher, Sarah Evans, Jobee Sinclair, Dohrman Sinclair III, Bob Evans, Mary (Minor) Evans, Dohrman Grant, Julie Reicenborn, Matt Evans, Carolyn and Peter LeVan.

1994
Renee Jacobson, Alan Evans, Sarah and John Evans, Mary M. Evans, Matt Evans, Katharine Minor, Katie Evans, Howie Minor, Keekee Minor, Barbie Evans, Paul Minor, Evan Minor, Mike Minor, Joey Evans, Howard and Pauline Minor, Bob Evans.

and pizza, golf and tennis, walking and visiting, and a formal concluding meal where Matt Evans announced his engagement to Julie Reichenborn.

In her Christmas letter to friends that year Katharine wrote,

> *Christmas comes earlier each year and we know we're getting older when we get winded playing chess and dialing long-distance wears us out.*
> *It has been a good year for me. I took my annual trip to*

Thibodaux, Louisiana in the spring to visit daughter Margaret, where she teaches at Nicholls University.

Also this spring, I visited Keekee in Rockville, Md. (Washington, DC). I'm so glad she's back from her trek in the Marshall Islands.

Mary was here in the spring for a week and this fall I flew to Minneapolis and Duluth to visit her and Bob and to see my five great-grandchildren and their parents. Mary and Bob will be in Florida for Christmas and they will be in Birmingham, England for the 1995 spring where Bob will teach for a quarter.

This summer, I was back in good old Chautauqua. Howard and his four boys were there, and I visited Howard and Pauline and the boys in Erie, Pa. for Thanksgiving week. Howard Jr. is a sophomore at Pitt University.

We also celebrated a Sinclair reunion at Oglebay Park in Wheeling in August. The family members flew in from Oregon, Louisiana, California, and Connecticut and drove in from Minnesota, New York, Pennsylvania, and the District of Columbia. A good time was had by all. After reading the above, I think we must have a little Gypsy blood in our veins.

May you be enveloped in the true meaning of Christmas and enjoy a happy, healthy and peaceful New Year.

Affectionately, Katharine

Keekee, Margaret, Katharine, Mary

The Minor Family 1990
Howie, Howard
Mike, Paul
Pauline, Evan

The Evans Family June 23, 1996
Floor: Barbara and Joey; Bench: John, Bob, Mary, Jim holding Sam, Maria holding Lucy; Standing: Katie, Sarah, Renee holding Silka, Alan, Matt and Julie.

The 90's brought more great grandchildren and the marriages of grand-sons. In 1990 Alan Evans married Renee Jacobson in LaMoure, North Dakota. Katharine flew into Duluth and drove with her daughter Mary and husband Bob to North Dakota. The groom's dinner was held in an old-time bar/restaurant, and before dinner people took rides in a covered wagon. The wedding was held in a Lutheran church which stood alone in the fields. Alan and Renee arrived in a stretch limousine and later at the reception people were able to take rides in it.

Lucy and Sam were born to Jim and Maria Evans. Lucille Daniella Evans arrived in Minneapolis, Minnesota in 1992, and her brother, Samuel Robert Evans, was born in 1994, in Minneapolis. In 1995 Matthew Minor Evans married Julie Reichenborn in Coon Rapids, Minnesota. Katharine and her daughter Margaret flew into Minneapolis for the occasion. Matt and Julie's wedding and reception were lovely. It was the only reception Katharine had attended where the RSVP cards were drawn from a box and awarded prizes. The next day all the family and close friends joined the bridal couple for a picnic. Silka and Kyra were born to Renee Jacobson and Alan Evans. Silka Josephine Jacobson Evans was born in 1996 in Beaver Dams, New York, and Kyra Alyssia was born there in 1998.

Chautauqua Activities

Chautauqua provided a wonderful summer place for Katharine. She served on the board of the Presbyterian House in Chautauqua for forty

1996

Katharine Minor holding great granddaughter Silka Jacobson Evans with great grandchildren Katie, Joey and Barbie Evans around her. Back: Daughter Mary, grandsons Paul Minor, Howie Minor, Mike Minor, Alan Evans and Renee Jacobson.

years. She took classes, enjoyed the evening programs and symphony concerts in the amphitheater, went to lectures, saw plays, attended operas, and appeared at some of the Boys and Girls Club activities when children and grandchildren were participating. The Chautauqua season in 1995 began in a very unusual way for Katharine Minor. At the first Sunday church service in the amphitheater she passed out in church and was taken to the Westfield Hospital. As she noted later, it was before the collection. A reading of her heart beat taken at the hospital showed that it was beating over 300 beats a minute. When she returned a year later she saw the same doctor and commended that he probably did not remember her. He replied, "Oh yes I do, I have your electrocardiogram on my dresser!"

Dohrman J. Sinclair Jr.

Katharine's brother, who had been at a nursing home in Sebring, Ohio, died on Wednesday August 21, 1996, at the age of 92 in Crandall Medical Center. The following appeared in the Steubenville *Herald-Star* obituaries:

> *He was born July 27, 1904, in Steubenville, son of Dohrman and Mary Donaldson Sinclair. He was preceded in death by his parents, two sisters, Marie Grant and Wilma Le Van Baker; and a brother, Frank.*
> *After his graduation from Dartmouth College, he worked*

at the Union Savings Bank and Trust Co., now UniBank, until the outbreak of World War II. He served as a lieutenant during the war and after the war accepted a position with the Civil Service Commission in Washington, DC. and later with the Air Service Command in Dayton as statistician officer, receiving training at Harvard Business School. He then moved to San Diego, California, as the regional officer of the Veteran's Administration. He later joined the Wells Organization, raising funds for churches and hospitals in the United States and Canada until his retirement.

He became interested in writing and painting, painting mainly seascapes and published several books on family history, the first called Sinclair Album, and the second called The Ancestors and Descendants of Dohrman J and Mary Donaldson Sinclair. He also published books written by his mother which he was able to get ready for print. These included Pioneer Days and Pioneer Times. His retirement years included traveling to Australia and yearly trips to Europe. Dohrman took a course from the American Genealogy Society and did a great deal on family history.

He was a member of First Westminster Church, Steubenville Art Association and was a past president of the Jefferson County Historical Association.

He attended Steubenville Public Schools and graduated from Lawrenceville Preparatory School in 1924 and Dartmouth College in the class of 1928.

Surviving are his daughter, Wilma Sinclair of Navado, California, a sister, Mrs. Howard (Katharine) Minor of Steubenville; and several nieces and nephews."

Steubenville's Sesquicentennial

In 1997 Steubenville, Ohio celebrated its 200th year birthday. Katharine with her wealth of historical knowledge was interviewed by the newspaper and was able to assemble a number of pictures and information including the newspaper published in 1897 which she provided so it could be included with the bicentennial booklet. She had pictures which she had stored for many years and which showed a Steubenville one hundred years younger.

Katharine was a person who graciously accepted a call from a reporter from Columbus to come and interview her or a knock at the door from someone who had been told Mrs. Minor could help her learn about the history of Steubenville. Her knowledge ranged from such subjects as the first professional 19th century black baseball player buried in the Union Cemetery, to her friend, Isabelle Lippert, who played for Dean Martin when he was beginning his singing career in the late 30's in Steubenville. She was never at a loss for stories about her father. She made him very real to her children by telling stories about his pranks. Once he pretended to be the gas man and called his mother-in-law to have her check to see if the gas light was burning outside her home. Another time he had the employees at the bank ignore the snake which he released from a cigar box when a habitual drunkard came into the bank. As the snake wound itself around the teller's bars the drunkard became hysterical and swore off drinking. Dohrman was good friends with the ticket master at the train station. Mr. Richards knew everything about train travel. One day Dohrman asked him for a ticket to Hezekiah. Usually the ticket master had a ready answer, but this time he said he would have to look it up. He never did find the town, for it was a name from the Bible.

There was much going on to celebrate the 200th birthday of Steubenville, including a parade downtown. Katharine was asked to be an

Steubenville, Ohio Bicentennial parade with
Katharine Minor as an Honored Citizen
August 1997

honored citizen and was driven in a convertible by David Di Bartolomeo. He told the following story to the author. David's wife was scheduled to drive in the parade and was unable to do so when the time came. David was a substitute and really was not looking forward to being part of the parade. However, he confessed later that it had been one of the best days of his life. David and Katharine spent the time talking about the history of Steubenville and sharing information. Katharine was also stopped during the parade to be interviewed by Eric Minor from the television station.

Query Club

In October 1997 Katharine was hostess of the anniversary luncheon for the 100th celebration of the Query Club held at the Jefferson County Historical Association Museum. A November 13, 1997 *Herald-Star* article written by Marian Houser stated,

> *Mary Minor Evans gave a resume of the 100 years that have passed since its formation. She gave a toast to past and present members and to the future of the club.*
>
> *"The men are tired of the Bric-a-Brac parties" was the quote that turned the wheels to form the club 100 years ago.*
>
> *Carrie Pettit Dohrman made this comment to Ellen H. Brown one autumn afternoon in 1897. Before the day was over, the Query Club came into existence, officers were elected and rules and bylaws were discussed.*
>
> *Rules were few but adamant. Meetings HAD to be held each Tuesday afternoon. To become a member, the applicant must be a sister, or near relative of a charter member, and an officer could not hold the position longer than a year.*
>
> *No refreshments were to be served, unless it was some-thing the hostess made herself, more often it was just a plate of candy.*
>
> *The first meeting was held at the residence of Mrs. H. G. Dohrman, president, on November 9, 1897. Nine members were present and each answered roll call with a current topic. Beatrice Kelly gave an interesting review of "The Master," by Zangwill and a game of "Noted American Char-acters" was played.*
>
> *During the first year, members visited the Klondike, Rus-sia, Egypt, Scotland, Japan, Ireland, India, and France through reviews. Music was introduced to the program at the request of May Sweeny and quite a number of the members*

proved to be efficient as soloists and duos on the piano.

There were book reviews of "Hugh Wynne," by S. Weir Mitchell "The Kentuckians," by John Fox Jr. and "Captain Courageous," by R.L. Stevenson.

The silver anniversary was held November 8, 1922, at the Fort Steuben Hotel dining room. Here is a brief summary of what occurred that day. Mrs. J. Easton McGowan, president and chairman, gave the welcome and welcomed the first president, Carrie Pettit Dohrman, who gave a history of the club from the beginning.

Dohrman said, "The Query Club is, in a sense, a legacy. Twenty-six years ago this Thanksgiving, a few friends got together and launched a kind of cooking club upon the social sea of Steubenville. The name of the club came about from the fact that there was a query box for members to draw out a question to be answered at the next meeting."

The ten original members were Abbie I. Sharp, Elinor H. Brown, Elizabeth McCandless Crawford, Amanda Crawford, Carrie Pettit Dohrman (married to Katharine's father's half brother Rash Dohrman), Clara Hammond Steinrock, Beatrice M. Kelly Sharpe, Maud Crawford Mooney, Isabelle Sarratt and Mary Hayes Spencer.

The club progressed over the years, delving into science, literature, art and circling the globe in imaginary travels. "We are very self contained, we never gossip, as everyone is everyone's relation. We have been social and had indoor and outdoor parties, Christmas parties and covered dish luncheons," Dohrman said.

For a short time, the Query Club was a member of the state federation, but not taking an active part in many of the activities, dropped out and is a club set apart under the jurisdiction of their own laws.

As time passed, the club celebrated a 50th-year birthday September 10, 1947, at the Williams Country Club. Five charter members were honored, Mrs. E.O. Smith, Mrs. C.P. McFadden, Mrs. George E. Sharpe, Ellen H. Brown and Isabelle Sarratt. A toast was proposed by Mrs. John Irvine to the older members and Mrs. C.P. McFadden proposed a toast to new members.

History was lost for a time as Mrs. George E. Sharpe's minutes were consumed in the Sycamore Hill fire.

The organization started during President William McKinley's term and has continued through the years. Thanks to those who kept minutes so meticulously, a more complete history is available. Over the years, members took imaginary trips through exotic countries via travel reports, lived out the stories written by famous authors, learned about science and had to be prepared to answer the questions drawn from the query box at the next meeting.

Winter Ills

The winter months of November and December 1997 found Katharine in and out of the hospital with pneumonia, cracked ribs, bloody noses, irregular heart beats, and medication adjustments. "Medication pills remind me of winding a grandfather's clock, the pendulum swings back and forth," said Katharine.

At Christmas time her daughters helped her send out over one hundred Christmas cards. She also managed to be hostess to her four children, five grandsons and her newest great granddaughter. Christmas 1997 was spent in Steubenville. Margaret came from Thibodaux, Louisiana; Keekee from Washington, D.C.; Howard and all his sons from Erie, Pennsylvania; Mary and Bob from Duluth, Minnesota and their son Alan with his wife and daughter from Corning, New York. The most excitement was getting an old ice box out of the basement with the help of five strong men.

May 1994
Margaret, Keekee, Katharine Minor, Mary M. Evans, Howard

In January 1998 the author drove her mother along N. Fourth Street from Franklin to Market Street and Katharine rattled off the names of those who had lived in each house on both sides of the street until Washington Street, and then she went on to name the stores that had existed so many years before and in some cases still existed.

During this time, all four childhood friends made contact. Virginia Pearce Glick sent a letter, Mary Peterson Chalfant talked on the phone to Katharine, and Eleanor Giles' news came from Martha Manor, just a few doors from the house where she had lived for so many years.

In March Katharine gave her children a scare by landing in the hospital and not being able to recognize people before going into a coma. With her unusual ability to rebound, she was soon making arrangements to leave the hospital. One evening her daughters arrived to visit after dinner and the nurse said, "Come and see our new head nurse." They went to the nurses' station to discover their mother in a wheel chair telling a couple of nurses about the first public hospital in Steubenville and how the Lacy Hotel had been used rent-free from Katharine's father before the Ohio Valley Hospital had been built. For three years and at a cost of over $5,000 to Sinclair, this temporary hospital served the needs of the community.

Katharine not only rallied but decided to fulfill her wish to visit and see Margaret's new home in Thibodaux. Her trip down and first week went well. Neighbors would stop by and visit when she sat out on the porch, and she gained more friends while Margaret taught. The second week found her again in the hospital. Lo and behold, her new doctor not only knew her Steubenville doctor, but they had gone to school together in Cleveland. In their calls back and forth, arrangements were made for the Steubenville doctor to see the Thibodaux doctor when he came to New Orleans for a meeting. The two doctors were also busy figuring out the best procedures for Mrs. Minor. It was then discovered that the night nurse had lived in Steubenville for nine years. Katharine always seemed to have interesting coincidental things happen wherever she was.

As Katharine kept track of the hospital entrances she kept her humor and was always treated well by the nurses. In July, when she was again in the hospital, her doctor said, "You must have turned a few heads when you were a teenager. You have very good features." Her children took turns visiting and found a wonderful person, Barbara Skidmore, to stay with their mother when she was home and they were not there. Katharine's next door neighbor, Cheryl Levite, found time to visit, bring her new grandson over and occasionally come for sherry. She was always there in an emergency with her nursing skills. The Ohio Valley Hospital nurses, especially Pudgie (Roberta Ennis), kept up Katharine's spirits when test after test was done to find the cause of her pain.

No matter where Katharine was, she kept track of the whereabouts of her family and friends. Communication had always been important to her. Katharine had watched the two-a-day letter delivery be reduced to one-a-day and had seen the slow boat letters now be delivered by air. Her comment on all this express way of communicating was, "I wish I had stock in e-mail." She did not have e-mail until one of her children decided it was a great added way to communicate with her and there was always someone around who could download the messages from her four children or eight grandsons. At nearly ninety she did not want to be left out of the loop.

Ninety

This book was written as a ninetieth birthday present and contains ninety years of Katharine Sinclair Minor's experiences. She made plans to spend the summer in Chautauqua but the hospital admissions got in the way. On July 17 she checked out of the hospital, ordered flowers for all the nurses and other staff on the fifth floor of the Ohio Valley Hospital, and went home. That evening she had great pain and was again admitted to the hospital. On Wednesday she slipped into a coma. Thursday was her birthday and the calls went out to the family coming for her birthday to come a day early. All her children arrived, plus her son-in-law and three of her grandsons. Two off-duty nurses who were her great friends and her minister also were at the hospital in her room. All of them stayed with her through that long night. At 10 p.m. she was told that her birthday was two hours away. Then as the time passed she was told it was one hour away,

Katharine's 90th Birthday cake

then half an hour and finally at midnight a dozen people sang *Happy Birthday* to her on her ninetieth birthday. As the sun rose in the morning her spirit rose. She had completed her four score and ten years to the day dying on Thursday morning July 23, 1998 just as she had been born on a Thursday morning ninety years earlier.

That evening fifteen family including two more grandsons and Katharine's first great granddaughter, plus her friends and care givers, gathered for her birthday dinner and to share her 90th birthday cake. Grandsons, Mike one night and Jim the next, took over fixing dinners with the help of brothers and cousins.

Katharine's obituary appeared in the Steubenville, Ohio *Herald-Star*, the Wheeling, West Virginia *Intelligencer*, and the Chautauqua, New York *Daily*. The family talked about her Scottish heritage and how she probably decided that it was better to die when everyone was already home so they did not have to make an extra trip.

Katharine Sinclair Minor dies at age 90

STEUBENVILLE - Katharine E. Sinclair Minor, 90, of 633 Belleview Boulevard, died Thursday, July 23, 1998, at the former Ohio Valley Hospital which her father help found.

Katharine Sinclair Minor

She was born, July 23, 1908, in Steubenville, the daughter of the late Dohrman J. and Mary Donaldson Sinclair. In addition to her parents, she was preceded in death by her husband, Howard Holland Minor, two sisters, Marie Grant and Wilma LeVan Baker, and two brothers, Frank Sinclair and Dohrman J. Sinclair II.

She attended the former Stanton Grade School; Mrs. Dow's School at Briarcliff Manor, New York; the Misses Eastman School in Washington, D.C. and graduated from Emma Willard Prep School of Troy, New York in 1927. She attended the University of Wisconsin and Columbia University in New York.

She was chosen Ohio Mother of the Year in 1972 by the American Mothers Committee, Inc.

Mrs. Minor has been an integral part of community life during all her years in Steubenville, being active in church and civic affairs. She was appointed by the mayor to be a board representative on the Citizen's Committee. She was a trustee of the Young Women's Christian Association; past president and life member of Steubenville Woman's Club; life member and board member of the Chautauqua, New York Women's Club; the Civic Music Association chairman; Salvation Army; Jefferson County Soil Conservation; and the College of Wooster Woman's advisory board. In 1997, she was an honored citizen in the Steubenville bicentennial parade.

Mrs. Minor was organizer and president of "Project Seven" which raised money and planted more than 1,000 forsythia bushes along the highway and had thousands of yellow crocuses planted in block letters 5-feet high spelling out "SPRING IS HERE." She was the organizer of the group that re-established the first Federal Land Office building. She was an organizer and founding member of the group that succeeded in establishing the Jefferson County Historical Association. She also was an organizer and first president of the Steubenville Junior Woman's Club, past president of Steubenville Query Club, a local organization founded in 1897. She was a member of the Steubenville Woman's Club American Home and Garden departments and the Bird and Tree Garden Club of Chautauqua, New York. She served on the Board of Meadowcroft Village in Avella, Pennsylvania.

She was past president of the Jefferson County Health Council, past member of the Ohio Valley Hospital Blossom Twig, past board member of Brother's Brother Foundation and a volunteer who vaccinated natives in Costa Rica. Mrs. Minor was a past president of McKinley Parent Teacher Association, an honorary member of Delta Kappa Gamma, past Jefferson County representative on the Board of the Ohioanna Library, a life member of the Chautauqua Literary and Scientific Circle, a member of the Jefferson County Genealogy Society, a member of the Steubenville Art Association and a member of the National Association of Parliamentarians.

She was a member and past registrar of the Daughters

of the American Revolution, a Page at the DAR National Convention, and later a delegate to the DAR National Convention in Washington, D.C. For many years she has been a member of the Laura E. McGowan Circle of the National Order of Kings Daughters and Sons.

Mrs. Minor was a member of the League of Women Voters and was the Ohio representative to the First National Convention of Young Republicans in Washington, D.C. and the first president of the Young Republican Club of Steubenville.

A member of the First Westminster Presbyterian Church of Steubenville, she was past board member and Clerk of Session and elder. She also was past president of the church's women's association, fellowship chairman, member of the choir and a Sunday school teacher. She was the Steubenville Presbyterian Representative to the advisory board of The College of Wooster, and a Board member of the Chautauqua, New York Presbyterian headquarters for 40 years.

She has traveled extensively across the United States, Europe and around the world, and has twice been the Woman's Golf Champion of the Steubenville Country Club. Many of her needlepoint articles adorn homes. Before she was married she sold life insurance during the depression.

Surviving are three daughters, Mrs. Robert H. (Mary Minor) Evans of Duluth, Minnesota, Katharine (Keekee) Minor of Rockville, Maryland, and Margaret S. Minor of Thibodaux, Louisiana; and one son, Howard S. Minor of Erie, Pennsylvania; eight grandsons, and six great-grandchildren.

Calling hours are from 2-4 and 7-9 p.m. Saturday and Sunday from noon until 1:15 p.m. at McClave-Chandler-Mills Funeral Homes, Inc., 611 North Fourth Street. Funeral services will be held at 1:30 p.m. Sunday at First Westminster Presbyterian Church, with the Rev. Leroy Dillener. Burial will follow at Union Cemetery.

On Friday, July 24, 1998 the Steubenville *Herald-Star* carried the following article:

Minor will be missed by friends, family
by Beaanne Banovsky, staff writer

On Thursday morning, Katharine Sinclair Minor, daughter of the late Dohrman Sinclair, celebrated her 90th birthday with her family. Family members said she watched the sun rise, and at 6:13 a.m. she died.

Jean Barren, Minor's friend for more than 50 years, said Minor was one of the first people she met when she moved to Steubenville. She and Minor were members of the same church, the First Westminster Presbyterian Church, and they belonged to a number of community organizations together.

Barren said her friend was a good motivator and had a kind spirit that affected everyone she met. "The thing about Katharine is she was a wonderful idea person and could get people motivated," she said.

As a member of one of the founding families of Steubenville, she devoted her life to preserving Steubenville and its history and her home was filled with books. Her father, Sinclair, built most of downtown and was responsible for starting a local bank. The Sinclair building named for him downtown is now home to Citizens Bank.

Minor's son Howard said he remembers his mother was much like her father. She had an ability to see the positive in every aspect of her life and strived to make it better. "She looked for and found the good that was there," he said. "And she was willing to look harder than most people were willing to look so she would always find some redeeming quality that was there."

Barren said there was a reason Minor felt so strongly about preserving the history of Steubenville. "I believe she felt history was something everyone should be aware of and that's why she was a part of the Jefferson County Historical Association."

Steubenville Fourth Ward Councilman David Fortunato said it was a pleasure working with Minor at the Historical Association. "Katharine Minor was a grand lady and a walking encyclopedia of the history of Steubenville," he said.

Minor's daughter Mary said one of her mother's many achievements during her life was getting the Union Cemetery in Steubenville recognized as a National Historical Land-mark. Margaret added, "There were people before who were unable to do it, but she said let's try it again, and they suc-ceeded."

Mary said one of the important things about Minor's life was the long lasting friendships she made, some lasting more than 80 years.

Keekee Minor said her mother continued to perform community services in the later years of her life and always cared about those who lived in her city. "She always amazed me," she said, "Even in her 80's, she wrote cards to shut-ins and visited the nursing homes taking magazines and other reading materials."

Many returned to Steubenville for the visitation and funeral. During the visitation the Daughters of the American Revolution members came to perform a memorial service, and later that day the Laura E. McGowan Circle of the International Order of King's Daughters and Sons conducted a memorial service. Nurses stopped at the house and more Minor and Evans family arrived.

Her funeral was held in the First Westminster Presbyterian Church with her grandsons serving as pallbearers. Rev. Leroy Dillener, Jr. gave remembrances of Katharine Sinclair Minor's life. He spoke of celebrating her life that God in His mercy had shared with us and linked it with the letters of her name.

K- KIND. Katharine was a kind, caring person, who thought of others and reached out to help and support.

A - AFFECTIONATE. She was most loving with family members and friends. She dearly loved her children, grand-children, and great-grandchildren. I remember very clearly when the great-grandchild was born and was a girl, and her name was Katherine. Yes, she was a loving "Mom" to many, and well deserved the "Mother of the Year" award.

T - TEACHER. She taught well, not only by word but by example. She was a good Sunday School teacher, and her students remember her fondly. Her four children have a wonderful story about being taught some table manners.

H - HOSPITAL AND HISTORY. These are two of her most cherished institutions. The Ohio Valley Hospital was one of her concerns. Her father helped to establish it, and her hus-

band, Dr. Howard Minor, helped to promote it and to use it. The Jefferson County Historical Association was a project Katharine helped to establish and to support.

A - *ARTISTIC.* She loved beautiful things, and flowers were a passion with her. She was a member of the Garden Club and did a lot to make Steubenville a place of beauty, with flowering trees and shrubs that were planted along Route 7. And one year she saw that the flowers proclaimed in words, "Spring Is Here." She did a lot of needlepoint, and these grace many homes here. She also did other craft work.

R - *RELIGIOUS.* Anyone who knew Katharine has to be aware of her deep and abiding faith. She loved her Lord, and was a loyal member and supporter of Westminster Presbyterian Church, where she served as elder and clerk of session. She informed others that she was a Presbyterian and proud of it. The Chautauqua Institute was very much a part of her religious experience and she looked forward to the worship services and the excellent sermons and music.

I - *INTUITIVE.* She seemed to sense a need and reached out to meet it, to help. She showed her love and concern. Katharine had a large correspondence list, and these were people whom she knew and for whom she cared deeply, and she seemed to know the right thing to write, to say, and to do.

N - *NEIGHBOR.* She was a good neighbor in every sense of the word. For her the whole community, indeed Steubenville itself, was her neighborhood. She inherited this concern from her father, Dohrman Sinclair, who did so much to promote Steubenville and environs, including the Market Street Bridge, and encouraging the Follansbee Brothers in the steel industry.

E - *EMPATHETIC.* Katharine cared for people deeply, and felt with them their joy and their sorrow, their hopes and their trials. Yes, she felt for others.

Katharine's grandsons Mike and Paul Minor played *Greensleeves* on their guitars and Katharine's neighbor Cheryl Levite sang *Amazing Grace.* Barbara Sweeney, a long time friend, was at the organ.

There were more than thirty cars which drove to the Union Cemetery for the final words. She was buried there with her husband, her parents, and her siblings. Afterwards her home was filled with her friends. Many shared their thoughts on paper about this special lady.

Peg Dillener wrote,

> "*Katharine told me the story of the man who was plant-ing the crocus bulbs to spell out Spring Is Here. She spoke in a gruff voice when the man asked for more bulbs (imitat-ing him). She had figured out how many thousand of bulbs would be needed. However, he ran out and said, 'Mrs. Minor, I need another 100 bulbs.' She said, 'How come?' but he said (again) 'I need another 100 bulbs.' Two days later the same scene repeated itself (word for word). By the time she finished the story I was laughing hard - I wish I could have seen the floral SPRING IS HERE.*"

> "*Katharine Minor was my second mother. To me she was known as* Mom *Minor. She invited all of us to love her and the love we had for her was returned.*" David Rietz

> "*I will remember Mom Minor as the friendliest person I ever met at Chautauqua - she made me feel welcome imme-diately - what a lovely lady she was. I will always remember her. Chautauqua has lost a wonderful neighbor. She will be missed sorely. I will always smile thinking of her 'attitude adjustment hour invitation.'*" Cindy Rietz

> "*My name is Pudgie and I was Katharine's Ohio Valley Hospital nurse. I am very thankful to have met Katharine and her family - it was a true blessing. Katharine was very dear and gracious. She was proud of her heritage, family, and community. I'll always remember my talks with her about the Ohio Valley Hospital. I'll remember coming around the corner of the nurses' station and my surrogate head nurse Katharine was telling the priest about the Ohio Valley Hospital - a true testimony for us RNs and then set him straight about her religion. I remember her smile, her laughter, and her favorite saying - 'Always remember the good things and forget the bad things.' I'll always remember my Katharine.*" Pudgie (Roberta Ennis)

> "*I met Katharine when I became a member of the Board of Directors of the Jefferson County Historical Association. I was very impressed with her knowledge, her kindness and*

her ability to become an instant friend to the people she met. I drove her home from several of the museum functions and enjoyed all her knowledge she shared. I will always remember a lady with a lot of class and kindness. I also remember her beauty and no wrinkles." Barbara J. Wilinski

"I remember how she cared for me when I was going through a very difficult time in my life. I also remember the 'ham loaf.'" Buzz (Frank Sinclair) She was famous for her ham loaf and the recipe can be found at the end of the book.

"Katharine always called when she went away and asked me to watch her house. When the nephew came I checked him out. I will miss my good neighbor." Lillian Weis

"Katharine was a very special person - 'One of a kind.' I will miss my visits with her very much." Brock Hamilton

"Katharine was an 'instigator.' She would get some idea into her head then call you up and say something like, 'You know, I think you should .... or why don't you ....? and damn it, you just couldn't say 'No!'" Howard Brettell, Jr.

"I remember Katharine Minor best from the way she showed her disappointment, she never lost her cool - she did it in a very lady-like way. When I had occasion to be in some craft classes at Westminster Presbyterian Church, she always made sure each one of us had the material we needed for the class. On the last Sunday she lived, my son Frank called to say he had shingles. I told him that Mrs. Minor had them too." Felicia Borkowski

"Shortly after Doug and I were married and had one year old Cathy (with us today at 47) we often came from Pittsburgh to Steubenville for Sunday dinners with Aunt Kay and Uncle Howard (early 50's). Also we often came for Sunday services in Chautauqua from Cleveland and from our Adirondack home in Star Lake. We remember Aunt Kay as a gracious and charming hostess, very efficient too - she always assigned everyone chores.

I remember my father, Earle spending hours on the

porch in Chautauqua because Aunt Kay wouldn't let him smoke in the house. Earle came home from Aunt Kay's and Uncle Howard's raving about her wonderful coffee. We never told him it was instant which had just been invented."
Lynn and Doug Mead

"Katharine Sinclair Minor developed in her lifetime's general persona, a 'fertile ground aura' in which community progress or preservation could grow or be maintained. This - in a manner most friendly and congenial, as well as lovely - matched her face and admirable presence always. A very valuable, priceless commodity to the community for most of her 90 years was her contribution within humanity here within Steubenville, Ohio, the Ohio Valley and beyond to such places as Chautauqua." William F. Millart, Brilliant, Ohio

"As I sat in the recently remodeled sanctuary of West-minster Church, I was reminded again of how hard Katharine lobbied to have me come to Steubenville and become pastor of that church. It seemed that God was calling me to this ministry and that Katharine was his prophet. My coming never came to pass, but this failure was not due to her belief that this was God's will for the church she loved so much." Richard Anderson

"Mrs. Minor was timeless...she related to everyone...she found a common ground and established communication. She bridged the generational gap with two high school freshmen...discussing her boarding school days...playing basketball against Julia and Jenny's school 'Miss Madeira's School'. There was an exchange of game experiences...she mentioned that her school always lost to 'Model School.' Jenny and Julia were amazed ...that had been their very same experience. Mrs. Minor became a favorite with them just as she has been with their parents and we will all miss her." Fay Stover Indicello.

"I remember her smile, her generosity, and her attention to your matters when she engaged you in conversation, which she always did. I remember her fondness and love for Keekee, even though they didn't see all things in the same

way. She was a wonderful person, 'wonderful' being one of her favorite words." Al Indicello

"Our strongest memory of Katharine is as a role model for all of us. She made everyone feel special - that what we were doing was important and of interest to her. Here was a woman who was actively engaged in important issues - who made good things - small and large - happen. She made us want to emulate her - to make our own world more caring, meaningful, 'civilized' in the very best sense of the word, and to build a sense of community no matter where we were." Susanne Lee and Bob Archer

"I remember sitting on the bed every morning in Chautauqua with Tutu having her coffee and everyone would come in and out planning their days. Often while in there I would go into the linen room off her bedroom and look to see if I had grown overnight. More often than not I hadn't." Matt Evans (The children, grandchildren, and great grandchildren all have growth lines marked on the wall.)

"From the very first memories of Chautauqua vacations, Tutu has been a most inspirational person. Growing up was a great experience because of the generous love she provided for my family. I learned more from her than I ever realized about caring, kindness and sharing. Many memorable Christmases have been spent with her at her home giving me a very special childhood. Her warmth at Chautauqua will be with me always." Howard Minor Jr.

"One of my favorite memories of Tutu is when I was just a little tiger. I was in Chautauqua trying to finish one of my dinners. I was completely stuffed and said that I couldn't finish my meal. Tutu turned to me and said, 'I think I can find a little room for you...right here!' And she pinched my tummy, and it tickled me. I laughed and then finished my meal." Paul Minor

"I didn't know how I would feel when Tutu passed on, but when the sun rose that morning, I was comforted. She got it right. She knew that it was how you treated other peo-

ple that counted. 'Love your neighbor as yourself.' She excelled at that." Michael Minor

"The world is a little emptier without the joy and compassion of one of the last old fashion ladies. I have so many fond memories of good times ... around a ham loaf...Christmas in the Steubenville living room... Boys Club... and especially the summer I spent becoming a musician in Chautauqua. I'll never forget these special times and the woman who made it all possible." Alan Evans

"I will always remember Katharine when I think of Chautauqua. She had a presence there that few could rival." Renee Jacobson

"I don't remember much about Tutu before she got shingles ten years ago. From what people have told me she lost a lot of her energy and enthusiasm after that. From reading in the newspapers all the things she accomplished in her life I am amazed at what Tutu did. Spending my summers in Chautauqua with Tutu was great being able to learn about my ancestors and all they did." Evan Minor

"Tutu had her own style about being a gracious hostess. She made everyone welcome by presenting them with a list of things they could do once they arrived at the house in Steubenville or Chautauqua. She always went out of her way to make sure you were doing something." Jim Evans

"My grandfather's seventy-first birthday in Chautauqua was one of my most memorable experiences. Tutu's patience and cheerful optimism in caring for her husband will carry me through my life. She spent many years with him and his stroke, nursing him back to health with her vibrant energy, which was evident wherever she was. I will remember her sitting on the porch and inviting friends and strangers alike (of course there were no strangers for long for Tutu) and maintaining her dignity all the while. The last time I saw her was on her birthday. For someone who lived 90 years she accomplished a lot." John Evans

1998
Seated: Keekee Minor, Howard Minor, Mary M. Evans and Margaret Minor.
Standing: Jim Evans, Katie Evans, John Evans, Evan Minor, Bob Evans, Pauline Minor, Mike Minor, Paul Minor and Howie Minor.

In the *Herald-Star* the following appeared on July 27, 1998.

Area lost two strong women last week

The Steubenville/Weirton area lost two integral figures in their histories this past week.

Katharine Sinclair Minor of Steubenville died Thursday morning, her 90th birthday. And Tuesday, Inez Orler, 85, of Weirton, died. Both women made their marks in history in their respective communities.

Minor, a daughter of the late Dohrman J. and Mary Donaldson Sinclair, wife of the late Dr. Howard Holland Minor, was part of the family that built Steubenville.

Orler was one of the first female principals in Weirton, after serving as a first-grade teacher for 23 years. Just before retirement from schools, she started a new career as a historian, writing books on local history.

Minor's life was part of a bygone era of tea parties, carriages, only now found in history books. She grew up in what is now the town's Historic District. She devoted her life to church and civic affairs in Steubenville, from soil conservation, to planting forsythia bushes, to the Y.W.C.A., to saving the first Federal Land Office. At one point she even vaccinated Costa Ricans.

Her dedication to other affairs, along with the responsibilities of rearing her family, is not often found. Appropriately, because of her parents' involvement in building Steubenville's history, she helped establish the Jefferson County Historical Association. At home, her residence housed volumes and floors of books on every topic. The concern is what will become of those volumes so they're not tossed aside.

In her last interview with the Herald-Star for a Bicentennial edition last August, a reporter spent nearly a day at her home. Mrs. Minor had talked the reporter's ear off and filled her notebook with her wealth of information about her father's efforts to build Steubenville's parks, water works and, among other things, a bank before his untimely death. Her mother, too, had written Pioneer Days, an early history of Jefferson County, instilling in Minor the same sense of caring for the community.

Her highest honor was being named an honored citizen in the 1997 Steubenville Bicentennial Parade.

Orler was a noted author of the History of Weirton, published in 1976. At that time, she was named a Hancock County Bicentennial honoree.

These women made their marks with the dedication and devotion to improving the quality of life in the Steubenville/Weirton area.

People of their caliber can't be found again. We can only hope in some small way that someone carries out just a facet of what they started.

It seemed appropriate that the woman who wrote about the history of Weirton should be recognized with the daughter of the man who made Weirton possible by bringing business to Holiday's Cove.

Chautauqua Memorial

In Chautauqua a memorial service was held Saturday, August 8, 1998. It was never a question of not having one, for all her friends only asked when it would be. The day she died a sign appeared on her porch in Chautauqua announcing her passing. Anyone familiar with Chautauqua knew that was the best way to alert her friends. During the memorial service at the Chautauqua Presbyterian House, Mike Minor played his guitar, Clarissa Burgwardt played the organ and her husband Carl sang. Rev. Dr. Kent Ira Groff spoke about Katharine's father and how he had set a wonderful example for his daughter. He talked about Katharine's active life in Chautauqua as a life member of the Chautauqua Women's Club, on the Presbyterian House Board for forty years, a member of the Chautauqua Bird and Tree Club and a homeowner since 1945. Rev. Groff reminded the audience that Katharine was the Ohio Mother of the Year. He referred to her porch and all the good visits people had there. He related one of his porch experiences, saying that when he discovered a piano lay within the house he asked to play it. He chose to play Scott Joplin's *The Entertainer,* and it was this piece that was used to notify people that the end had come to the brief time given for exchanges among her friends. In the time allowed for sharing many spoke.

Wendy Vance John said, *"I don't recall knowing anyone else in my life who was as warm and genuinely friendly as Katharine. I will be left with pleasant memories of our growing years at Chautauqua."*

Trudy Patterson Colflesh spoke of *"a gracious, giving, compassionate woman who lived out the admonitions of scripture of love, hospitality, generosity, mercy, and kindness (Rm. 12:9-15). The Lord has prepared a place for her. It will definitely have a front porch - a place of giving, sharing, laughing, learning, and caring. She was interested in the details of people's lives, mailing birthday cards, calling to see how someone was doing, lightening up when they came by, and pulling up a chair on the front porch. She made a commitment to live her life to reflect God's love and grace."*

Joe Twist related the story of taking his daughter over for tea (attitude adjustment time) and having his daughter say that Mrs. Minor's tea was certainly different.
Then Jane Meade said, *"When my dog was in a play at Chautauqua, Katharine arrived with a ribbon and card for the show dog. At another time Katharine brought flowers over when my yard hadn't received a prize."*

Both Andrea Zarue and Batia Leiberman mentioned how much Katharine had helped them when they lost their mothers. Katharine was a good adopted mother.

Shorty Follansbee refered to how special the Minor's front porch was, both in Chautauqua and Steubenville, where Katharine had invited him to come to visit Follansbee. He had never been to the town and Katharine arranged with the mayor to give him a tour of the town founded by his ancestors.

Lin Winters told about her *"Mom" and "what a gaping hole her physical absence will leave in the many lives she graced. She gave so much of herself - her love, her interest in and caring for everyone around her. Being with her was always uplifting, worthwhile and fun. She had a way of making us feel special and cared about. She was in every sense an incomparable lady. I will always be grateful for the blessing of her in my life, for the role model she was that I can only aspire to, for the light she radiated."*

Liz Birmingham Wellman related, *"To me, she was my mother, too. I felt a certain security when I rode by on my bike and saw her sitting in her usual chair on the Minor porch. There was no moment in which she was alone on that porch, for she was always inviting people up. They seemed to converse easily with her and she seemed to listen well to them. In fact, she had more friends than I would ever hope for in a lifetime.*

If I were to describe her, I would say, she would do for others with no desire of returned favors."

Her favorite and only son-in-law said, *"She exemplified dignity."* Bob Evans remarked that he spoke for himself, for Pauline (Howard's wife) and Doc when he said that they all married into a formidable family. *"Yet, because of Katharine's graciousness they could talk about and disagree on things, including religion and politics, in a civil matter. She was a Republican and I was a Democrat. Because of her gracious ways she made people feel at ease."* When emotion swelled up, Bob's wife reached up to hold his hand and he continued. *"Duty was a good 19th century value and Katharine exemplified this virtue. She gave to her family,*

her friends, her church, and her community. This commit-
ment to duty was always lovingly done by Katharine."

Helen and Glen Vance wrote, *"It is so hard to express*
our sympathy to you when we feel that we ourselves need to
be comforted at the loss of Kay. I certainly know she wasn't
very happy these past couple of years, for I share the same
discomfort, but she always had a smile for everyone. I know
of no one so gracious and so generous - a person everyone
will miss because of her kindness and cheerfulness. We feel
lucky to have known someone like Kay."

Katharine Sinclair Minor was a combination of ancestry, upbringing and the many experiences she had. She went by the names of Katharine, Kath, Kay, Mom, Tutu, Mom Minor, and Mrs. Minor. She answered to all of them and gave her all.

Although her father died when she was just seven, the note he wrote to her when he was in the car accident a few years earlier really was her guiding philosophy throughout her life. To keep a note in a lock box and a copy at home shows the value she placed on it.

❦

Katharine Sinclair Minor
1997

One of Katharine's most requested recipes was for her ham loaf. Many happy memories are associated with meals which featured it. So others may enjoy what her family and friends enjoyed, the recipe follows.

Ham Loaf

1 pound ham and 1 1/4 pound pork ground together
2 cups of Wheaties

1 teaspoon dry mustard	1 cup of milk
1 teaspoon brown sugar	2 eggs

Mold and bake two hours in a slow oven (300 degrees). Baste with the following sauce every 15-20 minutes.

Mix together and heat
1/2 cup of water   1 cup vinegar   1-1/2 cup brown sugar
1 heaping tablespoon dry mustard

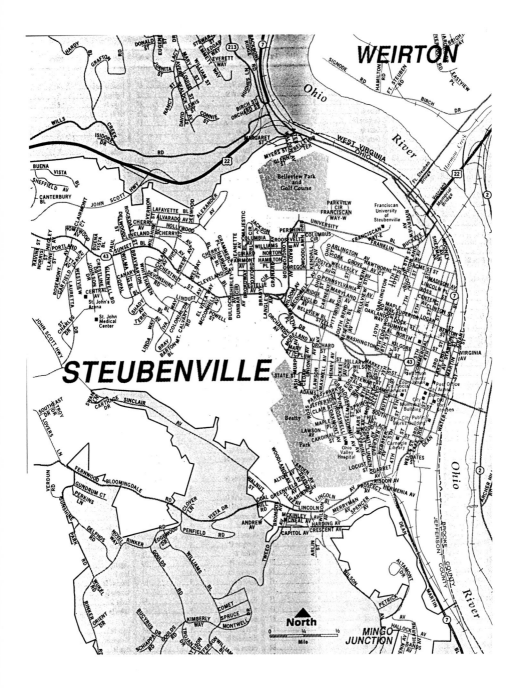

Notes